Higher Education: Some Newer Developments

Higher Education:
Some Newer Developments

Edited by SAMUEL BASKIN
Director of Program Development and Research in Education
Professor of Guidance and Psychology
Antioch College

Sponsored by The Association for Higher Education

MᴄGRAW-HILL BOOK COMPANY
New York, St. Louis, San Francisco, Toronto, London, Sydney

567891011 BP 109

Higher Education: Some Newer Developments

Library of Congress Catalog Card Number
65–15927

foreword

At this time of rising public awareness of the increasingly important role of higher education, the Association for Higher Education is pleased to have a hand in presenting this interpretive volume. In each of the past 19 years the association has sponsored a National Conference on Higher Education. Through this continuing forum the association has focused attention on key issues and creative approaches to critical problems in colleges and universities.

In anticipation of the Twentieth National Conference on Higher Education, the executive committee of the association decided that a fresh overview and evaluation of "some of the newer developments in higher education" would be especially appropriate. Fortunately, Prof. Samuel Baskin agreed to assume the editorship. Worthy of note is the fact that practically all the authors have contributed to previous AHE national conferences.

By way of explanation, the AHE is a national organization of faculty and administrators which is striving to improve the quality of teaching and learning in colleges and universities. AHE attempts to keep members abreast of current developments in higher education and to represent their interests through publications such as *Current Issues in Higher Education,* a report of the annual national conference, and *College and University Bulletin,* a biweekly newsletter, and through research projects, legislative liaison, committee work, and conferences. AHE is a self-governing department of the National Education Association, with more than 20,000 members.

The association is grateful to each author who has contributed to this volume and particularly to Dr. Baskin, whose determination never wavered and whose efforts went far beyond the normal call of duty. The association also wishes to express its thanks to Antioch College for its cooperation in the project by making time available to Dr. Baskin for the conduct of the study. Special thanks are also due to Mr. Richard Landau and Mr. James Gatten for their assistance in editing the manuscript and to Mrs. James Gatten and Mrs. David Muffler who prepared the manuscript for publication.

G. Kerry Smith, Executive Secretary
Association for Higher Education

preface

There are some who argue that the crisis of numbers in higher education may yet turn out to be the best thing that has happened to higher education after all. Clarence Faust, president of the Fund for the Advancement of Education, put the argument this way:

The flood of students we must expect in American education, I hasten to say, is not a misfortune, but a boon, and it may well be that under the pressure of necessity we shall correct some long-recognized weakness in our education system. Under the pressure of necessity we may do some things we should long ago have done but would not be likely to do even now, except under the spur of necessity.[1]

There is good evidence that more significant experimentation is taking place in higher education today than has ever taken place at any other time in our nation's history. This volume tries to do several things: to inform the reader of what has been happening; to provide case illustrations of various developments; and to view these happenings in terms of advantages, disadvantages, problems and issues posed, and implications for the future.

Many forces are contributing to the current ferment in higher education. Several have special significance: the much-discussed population upsurge, with the press it posed of educating an undergraduate student body that was expected to more than double in size between 1960 and 1970; the advent of Sputnik and the attention it focused on finding ways of better educating our populace, particularly in the sciences, mathematics, and languages; the revolution in the science of technology and the demand it created for people with training in new areas of competence; and the problems of financing higher education in an economy which saw the costs of the higher education enterprise rise from 2.9 billion dollars in 1953–1954 to 3.6 billion dollars in 1958–1959 and which was faced with a projected figure of 9.8 billion dollars by 1969–1970.

[1] "The Years Ahead for Higher Education," address by Dr. Clarence Faust delivered before Ohio College Association, Apr. 6, 1957.

The charge to the authors who cooperated in the preparation of this book read as follows:

The principal purpose of the study will be to present an overview of some of the newer developments in higher education ... the report is intended to inform, to evaluate and to suggest. We are assuming that we are speaking to an audience that is largely uninformed of, and wants to learn more about, these developments. Our job is to tell them as much as we possibly can about what has been happening. ... What is the nature of the development? How did it get started? What issues, problems, gains, advantages and disadvantages does it pose? How might others apply these ideas? What meaning do the developments hold for others and for higher education in general? ... The report should center on key issues and concerns in higher education today. It should inform and evaluate, but it should also challenge and open up ideas. ...

Coverage in a volume of this sort always poses problems of scope. For reasons of size and manageability of the project, the Committee of the Association for Higher Education, which planned this book, decided to limit it principally to developments in the four-year undergraduate liberal arts institution. Case illustrations have been drawn from a variety of settings to provide as representative a sampling as possible. Each chapter was planned as a unit by itself (although cross references are made throughout) so that the reader can turn to any one chapter without having to refer to any other.

Developments discussed include the "new" colleges (to include newly created colleges as well as new programs at already established institutions), the college curriculum, independent study, study abroad, programs for the superior or abler student, uses of new media and technology, buildings and facilities as they affect teaching and learning, the community as a resource for learning, programs for the improvement of college teaching and administration, year-round calendars, interinstitutional cooperation, and the financing of the college.

The book makes no claim of being an all-inclusive review of everything that is happening in higher education. It offers no formulas or grand solutions for higher education in the years ahead. Its intent is simply to inform, to evaluate, and to suggest. We hope that the reader will find this to be the case.

Samuel Baskin

contents

LEWIS B. MAYHEW

1

the new colleges

*D*uring the period 1961 through 1964, 146 colleges and universities were created in the United States.[1] These institutions were founded in response to a variety of stimuli: a dramatic population growth, a desire to attract new industry and to ensure economic growth, a desire by religious denominations to provide institutions under sectarian control, the development of new sources of risk capital, a wish to keep institutions small, the economic benefits to be derived from having a college campus in a given locality, dissatisfaction with older institutions, and the long-held dreams of men and women of building their own utopias in higher education.

[1] Leslie F. Robbins, Division of Higher Education, U.S. Department of Health, Education, and Welfare, Washington, D.C., letter, May 27, 1964.

This chapter describes some of these new institutions: the forces that have shaped their development, their goals, the programs and means they have employed, and the problems with which they have been faced. The selection made represents an attempt to provide a general understanding of a variety of examples and includes institutions from various parts of the country—public, private, denominational, and nondenominational.

BACKGROUND

The demands for higher education by a dramatically increased high school population have, of course, been a major factor in the establishment of new institutions of higher learning.[2] In Florida and California, states undergoing rapid growth, the need for more public colleges and universities is particularly apparent. However, even with the population upsurge in the background, other influences have been of importance in the development of these new colleges.

Some regions, notably the Southeast, have sought to upgrade the educational level of their people in order to attract the industry and commerce necessary to ensure a reasonable economic growth. As industry has come to these areas and as they have shifted from a rural to an urban character, the need for new facilities of higher learning became all the more pronounced. New industries have demanded highly skilled workers and technologists, and these individuals in turn have demanded more and better medical, dental, and other professional services; better teachers and schools for their children; and new outlets for their cultural and intellectual interests. Since existing facilities were inadequate and unable to meet these needs, new institutions of higher learning were sorely in demand.

[2] The number of students enrolled in degree programs in colleges and universities rose almost 60 per cent, from 2.3 million to 3.6 million between 1950 and 1960. Based on trend projections, which assume that whatever causal factors operated in the past will continue to operate in the future, the 1960 figure of 3.6 million is expected to rise to 7.0 million by 1970 and to 8.7 million by 1975 (U.S. Department of Health, Education, and Welfare, projections of the Division of Educational Statistics, June. 1964).

Intellectual forces have, of course, also been of major influence. Thoughtful men and women have been deeply disturbed by the relative impotence of many collegiate institutions. Changing a college or university that had existed without change for a century or more was difficult, if not impossible; the only real hope for improving higher education lay in starting new institutions. The feasibility of creating new institutions and experimental ventures in higher education had been enhanced by developments in the use of new methods, theories, and technology for teaching and learning; it was given impetus by public dissatisfaction with education when Russian technology surged forward in the mid-1950s, and it became a realistic possibility as major philanthropic foundations began to put risk capital into educational innovation.

In addition, several other forces have been operative. Some religious denominations, having seen a number of their institutions evolve into secular schools, sought to resume their role in higher education by establishing new colleges and universities. In some states, new schools were created to give expression to an educational philosophy rooted in a political system of values. In California, for example, the creation of many junior colleges, state colleges, and branches of the state university is partly the result of the belief of state political leaders that all young people should have an institution of higher education close to their homes. Similarly, some new institutions, which were really branches of a mother institution, have been created because of the belief that the values of higher education were being lost through the sheer size and complexity of the original campus. New campuses, or new configurations of older campuses, seemed a way of capturing the essence of the small college campus without losing the power and efficiency of a large organization. And sometimes simple historical accident has been involved, such as when a physical plant suddenly became available.

Without doubt the self-interests of men and of regions have also been involved. Although town and gown have coexisted with considerable tension, a college campus is still an economic asset, and chambers of commerce and businessmen have exerted significant pressure for the establishment of collegiate enterprises. Further, creating a new institution is a powerful ego stimulus, and this must be counted as one of the creative forces. And there is in the American character a missionary vein. Creating new institutions is one more way of carrying a particular message of salvation to those who need it.

Out of this welter of forces, causes, and influences have come the new colleges. Each has come into existence because of a specific coincidence of forces. Each has been born through the struggles and efforts of men and women. Each has encountered vexatious obstacles in its formative years, and each, at least in its written statements about itself, has glimpsed a vision of utopia.

THE CASE EXAMPLES

Presented here are examples of new institutions. The criteria for selecting them were relatively simple. They were to be of recent origin and should represent a serious attempt at uniqueness and innovation. They should be varied with respect to the types of institutions of higher education already in existence, and they should reflect the educational sentiment in at least a few of the fastest-growing states.

The University of South Florida, Tampa

Forces coincident to establishing the University of South Florida as a state university at Tampa were the impact of a burgeoning population, the philosophy of putting facilities where the people are, the need for general upgrading of educational levels, and the pull of business interests. The dream was to meld general education with professional preparation, all built on as sound empirical bases as possible.

Legislative enactment to create the new university followed a study of the state's higher education needs (college enrollment in 1960 was 68,112; it was expected to climb to 180,000 by 1970[3]) and the development of a master plan that called for the establishment of three new four-year institutions of higher learning and eighteen community junior colleges. The decision to locate the first

[3] John S. Allen, "Planning the University of South Florida," *Casebook on Campus Planning and Institutional Development* no. 667, p. 49, U.S. Office of Education, Washington, D.C., 1962.

of these new enterprises in the Tampa Bay region was determined in part by geographic need and in part by the persuasive efforts of Tampa merchants and industrialists, who saw the economic and cultural advantages of a new university. The institution, named the University of South Florida, opened its doors in September, 1960.

The University has been organized as a four-school university with a College of Basic Studies and separate Colleges of Education, Business, and Liberal Arts. The College of Basic Studies stresses general education during a student's first two years. The general education program continues in the upper-division college, although the focus shifts toward professional and other educational goals. To ensure that the program of the College of Basic Studies and those of the more specialized colleges are related, many courses and curricula have been developed as all-university programs. Whenever possible, joint appointments have been made between two or more of the colleges.

Institutional research has been assigned an important role in the life of the institution. Although the institution does not deny the place of faculty research in a university, it believes that the primary emphasis should be on teaching and on student learning. Every effort has been made to give a distinctly intellectual tone to the university. Buildings have been designed to encourage face-to-face confrontations with the faculty. The library is central in the life of the university, with the building itself located at the crossroads of the campus. It is revealing that the director of libraries was the first professional appointee of the newly appointed first president. Since students are expected to assume considerable responsibility for their own education, independent study is stressed. A relatively elaborate examination program with constant assessment of student progress has been developed. To avoid the evils of overspecialization, a divisional, rather than a departmental, organization has been employed.

The task of finding well-trained professors who were interested chiefly in teaching and who could serve at comparatively modest salaries posed a major problem. The concept of joint appointment of professors for both general education courses and more specialized courses also created complications. Through a process of serial review of credentials of candidates by the several administrative officers, however, a relatively well-trained faculty was appointed. Its members, 70 per cent of whom held the doctorate, had been trained for the most part in Southern, Middle Western, and Far

Western state universities. It was a faculty interested in teaching but interested, too, in research and scholarship. But even such a faculty, well oriented to teaching, has had some difficulty in understanding the purposes of general education.

The times themselves presented complications that had to be resolved. A new state university in the South after the 1954 United States Supreme Court decision was bound to encounter the desegregation problem. Also, creating an institution of higher learning that emphasized candid exploration of new ideas in a region of the country conservative in its religious, political, economic, and social beliefs produced other vexations.

A major problem, which was foreseen but not solved, stemmed from the way in which the planning was done. A small group of administrators, many of them old friends and colleagues, were together a full year before the first faculty member appeared. This was an essential activity, and yet it produced an administrator-centered institution in which faculty members felt like outsiders. This in- and out-group feeling was intensified when the chief academic administrators located their homes in one region of the city while faculty members spread themselves into many regions. However, consciousness of the problem has helped alleviate some of the worst consequences of a faculty-administration cold war.

At the beginning of its fourth year (1963–1964), the University of South Florida already had about one-half the number of students in attendance (4,600) that had been projected for 1970 (10,000). It had survived with few scars a major investigation by a legislative committee. This in itself is testimony of basic strength, for even the strongest of well-established institutions has quaked at the onslaught of legislative inquisitors. Its program can be regarded as an eclectic one with a strong base of general education.

Monteith College of Wayne State University, Detroit

Monteith College of Wayne State University was designed as an experiment to determine whether a large institution can, by creating smaller parts within itself, exploit the potentialities of a small college and yet utilize the resources of a large institution. Initial steps in the planning of the new college were undertaken in the fall of 1957 by a faculty committee. In April, 1958, the Ford Foundation made a grant of $25,000 to Wayne State University to help defray the cost of planning, and on December 12, 1958, the Foundation allocated $700,000 to help in the establishment of the new college.

Wayne State is a large, municipally supported school that came into existence during the Depression of the 1930s. It is almost a prototype of a "streetcar college," providing an education for those young people in the Detroit area who are not able to go elsewhere. Like all institutions of higher education in Michigan, it has continued to grow in size. Located as it is in the heart of a metropolitan area, it has been plagued by an impersonality that is characteristic of the large and complicated institutions.

Monteith College admitted its first class, a total of 314 students, in September, 1959. It is presently admitting about 250 to 300 students per year and plans on a total enrollment of 1,200. Its student body is similar in most respects to that of the University itself, and the College appears to be firmly established as a separate unit within the University.

The program gives major stress to general education or liberal studies. The general education program consists of a program of basic studies which includes a five-quarter sequence in the social sciences, a six-quarter sequence in the natural sciences, a five-quarter sequence in humanistic studies, and a senior colloquium. The latter has been designed as a two-quarter course in which students read and discuss critically a series of books interpretative of the fields covered in the other three basic courses. Independent study and inquiry are stressed through freshman research projects and the independent study requirements of the basic studies program and the senior colloquium. Thus, during his early years the student is expected to take the terminal segment of one of the basic general education courses without attending the discussion groups of the course. During his senior year he is expected to complete about half of his work in the senior colloquium through independent study. To earn his Monteith degree, a student must complete 84 quarter hours in the basic studies or general education program (of a total of 180 quarter hours required for graduation) and write a Monteith essay. The student takes most of his remaining course work in the other colleges of the University.

Of major importance in the College program is the Monteith Center. The Center is the hub of many of the College's activities, including informal meetings and conversations between students, faculty, and guest speakers; concerts; and social affairs. Serving as a central gathering place, it has the effect of bringing both faculty and students together in a unit which they can identify as their own. At present Monteith is making use of an old renovated building for its Center. A recent Danforth Foundation grant will enable Monteith to build a new facility for use as the Monteith Center.

Monteith has undertaken extensive research of its new program. This research includes follow-up studies of its students since their time of entrance and a comparison of Monteith graduates with College of Liberal Arts graduates of Wayne State and with national groups where normative data were available. Comparisons were made on such measures as the Graduate Record Examination, the Omnibus Personality Inventory, the College Characteristics Index, and the Test of Critical Thinking, developed by the Committee on Measurement and Evaluation of the American Council on Education. Of particular note were the results on the Graduate Record Area Examinations, where Monteith seniors were markedly above national norms and those of the College of Liberal Arts in each of three areas (humanities, social sciences, and sciences) measured by the examination.[4]

New College at Hofstra, Hofstra, Long Island

Dreams of an "ideal" small college were entwined with the planning that resulted in New College at Hofstra College. With the aid of a grant from the Ford Foundation, a planning group set to work to design a college within the context of its parent institution.

The new institution opened in the fall of 1960. New College was conceived of as a one-year academic program for the commuting student of "good-average" ability. The student body was to be limited in number to from 100 to 120 students, to be taught by a faculty of six teaching fellows. An extended academic year of approximately forty weeks was planned in the hope that a good number of students would be able to enter the junior year in one of the regular curricula of Hofstra, after the completion of their New College year, or at least to complete their undergraduate program in three years through additional summer work. As originally planned, students were to attend school four days a week,

[4] For a full review of this research, see *Monteith College: A Report to the President,* Monteith College, Detroit, Mich., December, 1963.

Monday through Thursday, with a long weekend available for outside employment.

A number of the ideas incorporated in the program were similar to those that were adopted at Monteith: interdisciplinary and liberal arts experiences designed to provide students and faculty with a common universe of discourse; independent study as a part of the student's regular college experience; discussion and seminar-type experiences; close student-faculty relationships; and New College's projection of itself as a small college within a larger college, with an identity of its own.

All students at New College take a year-long course called Introduction to Science and Humanities. This course encompasses the disciplines of literature, mathematics, philosophy, physical science, fine arts, and social science. In addition, students can elect one specialized course that they follow for a half year, at which point they can elect to continue or choose another course. All six teaching fellows participate in and attend all the lectures of the required course. The morning program at the College is devoted to the year-long science and humanities course and to work in discussion groups; afternoons are spent in specialized or field courses, in independent study, and in individual conferences with instructors and advisers.

Several problems that the College experienced were predictable in advance. Additional courses had to be added to the curriculum to meet student pressures for more variety of course offerings and course needs in special areas. Special arrangements had to be made to meet the course requirements of students in premedicine and education, and a new sequence of offerings has recently been introduced for students planning to major in chemistry, music, and theater arts. The plan of having six teaching fellows present at all lectures of the basic science and humanities course has posed burdensome time problems. The independent study period had to be modified to provide more faculty direction and guidance, and the three-day weekend proved to be too long (with not enough students taking advantage of this period for employment). This pattern has now been changed to a Monday-Tuesday-Thursday-Friday class schedule, with Wednesdays used for remedial work, conferences, independent study, and occasional meetings of the science and humanities course.

New College's retention rate has been a strong one, exceeding

that of the parent institution. Of the eighty-one students who registered during the first year (1960–1961), seventy-two completed
the New College program, and a similar rate has prevailed since.
While enrollment has not reached the figure of 120 originally
contemplated, the school has been able to attract an increasingly
more able student body. As originally planned, a number of students have been able to complete their programs in three years.
Perhaps the strongest evidence of New College's success is the
fact that the College has been authorized to establish a full three-
year degree-granting program of its own. This new three-year
program was begun in the fall of 1964.

Oakland University, Rochester, Michigan

The need for additional facilities for higher education in the state
of Michigan was dramatically illustrated by the phenomenal
growth that occurred at Michigan State University, where the
number of students enrolled had increased from a few thousand
just before World War II to almost twenty thousand by 1957. The
immediate impetus for the development of the new state university
at Oakland was a gift of land, buildings, and 2 million dollars in
cash made to the University by lumberman Alfred G. Wilson and
his wife.

Michigan State University, Oakland (now Oakland University),
opened its doors to its first freshman class, 570 students, in the fall
of 1959. While planned as a branch of Michigan State University,
it was to be developed as an autonomous unit with its own campus.
The plans for the University were developed by a number of study
groups, formed to make recommendations regarding the University
program. Among those participating in the discussions were Milton
S. Eisenhower, president of Johns Hopkins University; Lee A.
DuBridge, president of California Institute of Technology; pub-
lisher Henry R. Luce; and anthropologist Margaret Mead.

The program at Oakland is designed to provide a liberal education for all students. At least half of a student's four-year program
is in the liberal arts. All students are expected to take one-year
courses in English literature and history, the history and development of Western civilization, the history and philosophy of science,

and contemporary non-Western cultures. In addition, all students are expected to master a foreign language. In some cases, students may substitute a sequence in mathematics, beginning with calculus, for language study, although they are also encouraged to study languages. A number of courses stress independent studies and research. A major strand in the curriculum is directed toward developing international understanding. Courses in non-Western cultures give emphasis to the study of the Far East, Africa, and Latin America.

Oakland University graduated its first class in June, 1963. While the size of its freshman classes has increased significantly over the years, the University has been able to attract an increasingly stronger student body. Thus a comparison of student test scores on the College Qualification Tests, given at the time of entrance, shows a continued increase in the students' measured ability levels for the years 1959 to 1963. Most significant is the improvement of scores at the lower levels.

In September, 1961, Oakland shifted its calendar from a regular two-semester plan to a year-round program of trimesters of fifteen weeks each, thus making it possible for students to graduate in 2⅔ years. A number of new courses have been developed to give attention in the students' programs to education for world affairs. A major program of continuing education has been inaugurated. The University has sought to maintain stringent standards of academic achievement, so much so that it found, at least in its first years, that some of the demands being made by faculty were unrealistic and resulted in a higher rate of failure in certain course areas than was expected.

Although no formal study has been made of the University's experience under its initial curriculum, several college committees have been at work evaluating particular aspects of the program and studying ways in which the program might be improved. While seeking to maintain the emphasis on liberal education, a number of proposals have evolved, designed to permit greater freedom of course choice and to give more flexibility to the student's course program. In March, 1963, the Academic Senate approved a number of program changes designed in part to achieve this greater flexibility. The changes are to remain in effect until the fall of 1965, at which time additional study of the program and curricular offerings is planned.

Florida Presbyterian College, St. Petersburg, Florida

Churches in America traditionally have assumed leadership in creating new institutions of higher education. Since there was no Presbyterian college in Florida, and mindful of Florida's continuing need for higher education facilities, the Presbyterian Church in the United States and the United Presbyterian Church in the United States of America, with the approval of the two Florida synods, planned the establishment of a new institution at St. Petersburg. Appointed as president for the new college was a minister; as academic dean, a professor of psychology. These two men spent considerable time during their first year studying new educational ideas and seeking men and women who could put these ideas into practice.

Florida Presbyterian College admitted its first students in the fall of 1960. The college expects to be able to accommodate 1,400 to 1,500 students by 1968. Approximately 60 per cent of its present student body comes from Florida, and the remainder come from other states and other nations.

The curriculum at Florida Presbyterian College emphasizes both interrelatedness of knowledge and independent study in a four-year core program required of all students. The first two years of the program deal with Western civilization, the third year with Asian studies, and the fourth year with a course called Christian Faith and Great Issues. The great issues course is not intended as an indoctrination course but rather as an examination of key issues from the perspective of each individual's basic beliefs. The core-program is taught mainly through large lectures and small discussion groups. In the first year, ten men, each from a different academic discipline, teach the course. The second and fourth years are similarly staffed and structured.

During his first year, in addition to the core course, the student is required to take one course in mathematics or logic and one in science. He also takes one elective. As the student moves beyond the first year, his program allows more electives and field courses. A total of eighteen areas of specialization has been developed.

A special feature of the Florida Presbyterian program is the winter term. During the month of January there are no classes, and all students, *including freshmen,* are engaged in individual research and study on a major problem under the guidance of one of the professors. Project possibilities are posted in the college library well before the Christmas holiday, students rank their preferences in a one-to-five order, and the registrar assigns them according to one of these preferences. Students may work alone on a project or with another student or a group. Students are encouraged to choose a topic outside their major field of interest during their first two years and to work in their major field during their junior and senior years. They are expected to put in fifty to sixty hours of weekly study and work on their projects. Each professor serves as adviser to from twelve to fifteen students during the independent study period. The program continues throughout the student's four years at college.

In addition to the winter-term independent study program, capable students are eligible to take any course in the college curriculum by independent study. Placement and comprehensive examinations are being developed in various areas to permit students to earn credit by examination and advance to their proper place in the curriculum.

Florida Presbyterian began its program on an interim campus and moved recently to its new campus in St. Petersburg. At present, its buildings have an estimated worth of 7 million dollars and include a library, a humanities and science complex, an auditorium, a college union, dining facilities, an infirmary, and housing for 700 students.

Florida Presbyterian College appears to be off to a strong start. It has worked through a number of early problems that had been posed by its opening in temporary quarters. After some initial difficulties with the independent study program due to too rapid introduction, it has developed a strong program in independent studies. Despite the fact that its first freshman classes were somewhat smaller in number than anticipated, the College has ended each fiscal year in the black. It is one of the few institutions that have tried to put into effect the curriculum-fiscal notion, advanced by Ruml and Morrison, that tuition should be used entirely for salaries.[5] The average faculty salary for the year 1963–1964 was $10,180 for a nine-month period, with a range from $6,500 to $14,000.

Perhaps the biggest problem facing the College is that of main-

---

[5] Beardsley Ruml and Donald H. Morrison, *Memo to a College Trustee,* McGraw-Hill Book Company, New York, 1959.

taining its stance in level of students attracted, program, standards, and faculty salaries.

St. Andrews College, Laurenberg, North Carolina

Problems of economy, duplication of facilities, and maintenance of standards were of principal importance in the creation of St. Andrews College.

Over the years, the Presbyterian Church had given its support to seven colleges in North Carolina. Concern over the fact that there were so many small colleges in the state came to a head in 1953, when a survey commission was appointed by the synod of North Carolina to study the existing Presbyterian institutions in North Carolina and to make recommendations for a pattern of Christian higher education that would hold the greatest promise for the future. After eighteen months of study, the committee recommended that three of the institutions—Flora Macdonald College (a four-year liberal arts institution), the Pace Junior College, and the Presbyterian Junior College (both two-year institutions)—be consolidated and opened as a new college at a new location. Despite several lawsuits instituted by individuals who saw loss in the change, the new institution opened its doors in September, 1961, in Laurenburg, North Carolina, as St. Andrews Presbyterian College. The basic plans for the institution were developed by a study group financed by the Fund for the Advancement of Education.[6]

St. Andrews College has been designed as a four-year coeducational liberal arts college. It opened with a student body of about 500 with the expectation that it would grow to 2,000 students. Its program is guided by a philosophy of Christian belief. The curriculum includes a large segment of general education courses, covering about half the student's total time at the college. The general education or basic liberal studies include a multidisciplinary course called Christianity and Culture (which continues throughout the student's four years) and courses in natural science and mathe-

[6] Members of this group were William Taeusch, dean of the College of Wooster, Wooster, Ohio (chairman); Ruth Eckert, professor, University of Minnesota; Sidney J. French, then dean of Rollins College; Price H. Gwynn, Jr., dean of Flora Macdonald College and first dean of the faculty of St. Andrews; Jameson M. Jones, dean of Southwestern University at Memphis; and René de Vismé Williamson, professor, Louisiana State University.

matics, the humanities, and foreign languages. During the upper-class years, the student's program allows for greater choice of electives and professional and cognate courses. The Christianity and culture course is taught by a team of professors representing the fields of religion, philosophy, history, sociology, anthropology, literature, and the arts. Five or more professors are present at each meeting of the course. Each student is expected to carry an independent study project related to his liberal arts studies during his early years and to his major field during his last two years. Every effort has been made to maintain economy of operation by avoiding proliferation of courses and departments.

St. Andrews is now in its fifth year of operation. It has had to face a number of problems not characteristic of other new institutions. Merging the finances, staff, and some of the special programs of the joining institutions (such as the Flora Macdonald music program) has proved vexatious. Faculty recruitment has been difficult because of the problems of finding staff who not only were well-qualified teachers but also were communicants. Funding continues to be a problem, as it does in most schools of this type. However, despite these difficulties, St. Andrews has been able to develop its program fairly well along the lines envisioned by its planning group.

OTHER NEW INSTITUTIONS

California, the fastest-growing of the states, has one of the fastest-growing educational complexes. The state system for higher education is divided into three sectors. The University of California, with its multiple campuses, is one element; the state colleges represent another; and junior colleges represent the third. One of the more interesting developments in California is the Santa Cruz branch of the University of California. It will consist of fifteen to twenty-five residential colleges, each enrolling from 250 to 1,000 students. Each of these colleges will be semiautonomous, serving as the basic unit of academic administration, and will provide about half of the curricular needs of the students. Each college will have a unique academic emphasis, although all will provide a liberal arts education. Classes are intended to be small, and considerable tutorial work will be done. In addition to the small residential colleges, there will be university-wide programs of specialization based upon more traditional divisions of the disciplines. The university-wide programs will also provide the space and equipment needed by the residential colleges.

The small-college organization within a larger institution finds another clear expression in the Raymond and Covell Colleges of the University of the Pacific. The Raymond College opened in 1963 in a new series of dormitories, classroom buildings, faculty offices, and lounge facilities on the edge of the parent campus. It is staffed with a relatively young faculty and offers a rigorous liberal arts curriculum to a small student body. When all four classes are in residence, it will enroll 250 students, whose principal educational activities will be contained within this campus. The Covell College is a similar unit but features inter-American studies. Both its faculty and student body will be composed of North and South Americans, and instruction will be in both English and Spanish. The emphasis in both these colleges is on close faculty and student relations and considerable use of tutorials, discussion, and independent study. Perhaps the single most critical problem to be resolved is whether the cost per student credit hour in this highly individualized education can be kept reasonably consistent with the costs in the rest of the institution.

Of a different conception, since the demands are so different, is the Chicago Teachers College–North, which opened in 1961. This is a nonresidential college that hopes to infuse the education of teachers with heavy doses of general and liberal education. Thus all students are required to take courses in the humanities, behavioral and social sciences, natural science, and mathematics. The institution is housed in a unique building complex of contemporary design. Classrooms are flexible; they can be used by large and small groups. Interiors are designed to encourage interaction of students and faculty. Many new technological aids will be employed: language laboratories; telemation, which will permit the instructor to program his lessons to more than six hundred students; and closed-circuit television.

Grand Valley State College, in Allendale, Michigan, is a state-supported institution that owes its creation to the diligent efforts of Grand Rapids citizens who saw the values of a state college and who were willing to make contributions of land and money to assist in starting it. The College, which opened in the fall of 1963, plans to be relatively small. It will operate year-round and thus will be able to function with a modest physical plant. All students at Grand Valley take a core of foundation studies in general education, including courses in the humanities, social sciences, natural sciences, mathematics, and languages. Specialization begins in the second year, and all students are required to take some general education for each of the four years. A major innovation of the college is the heavy reliance on tutorial education, with each student meeting at least once each week with his tutor. The cost of this is partly offset through equally heavy reliance on large lectures and television and considerable independent study. The library has many of the attributes of a learning resources center and provides carrels wired to central reserves of tapes and records. The institution is chiefly a liberal arts college, although teacher preparation receives major emphasis.

Two Florida institutions, New College at Sarasota and the Florida Atlantic University at Boca Raton, opened their doors in the fall of 1964.

New College plans to adapt to the undergraduate setting some of the most desirable aspects of graduate education. Major emphasis is on individual study under the guidance of tutors. The three-year program is built around an eleven-month academic calendar; twelve-week terms now alternate with four-week independent study and reading periods. Students will take comprehensive exams at the end of each academic year. During the reading periods, students are able to do individual research, go on field trips, or study abroad.

The first-year program is designed to acquaint students with the natural sciences, the humanities, and the social sciences; at the same time, they will have an opportunity to pursue in depth the study of their major areas of interest. In their later years, the students will specialize in major and minor fields through tutorials, seminar and discussion groups, and field projects.

Students and faculty live in residential dormitories, much like those at Yale and Oxford, to encourage informal encounters between them.

Florida Atlantic University is a senior college providing the upper two years and graduate work to students who have completed their first two years of junior college work or have transferred in from a four-year institution. It will not have a freshman year or sophomore year program of its own.

Operating on the assumption that it will draw a more mature

student (inasmuch as the student will be in his third year when he enters the University), Florida Atlantic plans to make considerable use of independent study. It will also give major attention to the use of the new media and technology in teaching and learning. Its learning resources center will serve as a core unit in the instructional process.[7]

Although this chapter deals essentially with new institutions, several new developments at existing institutions merit attention here. For five years Stephens College has conducted a house-plan experiment. This involves 100 freshmen taking a core of required general education courses from the same group of faculty members within a single residence hall. Faculty offices are in the residence hall, and much of the instruction is carried on there also. Considerable use is made of the natural cohesiveness of the small residence hall to further educational ends. Libraries of paperback books are retained in the house, and a flexible schedule is employed to permit fieldwork and trips to various settings.

A similar, although much larger, effort is being made at Michigan State University. Large residence-hall complexes are being created on the edge of the major campus. The halls include classrooms, offices, and laboratories and are staffed by faculty from the University College. Students take their basic general education courses in the halls and even some of their specialized work. For their advanced work they go to the other parts of the campus. Eventually such residences may be created for specialized curricular groups, so that the end result will be small, single-purpose institutions operating with the advantages of both smallness and large size.

Since this book is principally concerned with developments in the four-year undergraduate institution, no attempt has been made here to review developments in the two-year colleges. It is important to note, however, that a large number of the newly created institutions are two-year community colleges. As originally conceived, the community college was called a "junior college" and was intended to provide the first two years of a typical four-year collegiate program. Within the last few decades, however, these institutions have been highly innovative in the number of new programs they have added in order to meet the growing educa-

[7] For a fuller report of this institution, see *Reports and Recommendations of the Planning Workshop,* Florida Atlantic University, Boca Raton, Fla., Sept. 4, 1963.

tional needs of their communities: two-year terminal education programs of a technical or vocational nature, two years of general education, adult education, and cultural centers for the supporting community.[8]

MAIN EMPHASES

These new institutions demonstrate several new or renewed trends in higher education. First, they generally reflect a desire on the part of educators to capture some of the educational potential of small colleges without yielding the undoubted virtue of large size. Thus Monteith, New College at Hofstra, Santa Cruz, the University of the Pacific, and Michigan State have all been attracted to the college-within-a-college concept. And this appears to be no passing fad. Several of the largest universities, although not described here, are exploring ways of subdividing enormous enrollments, especially in colleges of liberal arts and business, to ensure close relations between students and faculty. A few schools with commuting students are also searching for ways to regroup students more effectively.

Related to this quest for integrity through size is the equally prominent search for integrity through curriculum. Each one of these new colleges is seeking, through some variant of the liberal arts or general education curriculum, insurance against undue specialization or fragmentation of educational experience. Each planning group assumes that all students, regardless of ultimate vocation, should be exposed to the broad outlines of human knowledge. Some have valued this goal so highly that they loaded the four years with general education. Others provided for the option of a bachelor's degree in general education or in a more restricted major. But all struggled to reinterpret in modern idiom the liberal arts and sciences.

A number of new colleges are giving major attention to the use of automated instruction, tapes, and the like to enrich instruction and to make it more economical. Again a range is present, with

[8] For a fuller review of developments in this area, see B. Lamar Johnson, *Islands of Innovation: A Report of an Exploratory Survey of the Utilization of Junior College Faculty Services,* Occasional Report no. 6, Junior College Leadership Program, School of Education, University of California, Los Angeles, Calif., March, 1964.

Florida Atlantic University demonstrating the most elaborate provision for their use and Oakland State University perhaps standing
at the opposite pole. It is still too early to tell whether these new
media will be firmly woven into the fabric of higher educational
practice, but some of these institutions seem to be making definite
architectural provision for long-term use.

In contrast to the recent trend toward an elitism in higher education, these new colleges, with few exceptions, seem to be based on
a moderate theory. They want to attract well-prepared, able students, but they are not searching for only the top few from the
ability range. The Hofstra policy has exemplified the prevailing
view that the new colleges should educate the good-average student.

This same interest in good-average students is involved in the
general preoccupation with variants of independent study. Honors
programs have been typically based on some conception of the
student's responsibility for his own education. These colleges seem
to be saying that the same techniques that worked with honors
students can be made to work with a cross section of the student
population. Thus the University of South Florida has a credit-by-
examination system, as will Florida Atlantic. Several of the colleges
have created a term during the academic year free from formal
classes. The creation of carrels in some of the new buildings is
visible evidence that independent work is to be the rule. The
reasons given for this are mixed, with some educators candidly
remarking that independent study can enable limited faculty talent
to be spread further and more effectively. However, most of the
rationales presented are based on the educational assumption that
no one teaches another anything. Rather, change comes about
when an individual learns something on his own. These provisions
for independent study are intended to facilitate that learning.

But independent study could become sterile done in the absence
of a vibrant, intellectual climate. Thus each of these new institutions has sought deliberately to create a feeling of an intellectual
community. The University of South Florida made the creation of
an appropriate intellectual tone one of the keystones of its educational arch. It was hoped that the Stephens house plan would
make academic and intellectual matters the focus for living. The
residential colleges at Santa Cruz, it is hoped, will do the same
thing, as does the Center at Monteith and Hofstra's New College.
New College in Sarasota has been recruiting distinguished scholars
in residence to help create the desired climate for learning.

Most of the new colleges reveal an acute consciousness of the need to keep the curriculum within safe and economical bounds. Several are experimenting with quite large instructional groups for some purposes, especially transmission of information, so that the institution can afford to provide tutorial and small-group education for all its students for other purposes. Closed-circuit television, tape recording of lectures, and large in-person lectures figure in the programs to handle the prescribed liberal or general courses to be taken by all students. As one means of keeping the curriculum in bounds, these colleges have experimented with forms of academic administration other than the disciplinary department. Santa Cruz sees the residential college as the basic administrative unit, and the University of South Florida is attempting to exploit a divisional structure, as is Oakland University. Monteith and the two New Colleges operate as single units that deal with several disciplines as interdisciplines. Each college has quickly experienced the pressures for departmentalization, and as the colleges increase in size they may yield to the pressures. But at the moment a valiant effort is being made to conceive of the curriculum and the college in broader terms than has been customary in the past or is typical in the majority of well-established institutions.

One last emphasis needs mention. In one way or another these colleges are seeking to emphasize internationalism. Area studies, centers for Latin-American studies, contrived research abroad, and language study all are attempted. And a few of the new institutions not described in detail here, such as Friends International University, make a concern for worldwide matters a chief preoccupation.

COMMON PROBLEMS

The new colleges share not only innovation but also common problems. A major one of these is recruiting a faculty that can adapt to even the modest new ideas being incorporated into the plans. With a few administrators and a group of consultants who are chosen because of the congeniality of their beliefs a consistent scheme of education can be evolved that all who worked on can know and understand. With each new appointment, the concepts must be reviewed; as new people add their ideas to the pool, a regression toward the traditional is almost bound to occur. Eventually even the most glowing of innovations runs the danger of being reinterpreted in terms of the familiar experiences of the growing faculty.

Several institutions have tried to prevent this reinterpretation by appointing quite young faculty members, who presumably have had less opportunity to solidify their opinions. Unfortunately this has dangers, too. Young faculty members have notions about students formed in graduate schools. They are inclined to expect too much from the first classes, especially in new institutions. The experiences of New College at Hofstra (in its use of independent study) and Oakland University are illustrative.

Although these institutions have emphasized the primacy of the liberal arts and sciences as a way of preparing people for life, pressures begin to mount when the first student asks that vocational courses be added. At Hofstra and Monteith, for example, the core general education requirement was modified for the sake of engineers, those preparing to teach, and premedical students. At the University of South Florida, science students and faculty began applying pressure almost at once for some elective principle regarding the general education science courses. With each passing year these demands increase and apparently will be met, unless an institution does as St. John's College did and simply says that there is only one form of education professed here.

Just as students demand vocationalism, so faculty members demand departmentalization. A number of these new institutions have organized themselves along some divisional line. This has been done in the belief that a division can offer a more broadly conceived program and can better maintain "contact" between the disciplines. Faculty members are intrigued by this at the beginning but gradually come to feel that professionally they are losing out unless they are affiliated with a department or are teaching departmental courses. In American higher education, relatively few institutions have an arrangement by which teachers of broad interdisciplinary courses can have their entire careers in that context. This very fact encourages faculty to attempt to translate the experimental courses into some more familiar and, they hope, personally profitable mold.

Still another problem is that of remaining flexible. Each college has emphasized flexibility for such things as independent study, acceleration, terms off, and the like. Unfortunately, when dealing with large numbers of people, flexibility is not attained this side of chaos unless machinery is created to ensure it. The very creation of machinery builds in a tendency for the program to grow inflexible. As faculty vested interests increase in some innovation, it becomes difficult indeed to modify that innovation. Education becomes fixed in the mold in which it was most recently cast.

EVALUATION

Obviously it is still too early to attempt an assessment of the new colleges; nor would such an effort be appropriate here. Further, the faculties have generally been so occupied with the problems incidental to creating a new enterprise that careful evaluation has yet to be done. There are, of course, some notable exceptions. Monteith and Hofstra have collected valuable data about their programs. The University of South Florida is gradually accumulating evidence that when fully collated will yield a reasonably clear picture of the strengths and weaknesses of the program.

Several evaluative comments, however, might be made. These colleges are attracting considerable attention from the profession at large. Their leaders are much in demand to describe their innovation, and their experiences are cited in virtually all the books about higher education now flooding the market. As these descriptive statements come to be reinforced by solid research evidence, they can be expected to make a substantial impact on the thinking or theories of higher education.

Whether or not they make a similar impact on the practice of education, particularly in the larger institutions, will depend on other and quite independent factors. American higher education is a prestige and status system along with its other characteristics. There are a small number of institutions that often set the style that most other institutions seek to emulate. While one does not expect to find any single listing or fully agreed-upon grouping of the leading institutions, generally the names of Harvard, Columbia, Stanford, Princeton, Chicago, Michigan, and California come in for mention. One measure of the likelihood of spread of the innovations that currently characterize the new colleges will be found in the degree to which these innovations find acceptance and use in these and other top-quality institutions. Time alone will tell whether this will be the case and whether the new colleges will provide the ideas out of which future leadership will be fashioned.

In order for the profession to judge wisely, more evidence from research is needed. Most of the assumptions on which the new-college thinking has been based need empirical validation. Are small colleges more effective than large complexes? Do students need tutorial experience? Do interdisciplinary courses produce different results from those produced by specialized departmental courses? Can an intellectual tone be contrived and then grow into natural and self-sustaining power?

There are other matters deserving attention. More research needs to be done concerning how buildings and equipment actually affect learning. There should be studies of learning centers, student use of carrels, long-term effects of language laboratories, and the effects of architecture on the holding power of a college or university.

Another broad problem for research involves finding out how different students react to various educational structures. From the Stephens house plan a strong suggestion emerges that some students take to this personal, intimate kind of education, while other students find it stultifying. Some will take to a Monteith or a New College, but others will not. The profession needs to know more about such matters if the lessons from the newest colleges are to be fully exploited.

And cost needs study. Some new configurations of faculty time are being explored. Although higher education is not a business, it still must observe some business practices if it is to remain viable. To this end the profession needs to know whether a private liberal arts college can keep per unit cost low enough to support reasonably high faculty salaries. It needs to know whether an upper-division college can keep its per unit costs comparable to those of sister institutions having freshmen and sophomore courses to help subsidize upper-level ones. The profession will want to know about the costs of small colleges within large universities as compared with some other systems of organization.

Finally, research is needed that can lead to principles for creating new institutions of higher education. Although the number that will be created between now and the end of the century has been variously estimated, it will probably be somewhere between 500 and 1,000. The people planning those institutions quite properly will look to the experiences here described for lessons and applications. These will be available only if such matters as lead time for building, faculty personnel policies, and curricular planning are studied and if generalizations are produced.

As to the future, one still sees through the glass but darkly. Several items are, however, emerging with some clarity. It seems likely that American youth will be educated in greater and greater numbers in the largest institutions. Three-fourths or more of college students can expect to receive their education in less than one-fourth of the institutions. Thus the experiences of Michigan State, California, Monteith College of Wayne State, and Florida are likely to be the most instructive.

It also seems clear that most students will live in urban areas and will attend urban institutions as commuting students. Thus the Hofstra and Monteith experiments should be of considerable relevance.

The emphases of these newer institutions have appeared to be eclectic rather than based on some substratum of consistent theory or philosophy. They may be contrasted with the experimental colleges created in the 1920s, which seemed to reveal in their practices a strong affinity for the educational philosophy of John Dewey, modified by Freudian psychology. There does not seem to be a similarly transcendent philosophy at present, although the profession seems clearly in search of one. It seems reasonable that a new synthesis will emerge and that its assumptions will be tested and modified by the new colleges created in the decades of the 1950s and 1960s.

SOURCES FOR FURTHER INFORMATION

Baskin, Samuel: "Quest for Quality," *New Dimensions in Higher Education*, no. 7, U.S. Office of Education, Washington, D.C., 1961.

Decade of Experiment, Fund for the Advancement of Education, New York, April, 1961.

Ferrer, Terry (ed.): *Classroom Revolution,* The Herald Tribune, Inc., New York, 1963.

Harris, Seymour E. (ed.): *Higher Education in the United States,* Harvard University Press, Cambridge, Mass., 1960.

Hatch, Winslow R.: "The Experimental College," *New Dimensions in Higher Education,* no. 3, U.S. Office of Education, Washington, D.C., 1960.

Innovation and Experiment in Education: A Progress Report Presented by the President's Science Advisory Committee's Panel on Educational Research and Development, U.S. Office of Education, Washington, D.C., March, 1964.

Miles, Matthew B. (ed.): *Innovation in Education,* Bureau of Publications, Teachers College, Columbia University, New York, 1964.

Sanford, Nevitt (ed.): *The American College: A Psychological and Social Interpretation of the Higher Learning,* John Wiley & Sons, Inc., New York, 1962.

―――, Martin A. Trow, R. Snyder, and David Riesman: "Symposium on Undergraduate Environment," *Proceedings of the Symposium on Undergraduate Environment,* October 18–19, 1962, Bowdoin College, Brunswick, Maine, pp. 32–33, 1963.

Silberman, Charles E.: "The Remaking of American Education," *Fortune,* April, 1961.

Traxler, Arthur E. (ed.): *Keeping Abreast of the Revolution in Education: Report of Twenty-eighth Educational Conference, New York, October 31, 1963,* American Council on Education, Washington, D.C., 1964.

EARL J. McGRATH
L. RICHARD MEETH

2

organizing for teaching
and learning:
the curriculum

*N*early two hundred years after the establishment of Harvard
College the curriculum of that institution consisted of some thirty-
odd courses, all of which had to be successfully pursued by each
student who expected to receive the bachelor's degree. Moreover,
all the teachers had mastered these subjects and could switch from
the teaching of one to another without difficulty. While some minor
variations existed among the other colleges, it is an accurate
generalization to say that the curriculum of one mid-nineteenth-
century college was much like that of another, consisting of a
limited number of courses in ancient languages and literature,
philosophy and religion, and mathematics.

   Such a simple curriculum predetermined certain other characteristics of institutions of higher education. Since the curriculum was

*not composed of a score of separate subject-matter units, the intel-
lectual interests were not narrowly limited, as they are today, by
requirements in a major field or even a subdivision thereof. The
faculty consisted of men whose learning was broad in terms of the
knowledge of the day and whose professional activities were quite
unspecialized. And since the large, public universities had not come
on the scene, education was still largely limited to the select few.*

*No characteristic of American higher education has undergone
more rapid and basic change than the curriculum. These changes
have raised serious questions regarding the nature and organization
of, and procedures to be employed in, the curriculum and have
presented trying problems with which faculties and administrators
are now trying to deal. This chapter reviews developments in this
area.*

CURRICULUM CHANGE: SOME FACTORS IN THE DEVELOPING PATTERN

Since the latter part of the nineteenth century, American institutions of higher education have undergone profound changes. These
changes are most sharply reflected in the organization of the colleges' instructional programs, in the range of services offered, and
in the type and quantity of instruction. There were several influences making for these changes: rapid growth of new knowledge;
evolving conceptions of the purposes of higher education; and
developments in industry, commerce, and technology that have created new job demands and career opportunities.

The rapid growth of knowledge

Though knowledge began to expand before the establishment of
universities in this country in the late nineteenth century, 1876, the
year that Johns Hopkins was founded, may be taken as the date
when university work, with its emphasis on research and extensions
of boundaries of learning, began to be the ideal for institutions of
higher education. The influence of scholars returning from German

universities and a public demand for other types of instruction caused many new disciplines to be introduced into our institutions of higher education. The curriculum of the liberal arts colleges underwent a transformation, and soon thereafter entirely new university divisions were established, such as schools of engineering, agriculture, and business administration. Under these influences, specialization in learning soon became the order of the day. The omnibus courses in natural history and natural philosophy, for example, soon broke up into departments of physics, chemistry, geology, botany, astronomy, and others. Ancient history was soon superseded by specializations in the history of Europe, the history of the United States, the history of England, etc., and a great host of social sciences little known a few years earlier, such as sociology, anthropology, economics, psychology, and political science, assumed their places in the college curriculum among their older subject-matter peers.

With this rank growth of instructional units, it soon became obvious that students could no longer be required to pursue one common curriculum. The alternatives devised to take care of this problem were the elective principle in the liberal arts colleges, under which students chose various courses in accordance with their own peculiar interests and abilities, and the establishment of new professional schools with quite different programs of specialized instruction. Neither of these solutions proved entirely satisfactory, and they have left residual curriculum problems that will be discussed later.

Education for all

A second factor in the evolution of the curriculum which is causing current problems springs from a social rather than an educational source. The celebrated Harvard historian, Samuel Eliot Morison, in speaking of the social selectivity of the early American college, has this to say:

Children must learn to read the Bible, that they might know God's truth, and to write and cipher, as an aid to honest living; chosen boys must be taught the learned language in which the world's best thought and literature were still to be found; and a smaller selection of youths must be given university training, in order to furnish the

State with competent rulers, the Church with a learned Clergy, and society with cultured men.[1]

For the past 100 years, however, the conviction has grown among our leaders and our citizens generally that education is not only the avenue to personal success but also a social necessity in a democracy in which all the people decide the general social, economic, and political welfare. Consequently, there has been a constant extension of educational opportunity. As a result of the widespread recognition of the value of education, many youths who achieve a high school education today wish to attend some institution of higher learning, causing college enrollment to continue to grow at an accelerating speed. In 1900 only one young person of college age in twenty-five attended an institution of higher education; today the number is about one in three, and in some communities 80 or 90 per cent of the high school graduates go on for advanced study at a college or university.

This tremendous increase in college and university attendance has been accomplished by increasing diversification of student abilities, interests, and vocational objectives. Though little reliable information exists with regard to the scholastic aptitude of students 100 years ago, the facts available today show an enormous range in ability among those who seek a higher education. The complex combination of abilities and vocational objectives is a matter with which those who have responsibility for the design of the curriculum today must necessarily concern themselves.

New career possibilities

There has also been a change in occupational opportunities open to college graduates. In the early days of the Republic, the vast majority of young men who were fortunate enough to attend college were destined to become members of the professional or white-collar classes—lawyers, statesmen, doctors, ministers, or leading businessmen.[2]

Now, however, hundreds of occupations cannot be entered with-

[1] Samuel Eliot Morison, *The Founding of Harvard College,* Harvard University Press, Cambridge, Mass., 1935, p. 150.
[2] For a fuller discussion of this subject, see Earl J. McGrath, *Liberal Education in the Professions,* Bureau of Publications, Teachers College, Columbia University, New York, 1959, chap. 1.

out a higher education. The rather simple society that existed in this country even as late as 1900 placed few demands on colleges and universities for specialized instruction. Today, however, industrial and commercial enterprises have expanded and diversified to the extent that literally hundreds of new vocations exist that require some specialized training, and those who have studied the matter report that these occupations increase at the rate of ten or more a year.

Moreover, other agencies such as libraries, welfare organizations, schools and technical institutes, the church, and a host of other social organizations now demand types of specialized higher education totally unknown at the turn of the century. The government itself, as it has become larger and concerned with many more aspects of American life, now requires a large corps of highly educated persons to manage and carry out its various functions. Recent activity in space science is only the most dramatic of government participation in new fields. All these developments in American society require that institutions of higher education consider whether or not their present curricula adequately serve the society that sustains them and, if not, what changes need to be made.

This necessarily limited background must serve as the point of departure for a consideration of the present character of the curriculum in institutions of higher education and as the basis for an evaluation of changes now being made or contemplated to improve the services of these institutions. This chapter obviously cannot survey in detail all the curricular changes occurring in the entire enterprise of American higher education. Consequently, the primary concern will be with the curricula of the undergraduate liberal arts colleges and the undergraduate professional schools; and even in these institutions, only a selection of innovations and modifications can be considered.

DEVELOPMENTS IN LIBERAL ARTS COLLEGES
Focus on general education

Though recent curricular developments in the liberal arts college and the undergraduate professional school have been somewhat different, they have one thing in common. In the past twenty-five years, faculty members in both liberal arts colleges and other undergraduate divisions, such as business administration, engineering, nursing, and pharmacy, have shown a growing interest in the general education of their students outside their major field or professional specialization. This concern has resulted in the development of a great variety of programs of general education, the primary purpose of which is to introduce the student to a broad range of intellectual disciplines outside the field of his own specialization. So many books and articles have been written on this subject in justification of the attendant curricular modifications that no detailed review is needed. Suffice it to say that there is hardly an undergraduate institution in the country whose faculty has not changed its purpose and program to some extent to provide a more ample general education for its students. This trend toward liberal or general education is even more sharply reflected in some of the new college programs, such as those at Monteith College of Wayne State University and Florida Presbyterian College at St. Petersburg, where there is a decided emphasis on continuing the student's general education throughout his four years at college (as contrasted with most programs, which tend to limit these experiences to the student's first two years of college). Chapter 1 describes these new college programs in greater detail.

The most common of the earlier arrangements to provide a general education was to have a group of required survey courses, which included a great range of information drawn from many specialized disciplines. A few years' experience with this kind of curricular structure, however, revealed serious defects. The most frequent criticism was that faculties attempted to include too much subject matter from the various constituent disciplines, which resulted in superficiality and excessive fragmentation. It was contended that even though students may acquire a considerable array of knowledge, they have been so concerned with the acquisition of facts that they fail to penetrate any subject in sufficient depth to understand its major generalizations or to master its intellectual methodological processes.

Accordingly, institutions that now retain requirements in general education have commonly reduced the scope of material covered in the various courses in the social sciences, the natural sciences, and the humanities, and the topics retained have been more intensively studied. For example, the early survey course in literature, which commonly covered the entire range of literature from *Beowulf* to Virginia Woolf, has now been changed into a course that treats intensively a few great literary works. Moreover, these masterpieces are generally not chosen solely from the English language but, rather, include such great writings in translation as the works of

Aristotle and Plato, Goethe, Dante, Thomas Aquinas, Cervantes, and others.

Similarly, courses in the natural sciences now generally stress selected experiments that led to unusual advances in the various branches of science. An example is the course James B. Conant taught at Harvard, the content of which he has collected in the volume *Science and Common Sense*. In this general course and in others like it, no attempt was made to treat the subject matter of a single discipline systematically, as is done in an elementary course in chemistry, physics, or biology which serves the purposes of students intending to major in the field. Instead he used a series of "case histories" to illustrate what he calls the principles of the "tactics and strategy" of science.[3]

The idea of the general major

One feature of the general education movement of special and continuing significance is the general major, which has become more common in recent years. American civilization is one such major that involves courses, and frequently individualized instruction as well, in American literature, philosophy, and history. In such a major, the student has a better opportunity to observe the evolution and the dominant characteristics of American culture than he could if he concentrated in any one of the constituent departments. The University of Florida has several general majors in its College of Arts and Science, such as American area studies, social administration, and international affairs.

Some institutions have inaugurated optional majors in natural science. Muhlenberg College, for example, offers a program of this type, which requires the student to take instruction in physics, chemistry, biology, and mathematics rather than concentrate in any one of these four fields. The popularity and success of this program at Muhlenberg are attested by the fact that in a recent graduating class of 150 students, 32 elected this natural science major. This kind of broad major is peculiarly adapted to the needs of students preparing for admission to a professional school, such as a school of medicine, law, dentistry, or social work, but it is equally valuable to the student who does not want to concentrate heavily in a single department.

[3] James B. Conant, *Science and Common Sense,* Yale University Press, New Haven, Conn., 1961, preface to paperback edition.

Another type of general major relates to non-Western civilizations. Though these new programs cover various areas of the world, they deal preponderantly with Asiatic culture. Instead of majoring in economics or history or geography and concentrating on a certain country or region, the student interested in a particular area pursues a major that customarily combines courses and supporting individualized instruction drawn from the social sciences and humanities of that region. The Latin American Study Program at the University of Florida and the Asian Studies Program at the University of Hawaii, in the latter of which students concentrate in three of the fields of anthropology, art, geography, government, history, philosophy, and sociology, are leading examples of this emerging general major.

Ordinarily, institutions do not establish one set curriculum in these areas but, rather, design each student's program in accordance with the availability of instruction in several departments and the student's own individual interests. Frequently, such curricular options have a practical or vocational objective; that is, the student pursues the area major to prepare for employment as a foreign service officer in the State Department or for employment in an American firm such as an oil company that needs staff members to work in other sections of the world.

In spite of the broad realization in the teaching profession of the value of a comprehensive general education, it should be noted that the pressure for specialization continues and that in some quarters the representatives of specialized learning have had some success in weakening programs of general studies, even those established for years in prominent institutions.

Do colleges have a responsibility to provide a general education that, like its precursor, the traditional liberal arts curriculum, prepares graduates for an intelligent private and civic life, or are they to become in fact professional schools, concerned primarily with vocational preparation for the world of scholarship, business, and industry, or the other professions? Some institutions seem to be moving toward the former goal and others toward the latter, and some fortunately have been able to achieve both. It would seem to be in the best interests of our culture at large to have institutions provide both a broad base of knowledge in the major areas of learning and enough specialization to accustom the student to intellectual work of a high order within a narrow branch of scholarship or to prepare him in the specialized activities of the practice of a profession such as law, medicine, or engineering. The achievement of both these purposes affords an extraordinary challenge to faculties to design appropriate programs of studies.

Education for world affairs

Another significant development in the curriculum of liberal arts colleges relates to the need for all educated Americans to know more about other cultures and other peoples. In a recent volume, Percy W. Bidwell says: "Higher education in the United States is more provincial than in any comparable country. . . . Seniors emerge from our colleges with hardly any more acquaintance with foreign affairs than when they entered as freshmen. . . . College graduates are not adequately informed, interested, realistic, sensitive, and responsible so far as events and conditions outside the United States are concerned."[4]

This serious indictment of instruction in our colleges and universities concerning other areas of the world is based upon a very careful analysis of curricular offerings in representative institutions and on a test actually administered to students in these institutions. It is significant that the average student tested could answer correctly only 55 per cent of the questions asked.

Chapter 4 reviews developments in undergraduate programs of study abroad. Where well conceived and well directed, these programs contribute importantly to this objective of education for world affairs. Much, however, needs to be done within the undergraduate curriculum itself if our college graduate is to be adequately informed and responsible about the world beyond the United States.

While recognizing that some very good courses are offered in various aspects of international matters, Dr. Bidwell points out that these are usually elected by only a few students and frequently by those who are going to enter an occupation related to such studies. He expresses the considered opinion that if our young people generally are to gain an understanding of what is going on in the world outside their own country and culture, the colleges must provide courses in international affairs at the freshman and sophomore levels. These courses must not be specialized instruction, which might be the preoccupation of the professor devoting his time to systematic and intensive study of some area of the world, but rather

[4] Percy W. Bidwell, *Undergraduate Education and World Affairs,* King's Crown Press, New York, 1962, pp. 4–5.

general courses that introduce students to the economic, social, anthropological, political, and cultural problems that now exist in various parts of the world.

A few colleges and universities sympathetic with Dr. Bidwell's views have launched general courses in non-Western civilization for lower-division students. Columbia College, for example, has a two-year sequence in Oriental civilization, and Harvard has another entitled Far Eastern Civilization. The University of Minnesota offers a course called the History of Asia, in which two-thirds of the students are drawn from the lower divisions of the university. The University of Michigan has introduced a course in Asian civilization open only to freshmen and sophomores.

More so than ever, faculties are concerned about curricular arrangements that will enable the majority of undergraduates to gain an understanding of the peoples of other lands, who now, because of increased communications and rapid transportation, are really our neighbors. It can be expected that within the next few years, most colleges will offer instruction for the nonmajor in non-Western civilizations as well as constellations of more specialized courses in international affairs for those who wish to take a general major in this field.

Reduction in the number of course offerings

Recent studies show that the curricula of liberal arts colleges have become greatly proliferated and fragmented.[5] Institutional programs have been divided into eighteen or twenty departments, and the departments in turn have splintered their offerings into hundreds of courses, often with no justification other than the teacher's desire to pursue his own scholarly interests in research and publication. The elaborate fragmentation seems to bear very little relationship to the number of students served. For example, one college with 620 students offers 1,117 hours of different instruction (sections of the same course not counted), while another with 1,591 students schedules only 1,124 hours. The ratio of credit hours offered to the number of students in the first college is 1.80 but .71 in the second.

The total picture suggests not only that the offerings in many departments of many colleges are excessive but also that the pro-

[5] Earl J. McGrath, *Memo to a College Faculty Member,* Bureau of Publications, Teachers College, Columbia University, New York, 1961.

grams of the various departments have often been expanded for reasons little related to the needs of undergraduates. These extensive offerings could be justified in part if it could be clearly demonstrated that they constitute essential elements in a liberal education or indispensable preparation for graduate work. But the statements of department heads who preside over a small range of offerings warrant neither conclusion. When asked whether their majors had had a less than adequate liberal education, they almost uniformly answered negatively, and with one exception they expressed no desire to add more courses. When asked whether their students had encountered difficulty in gaining admission to, or maintaining creditable records in, reputable graduate schools, almost all these department heads asserted that few of their graduates had had any such difficulties and that when they did, their failures were ascribable to causes other than the narrowness of their preparation.

This extravagant offering of advanced specialized instruction in the various disciplines has had a deleterious effect on most institutions. In the first place, it has adversely affected the education of undergraduate students by permitting them to enroll for highly advanced and specialized courses that ought more properly to be offered in professional or graduate schools. Their undergraduate education is commensurately narrowed, since they are prevented from taking courses in fields outside their major.

Second, most undergraduate colleges do not have sufficiently high enrollment to provide classes of economically justifiable size at the junior and senior levels. Since most colleges suffer a student mortality rate of 25 to 50 per cent between the freshman and junior years, and since they usually have some fifteen to twenty departments, the number of student majors in most departments is necessarily small. When these few students are scattered among the usual broad range of optional courses in the various departments, classes often have fewer than ten and, many times, fewer than five students. Indeed, in one college studied, over 40 per cent of the classes scheduled during a two-year period registered ten or fewer students, often only two or three. Advanced instruction, therefore, becomes very expensive. The impact of these wasteful economic practices on institutional status is often severe.[6] Institutions are beginning to recognize that because of the expense of advanced instruction for few students, they are unable to provide salaries of

[6] For a fuller discussion of this problem of better use of staff and faculties, see Chap. 12, Dollars and Cents: Some Hard Facts.

suitable magnitude to compete with the larger institutions. The quality of their programs is correspondingly reduced.

Concerned about these problems of overspecialization and economy, a number of institutions with the aid of grants from the Fund for the Advancement of Education have undertaken studies of ways by which they might eliminate proliferation and duplication in their course offerings. Among these colleges were Lehigh University, Wellesley, Wabash, and Philander Smith.[7] In other studies, Franklin and Marshall College decided that eighty courses could be eliminated from its curriculum without any damage to the educational program; MacMurray College cut 200 courses from its program on the grounds that the college should avoid specialized offerings and center its efforts on a first-class liberal arts education; and Parsons College, in a reorganization of its program, cut its curriculum from 755 to 169 courses.

Few, if any, liberal arts colleges need their present comprehensive curriculum offerings. It can be expected that in the years immediately ahead, many other faculties will reexamine their offerings department by department and will determine whether or not they constitute an essential element of a liberal arts education or required basic instruction for advanced study in a graduate or professional school.

Improvement of course content

Special mention needs to be made here of a number of national commissions and study groups that have been formed in an attempt to discover ways by which subject matter in various areas of the curriculum might be better organized and presented. The National Science Foundation, the Carnegie Corporation, the Ford Foundation, and the U.S. Office of Education have been especially prominent in lending support to these efforts. While the great majority of projects undertaken thus far have been in the physical and natural sciences (with the exception of the U.S. Office of Education projects, which have given particular attention to languages and social studies), there is reason to hope that comparable studies may soon

[7] *Better Utilization of College Teaching Resources: A Report by the Committee on Utilization of College Teaching Resources,* Fund for the Advancement of Education, New York, May, 1959, p. 43.

be under way in the social sciences and humanities, where two such groups have recently been formed: the Social Science Education Consortium of Midwest Universities, under the Committee on Institutional Cooperation of the Big Ten, and the Commission on Humanities, under the American Council of Learned Societies.[8] While most projects undertaken thus far have been at the elementary and secondary school levels, a number of college-level studies are now under way. Two of the science study groups are described below.

The Commission on College Physics[9] was established in 1960 with the aid of a grant from the National Science Foundation. The committee describes its more immediate goals as (*1*) bringing together faculty members in physics to share ideas and experiences and to provide large-scale team efforts for the study of the structure or patterns by which specific course offerings might best be developed; (*2*) encouraging publication of review articles and books, designing laboratory experiments and apparatus and producing films designed to improve the quality and extent of physics instruction, and disseminating materials that will be of value in the early introduction of such topics as "Special Relativity," "Quantum Theory," and other "modern" topics into the undergraduate physics courses; (*3*) correlating work being done by separate groups to produce college-level films; and (*4*) arranging for the preparation and publication of articles that will make available to instructors information on new developments in physics. More recently the group has recommended the establishment of a new kind of curriculum which ". . . emphasizes the interpretation of physics and

---

[8] For a first report of work of the commission, see *Report of the Commission on the Humanities, American Council of Learned Societies,* New York, 1964.

[9] Headquarters for the commission is the Physics and Astronomy Building, University of Michigan, Ann Arbor, Mich. For the most recent report of the work of this group, see "Progress Report of the Commission on College Physics (June, 1962, to May, 1964)," *American Journal of Physics,* vol. 32, no. 6, pp. 398–440, American Association of Physics Teachers and American Institute of Physics, Lancaster, Pa., June, 1964. For a description of the work of various curriculum study groups (Biological Sciences Curriculum Study, Chemical Bond Approach Project, the School Mathematics Study Group, the Anthropology Curriculum Study Project, and others), see John I. Goodlad, *School Curriculum Reform in the United States,* Fund for the Advancement of Education, New York, March, 1964; and *ESI Quarterly Report,* Educational Services Incorporated, Watertown, Mass., Winter–Spring, 1964.

its re-integration with other parts of our culture."[10] The committee sees as one of its special concerns the problem of relationships between science and society. To meet the needs in this area, the committee is giving attention to the development of programs designed to provide broad but rigorous undergraduate training in physics for students who are planning to be physicians, lawyers, high school teachers, biophysicists, government officials, or public planners or administrators.

The Committee on the Undergraduate Program in Mathematics[11] is a division of the Mathematical Association of America. It is charged with making recommendations for the improvement of college and university undergraduate mathematics curricula. The committee is supported by grants from the Ford Foundation and the National Science Foundation. The committee has sought to stimulate curriculum revision through conference and study groups and the publication of suggested course outlines. It has also given attention to the development of programs for the mathematics preparation of engineers, physical scientists, social scientists, and other groups. An honors program for mathematics specialists in other disciplines has also been developed.

Other developments

Although separately treated in other chapters of this book, a number of other developments need mention here because they bear significantly on this question of the nature and organization of the college curriculum. Of special note are the new programs in independent study, programs of study abroad, honors programs, the use of the newer media (television, audio-visual aids, and programed instruction), and developments in the use of off-campus work and field experience.[12]

[10] "Recommendations of the Second Ann Arbor Conference on Undergraduate Curricula for Physics Majors," *American Journal of Physics,* vol. 31, no. 5, p. 329, May, 1963.
[11] Headquarters for the committee is P.O. Box 124, Berkeley 11, Calif.
[12] For a fuller review of these developments, the reader is referred to the following chapters: Chap. 3, The Student on His Own: Independent Study; Chap. 4, The Student Abroad; Chap. 5, The Abler Student; Chap. 6, Providing the Conditions for Learning: The "New" Media; and Chap. 8, Extending the Educational Environment: The Community as a Resource for Learning.

Independent study. While independent study programs have been in existence for many years, these programs have long been considered to be the special province of the superior or abler student. What is new in some of the more recent experimentation in the use of independent study is the attempt to extend these experiences to all students rather than regarding independent study as something to be reserved for the abler or superior student alone. Thus in recent years a number of colleges and universities, including both public and private institutions, have sought to employ this concept of independent study so as to include a wide range of students at all levels of ability. Of significance also has been the attempt to use these independent study procedures at the beginning or freshman year level as contrasted with the usual tendency to hold these experiences for the student's senior year.

Study-abroad programs. Mention has previously been made of the Bidwell report and the growing emphasis in our college programs on education for world affairs. The programs of study abroad represent one approach to this problem. These programs are bound to have an increasing effect on the undergraduate curriculum: in the amount of time to be devoted to the orientation of the student for study abroad; in the development of language and special-area courses needed to prepare the student for his experience abroad; and in the development of new course and seminar experiences designed to help him relate and more fully integrate his study-abroad experience. It is likely that a number of these experiences will be incorporated into the student's study-abroad program itself. It seems clear, however, that these programs will also have a significant effect on the undergraduate curriculum.

Honors programs. A great deal of attention has been given in recent years to the special needs of the abler or superior student. Of particular note are the many developments in the use of special honors courses and seminars within the framework of a total honors program. The work of the Inter-University Committee for the Superior Student at Boulder, Colorado, has been of particular importance in giving leadership to this movement and in setting guidelines for the development of effective programs for the honors student. These programs hold implications for curriculum change, not only for the abler student but for other students as well.

The new media. Much has been written about the role of the new technology in the organization of teaching and learning. Of particular note is the attention being given today to the development of a systems concept in the organization of the student's learning experiences and the growing employment of the learning resources center as a core unit in instruction. There are, of course, many cautions that need to be stressed in the employment of the new media. As William Clark Trow notes in his study on the teacher and technology: "The millennium for education will not be ushered in by the purchase of a truckload of teaching machines and another of television equipment."[13] There is little question, however, that when used sensitively and intelligently, television, audio-visual aids, and programed instruction can contribute markedly to enrichment of the curriculum. This is especially the case in such subjects as foreign languages and sciences.

Work and field experience. An increasing number of colleges are requiring work experience of their students as a regular part of the student's college program. The trend here is not so much toward a pattern which alternates work and study, as is the case with colleges under the cooperative plan, but rather toward the development of calendar plans that require or encourage the student to spend one or more quarters of his college career in some kind of work activity or field or other off-campus project. New programs recently instituted at Kalamazoo, Earlham, and Beloit Colleges are typical of these plans.

DEVELOPMENTS IN PROFESSIONAL SCHOOLS

The curriculum developments occurring in undergraduate professional schools are in many ways even more radical and therefore more significant than those occurring in liberal arts colleges. These changes are described below.

[13] William Clark Trow, *Teacher and Technology: New Designs for Learning,* Meredith Publishing Company, Des Moines, Iowa, 1963, p. 180.

Increase in liberal arts instruction

The first development is an increase in the amount of instruction in the liberal arts and sciences now embodied in the total education of undergraduate professional students. The studies made by the Institute of Higher Education of various professional schools, such as schools of business administration, engineering, pharmacy, and nursing, show that although there are considerable differences among these professions, all the schools are moving toward a larger component of liberal studies as part of their undergraduate curriculum. The leaders in these fields of professional education recognize that a broader base in the various academic disciplines is essential not only for an informed citizenship and a satisfying personal life but also as an essential element in professional competence and success. A recent study in schools of business administration, for example, shows that a very large percentage of these institutions either have already achieved or are approaching the ideal of 50 per cent of instruction in the liberal arts and science, that is, in courses related to the practice of business.[14]

The pharmacy schools offer another example of this trend. In 1960 the Association of Schools of Pharmacy imposed the requirement that all schools inaugurate a five-year program. One of the primary reasons for this extension of undergraduate education in pharmacy was to enable the schools to include a larger unit of instruction in subjects not related to the practice of pharmacy. A study conducted by the Institute of Higher Education of pharmacy schools shows that many took advantage of this opportunity to expand their nonprofessional offerings but that, regrettably, some increased the specialized instruction in the basic sciences or in pharmacy proper rather than in the nonprofessional subjects.[15] In engineering, a broadening of the liberal arts base of professional education also has occurred in recent years in such institutions as Massachusetts Institute of Technology, Carnegie Institute of Tech-

[14] From an address given by Earl J. McGrath at the meeting of the National Organization of the Council for Professional Education for Business, Dec. 27, 1962, entitled "Collegiate Schools of Business: A Further Appraisal."
[15] James Newcomer, Kevin P. Bunnell, and Earl J. McGrath, *Liberal Education and Pharmacy*, Bureau of Publications, Teachers College, Columbia University, New York, 1961.

nology, Rensselaer Institute of Technology, and Case Institute of Technology. Developments in these institutions are merely illustrative of similar developments that are taking place generally in the entire engineering field.

Core requirement of related studies

The second major curriculum development in professional education concerns the core of professionally related studies. Institutions are attempting to introduce students to the subject matter basic to advanced specialization through a required group of courses providing general facts and theory. In the field of business administration, for example, many institutions require all students to take a common program of studies in accounting, finance, management, and marketing, supplemented, of course, by basic instruction in the field of economics. This core of instruction combined with the 50 per cent requirement in general education outside the field of business provides the general body of fact and theory that the successful businessman will need, regardless of his ultimate choice of a specialized occupation. In engineering, the core commonly consists of instruction in physics, chemistry, mathematics, and often economics. Additional common courses include those in the various engineering sciences. Accompanying these developments is the practice of limiting the amount of instruction the student can take in a specialized engineering field. A considerable number of undergraduate professional school programs in other fields could be cited to reveal this almost universal trend toward requiring a core of instruction basic to further specialization in a particular occupation.

Reduction in specialized instruction

The third major development in the curricula of professional schools concerns a reduction in the amount of instruction offered within a given specialized area. Concretely, this means that instead of allowing the student to take forty or fifty hours of instruction in such a specialized occupational field as insurance or marketing in business administration, civil or chemical engineering in engineering, or drugstore administration in pharmacy, the schools are now considering reducing the permitted amount of instruction in these curricular specializations. To take the place of this early concentration, professional schools tend to require those who wish to advance into the upper levels of the profession to take specialized work at the graduate level. In engineering, for example, the undergraduate gets a sound general education, which includes instruction in the various engineering sciences in a core curriculum, but if he wishes to advance himself in the specialized branches of engineering, such as electrical or aeronautical engineering, he must be prepared to take further instruction in these fields after he receives his bachelor's degree.

Offerings by business, industry, and government groups

Another development in American society that has significant curriculum implications is continuing education pursued under the auspices of a firm or the government. Though such opportunities for advanced study cannot properly be considered part of the curricular developments in institutions of higher education, it is, nevertheless, appropriate to remark that much of the specialized instruction, which earlier would have been included in an undergraduate curriculum, is now offered in factories, other business enterprises, and government agencies. To understand the curriculum developments in professional schools, one must be familiar with two volumes recently published by Prof. Harold F. Clark, of Columbia University, entitled *Classrooms in the Factories* and *Classrooms in the Stores,*[16] which provide detailed and reliable information about postgraduate instruction that should have, and no doubt already is having, a profound influence on undergraduate programs of instruction.

It should be concluded from the foregoing remarks about the reduced amount of specialized instruction in the undergraduate curriculum that fewer specialties are offered. In some schools—for example, in the field of business administration—the number of majors offered has been reduced from seventeen or eighteen to five or six. On the other hand, new specialties are arising as economic

---

[16] Harold F. Clark and Harold S. Sloan, *Classrooms in the Factories,* New York University Press, New York, 1960; Harold F. Clark, Harold S. Sloan, and Charles A. Hebert, *Classrooms in the Stores,* Roxbury Press, Inc., Sweet Springs, Mo., 1962.

and social demands become more extensive and complex. Thus insurance has come to embrace a highly specialized group of occupations. It is not surprising, therefore, that one institution in New York City, the College of Insurance, has recently established degree programs in this important field of business enterprise. It is also significant, however, that this program includes both subject matter in the liberal arts and sciences and courses related generally to the practice of business rather than specifically to the activities of the insurance enterprise.[17]

In contrast to the practices in most European universities, these developments in specialized programs of study are consistent with our democratic, social, and educational philosophy of providing a diversity of instruction in our colleges and universities. They also are consistent with the developing needs in our culture for persons who possess specialized knowledge and skills as well as a sound general education for the manifold responsibilities of life outside a particular occupation.

SUMMING UP

One could sum up the developments in liberal arts colleges and undergraduate professional schools by saying that the whole enterprise of American higher education seems to be moving toward the ideal of preparing young people for the responsibilities of citizenship and private life and, at the same time, offering the basic instruction preparatory to entrance into a productive, gainful occupation. That this combination of general and specialized instruction meets the approval of most educators is evident from a survey of opinion conducted by the Institute of Higher Education. One study[18] showed that faculty members in the cooperating institutions believe generally that students should have a broad liberal education as well as technical instruction related to their professional field. Moreover, they believe that ideally these two types of subject matter should not be separated in the college years but, rather,

[17] See the catalog of the College of Insurance, 150 William St., New York.
[18] Paul L. Dressel, Lewis B. Mayhew, and Earl J. McGrath, *The Liberal Arts as Viewed by Faculty Members in Professional Schools,* Bureau of Publications, Teachers College, Columbia University, New York, 1959.

should run concurrently. This means that faculty members generally believe that instead of concluding liberal education and beginning a course of instruction in business, pharmacy, or engineering, instruction in the liberal arts subjects should preponderate in the early years of the curriculum, and specialized instruction in the later years. Thus the student would be able to see the relationship between the general instruction he is required to take and his long-range vocational goals. Hence, his motivation could be expected to increase commensurately in liberal as well as professional courses.

Curricula in institutions of higher education have been and continue to be in a fluid condition. It is a healthy sign that faculties are constantly reexamining the objectives of their programs, carrying on a great variety of experiments, and launching many curricular innovations calculated to improve the education that our young people receive. New developments in independent study, study-abroad programs, the use of the new media, work- and field-experience programs, and programs for the abler student are having a significant impact on the nature and organization of the college curriculum. These changes may be expected to expand and accelerate in the years ahead, and the end result will unquestionably be an improved higher education for all. Unlike the curricula of institutions in other lands, ours have been under constant reexamination for decades.

The responsiveness of our institutions of higher education in providing new types of instruction to an increasing diversity of American youth has resulted in some discomfort for those concerned and also occasionally in abortive efforts. On balance, however, it can be said that the ready adaptability of the curricula in institutions of higher education in the United States to emerging social conditions has been responsible, directly and indirectly, for much of our national prosperity and individual well-being.

SOURCES FOR FURTHER INFORMATION

American Council of Learned Societies and the National Council for the Social Studies: *The Social Studies and the Social Sciences,* Harcourt, Brace & World, Inc., New York, 1962.

Cole, Charles C., Jr., and Lanora G. Lewis: "Flexibility in the Undergraduate Curriculum," *New Dimensions in Higher Edu-*

cation, no. 10, U.S. Office of Education, Washington, D.C., 1962.

"Current Curriculum Developments," *NEA Journal,* vol. 52, no. 8, pp. 47–48, National Education Association, Washington, D.C., November, 1963.

Dressel, Paul L.: *The Undergraduate Curriculum in Higher Education,* Center for Applied Research in Education, Inc., Washington, D.C., 1963.

ESI Quarterly Report, Educational Services Incorporated, Watertown, Mass., Winter–Spring, 1964.

Gardner, John W.: *Excellence,* Harper & Row, Publishers, Incorporated, New York, 1961.

Goodlad, John I.: *School Curriculum Reform in the United States,* Fund for the Advancement of Education, New York, March, 1964.

Hatch, Winslow R.: "What Standards Do We Raise?" *New Dimensions in Higher Education,* no. 12, U.S. Office of Education, Washington, D.C., 1963.

McGrath, Earl J.: *Memo to a College Faculty Member,* Bureau of Publications, Teachers College, Columbia University, New York, 1961.

The New School Science, American Association for the Advancement of Science, Washington, D.C., 1963.

Report of the Commission on the Humanities, American Council of Learned Societies, New York, 1964.

The Scholars Look at the Schools: A Report of the Disciplines Seminar, Project on the Instructional Program of the Public Schools, National Education Association, Washington, D.C., 1962.

"Self-renewal in the Liberal Arts Curriculum," *CASC Newsletter,* vol. 8, no. 12, The Council for the Advancement of Small Colleges, Inc., Washington, D.C., August, 1964.

Thomas Russell: *The Search for a Common Learning: General Education,* 1800–1960, McGraw-Hill Book Company, New York, 1962.

Woodring, Paul, and John Scanlon: *American Education Today,* McGraw-Hill Book Company, New York, 1963.

BRUCE DEARING

3

the student on his own:
independent study

*A*lbert Einstein once said: "It is nothing short of a miracle
that modern methods of instruction have not yet entirely strangled
the holy curiosity of inquiry." The danger to that "holy curiosity"
comes not so much from bad teachers as from a rigid system of
instruction that attempts to satisfy curiosity only at a particular
time, in a particular place, and in a particular way. The joy that
should come from the satisfaction of intellectual hunger is too
often lost in a system of higher education which too often insists
that in order to learn, students must sit in classes for a set
number of hours over a set number of weeks. Education comes in
"packages," and while the size of the package may vary
from two or three credit hours to five credit hours, credit for
learning and learning itself are assumed to bear a close

*relationship to the number of hours a student sits in the college
classroom.*

*Pressed by the need for maintaining, if not improving, the
quality of the student's educational experience, a number of
colleges and universities have begun to seek out new ways of teaching and learning. Of particular interest are the attempts to make
greater use of independent study as a part of the teacher's
regular teaching procedures. This chapter describes some of the
uses of independent study on the American college campus.*

TEACHERS, STUDENTS, CLASSROOMS, AND LEARNING: SOME LONG–FELT CONCERNS

"It is not possible to teach anyone anything; it is only possible so
to arrange things that he may learn." So runs an argument that
appears to have increasing support in educational research and
inquiry. The surge toward innovation, which will place the student
more on his own to learn at his own pace things for which he has
an awakened interest and motivation, has many precedents and
antecedents. The textbook and the structured course of lectures,
directed discussions, and examinations demanding a patterned response are, after all, fairly recent phenomena. A persistent tradition in European education is an open situation in which a student prepares on his own through reading, travel, and attendance
at lectures as he chooses and through conversations with tutors,
fellow students, and perhaps even barmaids and idlers for a set of
examinations he will be permitted to undertake when he considers
himself ready. Surely this tradition at Oxford was in the mind and
experience of Frank Aydelotte, the Rhodes scholar who introduced
the honors program at Swarthmore and described the innovation
as "breaking the academic lockstep."[1]

The idea of moving as rapidly as one chooses through a prescribed curriculum and of sitting for examinations whenever one
is prepared, by whatever means, has been significantly essayed at
Johns Hopkins and at Chicago under Chancellor Hutchins. The

[1] Frank Aydelotte, *Breaking the Academic Lockstep,* Harper & Row,
Publishers, Incorporated, New York, 1944.

knowledge that individual persons learn at different rates and by different means and that learning has a great deal to do with such complicated matters as motivation, perception, organization, feedback mechanisms, and active participation rather than passive submission has been familiar to effective teachers at least since Plato and is not claimed as a fresh discovery by Dewey, Skinner, or any of the contemporary figures who have come to be associated with a trend toward independent study. What then accounts for the current interest in breaking out of the now well-established pattern of instruction in lecture-discussion groups of medium size, meeting at regularly specified intervals in a conventional classroom?

One answer, no doubt, lies in the recognition of the waste and inefficiency of a system geared to a tiny homogeneous minority, when we in America are committed to educating a vast and heterogeneous majority. Although independent study has been thought of most often as a release of the swift and able learner from bondage to a plodding pace, permitting him to leap ahead with joy, it may equally well be thought of as an emancipation of the slower but still respectable learner from a dizzying pace that leaves him baffled and defeated. Another factor in this recognition is the necessity for accommodation to a growing shortage of fully qualified teachers. The conventional classroom approach to learning must in very many areas give way before the intractable facts that there are already too few teachers and too few classrooms to accommodate the numbers entering college now, let alone the numbers anticipated in the near future. The Fund for the Advancement of Education has effectively dramatized this problem and has supported a great deal of the relevant experimentation.[2]

A second major impetus to the development of programs of independent study is the mounting evidence that mere acquisition of facts and abstract principles is far from enough to produce an educated person. For one thing, the body of fact, particularly in the sciences, is multiplying at a dazzling rate. Intellectual capital acquired during college and even graduate school years must be continually reinvested and augmented if one is to maintain effectiveness in a profession. A person who is expecting, or who is expected, to continue to learn throughout his active life must free

[2] *Better Utilization of College Teaching Resources: A Report by the Committee on Utilization of College Teaching Resources,* Fund for the Advancement of Education, New York, May, 1959.

himself from reliance upon the teacher and the digested text and perfect at least some of the tools of independent study.

A third force pressing in the direction of independent study is the growing conviction that learning is essentially an active rather than a passive process. Higher education should be something more than mere conditioning, and, to the extent that it is more, alert and active participation by the student in his own education appears to be most desirable.

The most familiar reason for academic failure in the first year of college is the sharp break between the expectations and demands of high school and those of college. Students appear to carry on from their recent experience habits of study that include a heavy reliance upon classroom instruction, dependence upon the teacher to indicate what is important in the texts, and often a disproportionate dependence upon the spoken word, rather than the printed word, in acquiring, evaluating, and demonstrating knowledge. If their first year of collegiate experience is cast in the same pattern, there are two unfortunate effects. One is the blithe assumption by students that they may expect the same measure of success from the same expenditure of effort. If the high school has been an unusually demanding one or if the college is unusually undemanding, this assumption may not be dashed. However, in most cases the end of the first semester constitutes a rude awakening to the new, different, and heavier demands for critical reading and creative synthesis in a framework of startlingly increased competition.

The second unfortunate effect, if college appears to proceed in the same pattern as secondary education, is the disappointment and stultification of the ablest students, who have arrived expecting something dramatically different and who feel cheated of the challenges and rewards they had anticipated. For both these reasons, it seems imperative to dramatize the break from secondary to higher education. It is less important that this break be between the twelfth and thirteenth years of formal education than that it occur and that it be recognizable.

A student needs to become an initiator as well as a participator if he is to continue his intellectual and cultural growth after he leaves the campus. All the evidence suggests that the inevitable effects of the current explosion of knowledge, the rapid changes and increased demands of many occupations and professions, and what may be either a blessing or a plague of increased leisure will place a premium upon the ability to continue the learning process throughout one's active life. If this is true, we surely cannot depend upon the conventional package of the course offering, where credit hours are calculated upon the number of hours the student spends in the classroom or the laboratory. For many reasons, we can be sure that there will not be enough classrooms, enough teachers, enough money, or enough assignable time to support this gigantic educational enterprise through the multiplication of conventional classroom courses of study.

Since it will be a necessity to devise other means of learning with a diminished emphasis upon instruction, is it possible to make a virtue of necessity? Can students assume a greater share of the responsibility for their own learning, with a net advantage to themselves or at worst no net loss? There is a good deal of evidence that they can. A wide range of experimentation in this direction has been undertaken within the past five or ten years.

INDEPENDENT STUDY: METHODS AND PROCEDURES

Independent study may occur in a variety of ways. It is easy to confuse by generalization, and it is important that in any discussion of independent study, the nature of the independence under consideration be made explicit. Sometimes a student may be following a course syllabus with directed readings but with little if any contact with the instructor, save for the initial setting of tasks and the final testing of accomplishment. Sometimes the student has the continuing help of a tutor or instructor but operates independently of a standard syllabus, pursuing his intellectual interests where they take him rather than retracing an intellectual odyssey of his instructor or his instructor's instructor. Sometimes the student is freed from attending a number of his regular class meetings but is expected to cover, either on his own or in teams or groups with other students, the material that might normally have been covered in the class sessions from which he has been excused. Sometimes the student, working with films, taped lectures, programed materials, texts, and assigned readings, is expected to accomplish almost completely on his own the goals usually supported by classroom procedures of lecture and discussion. And in some programs the student's independent work is expected to take place off campus, with the student pursuing an individual research project or extramural studies in which he seeks to make use of the resources of the field.

Programs of independent study thus include a wide variety of procedures, ranging at one end of a continuum from those which involve an open, often highly permissive relationship between student and instructor, in which the student is expected to define and develop his own course plans, to those at the other end of the continuum, involving what might be a highly structured and guided relationship. It may be, in some settings, almost a completely solitary enterprise, with each student operating as an individual person, setting and testing hypotheses by all the means available to him in the library and laboratory; it may in some settings center almost entirely on small-group or team approaches to independent learning; and it may in still other settings make use of a combination of individual work and small-group independent study, along with certain scheduled class or tutorial contacts with the teacher.

At its best, independent study may succeed in substituting the excitement of discovery for the dull routines of passive assimilation, and the habits of exploration for those of mere navigation. At its worst, independent study may be merely artless and undisciplined floundering and may be wasteful in that it abandons established means of economical covering of ground already well mapped in favor of a laborious and inadequate reconstruction of syntheses already completed by specialists.

INDEPENDENT STUDY AND THE AVERAGE STUDENT

There is, of course, nothing new about the idea that colleges might employ programs of independent study as a part of their undergraduate curricula. In a 1957 report on independent study programs, Bonthius and his colleagues listed a total of 334 such programs in 256 institutions.[3] Nearly all these programs, however, were designed for honors or superior students. What is new in some of the more recent experimentation in the use of independent

[3] Robert H. Bonthius, James F. Davis, and J. Garber Drushal, in collaboration with Francis V. Guille and Warren P. Spencer, *The Independent Study Program in the United States,* Columbia University Press, New York, 1957.

study is the incorporation of independent study as a part of the teacher's regular teaching procedures and the attempt to employ some form of independent study with *all* students in a particular course or program, rather than reserving these procedures for the superior or abler student only. Thus a number of colleges have instituted winter-term, or interim-term, programs of independent study in which all students are expected to take part. Similarly, a May, 1959, report of the Fund for the Advancement of Education[4] lists some sixteen institutions that have conducted experiments in the use of independent study as a part of their *regular* teaching procedures. Both the Fund for the Advancement of Education studies and the interim-term programs are reviewed in a later section of this chapter. A major implication of these new programs is that independent study can be used with a wide range of students. There is good evidence from programs already in effect that in some areas and for some purposes it not only is an acceptable substitute for conventional instruction for average and marginal students but also is actually *more* effectual. It appears that just as an able student may catch fire and speed ahead of his associates if freed from the rigid structure and standard pace of the classroom situation, a marginal student, if he is permitted to proceed at a pace consistent with his own needs and capacities, may gain confidence and mastery in dealing with materials that otherwise might defeat him. Surely, intellectual factors are important. The fruitful uses of independence, however, may depend quite as much upon the character and personality of the student, the nature of the field of study, and the educational goals sought as upon the intellectual capacity of the individual student. Thus a bold, imaginative, and responsible student with moderate ability may succeed in an independent study program, whereas a highly endowed student with an indolent, passive, or irresponsibly individualistic disposition may fail.

STRUCTURE IN INDEPENDENT STUDY

If we undertake to make a virtue of necessity by putting the student more on his own, it is evident from preliminary experience that we must also make something of a necessity of virtue, by imposing sufficient structure upon the experience to ensure against the

[4] *Better Utilization of College Teaching Resources.*

student's misconstruing his independence as merely freedom from demands or challenges. It seems evident that when a student is simply freed from class attendance in the general expectation that he will conduct reading, research, and informal discussion on his own, what he is likely to do is to devote the freed time to meeting specific demands of more highly structured courses or to lapse into idleness and sloth. A good deal of psychological experimentation has suggested that students learn best those materials upon which there is a clearly defined feedback. It appears to be a dubious proposition that a process of learning which is its own reward and which has no outside accountability will be either efficient or effective.

Most programs of independent study provide for some kind of instructor-student contact or follow-up during the student's periods of independent work. These may take the form of tutorial meetings; progress, research, or project reports; or regularly scheduled individual, small-group, or class meetings. In addition, a number of institutions have given attention to the problem of preparing the student for independent study and have developed guides and other training aids to help students in working on their own. These aids often include lists of selected reference materials, study questions for individual work, sample copies of "model" solutions to laboratory problems, and lists of procedures to be employed in evaluating essay and written work.

USING GROUPS IN INDEPENDENT STUDY

Much of the increasing body of lore on group dynamics can be codified and provided in leadership manuals and instruction guides. However, as any participant in a *T group* (a purposefully unstructured "training group" whose amorphousness most neophytes find uncomfortable in the extreme) can testify, it is far more dramatic and impressive to experience at firsthand the emotions, the frustrations, and the initially unaccountable behavior of an unstructured or ambiguously structured group under stress, and afterward to be afforded the insights and explanations of the psychologist, than it is merely to have these matters explained and interpreted, however lucidly, without first having had the experience. This is in itself a comment upon the difference between teaching and learning.

A number of programs of independent study have sought to make use of small-group or team approaches to independent study. Under these programs, the student's independent work takes place in groups which may range in size from four to twelve or more. The groups are student-led, with the students charged with the preparation, conduct, and order of the group meeting. Chairmen and recorders for the meetings are designated by the teachers or the groups themselves. These small-group study procedures have usually been combined with regular meetings with the teacher, so that a student might spend a portion of class time in group independent study (perhaps from 20 to 40 per cent of his regular class time) and the remainder of his class time in regularly scheduled class meetings with the instructor.

Group independent study is not, of course, to be equated with a T-group experience. In many ways, however, small-group independent study seeks to capitalize on the gains that can be achieved from small-group process and interaction. In effect, small-group independent study seeks to place the student in a new kind of "environmental press" in learning. It is a press which, because of the very nature of its situation and the kind of responsibilities for learning it imposes on the student, seeks to involve the student in a more intimate and direct way with the materials to be learned than might be the case were he only to hear or read about the subject.

Leading an effective small-group discussion is a difficult enough task for an instructor, let alone a student. If these procedures are to be effective, it is important that adequate attention be given to the preparation and training of students for working in small groups. It is equally important that students receive adequate feedback on their small-group meetings.[5]

[5] *Antioch College Reports,* numbers 2 and 5, describe a variety of training aids employed by Antioch faculty members in preparing students for small-group independent work and providing feedback to the group members. Among the aids developed at Antioch were study guides for chairmen on leading a discussion, suggestions for discussion recorders, and suggested study tactics for individuals working in small groups. In addition, some instructors conducted demonstration sessions on effective and ineffective work in small groups and held postclass conferences with chairmen and recorders of groups. For a fuller report of these experiments, see "Experiment in Independent Study 1956–1960," *Antioch College Reports,* no. 2, March, 1961; and "Using Groups in Independent Study," *Antioch College Reports,* no 5, June, 1963.

PROGRAMS

Fund for the Advancement of Education studies: new arrangements in the use of instructor-student contact time

Aided by grants from the Fund for the Advancement of Education, a number of institutions have sought to examine their ongoing instructional procedures and to test new arrangements in the use of instructor-student contact time. The principal purpose of these studies was to see whether students, through independent study, could be helped to assume a greater share of the responsibility for their own learning. Sixteen institutions participated in these studies. They included Antioch, Carleton, Goddard, Grinnell, Morgan State, and Oberlin Colleges; the Women's College of the University of North Carolina; Duke, Marquette, Pennsylvania State, Rutgers, and Vanderbilt Universities; the Universities of Colorado, Michigan, and Omaha; and the State College of Washington.[6]

The independent study programs conducted under the Fund for the Advancement of Education grants differed from institution to institution. The Oberlin College experiment was designed to test the hypothesis that students participating in freshman courses in mathematics, zoology, and psychology and working independently of their instructors for one-third of their regularly scheduled class time would learn as well as a comparable group of students who met with their instructor the usual number of times. The Antioch College experiment covered a total of nineteen different courses in each of the major areas of instruction: the humanities, the social sciences, and the sciences. Student class time in the Antioch experiment was reduced by amounts ranging from 20 to 60 per cent, depending on the particular course in which the independent study procedure was being employed. The experiment at Vanderbilt University involved a total of twenty-one faculty members from a total of fifty-four summer faculty members. Class-contact time in the Vanderbilt experiment was reduced by amounts ranging from 25 to 50 per cent. Other institutions used still other combinations of independent work and instructor-contact time.

[6] *Better Utilization of College Teaching Resources.* For an excellent review of these studies, also see Samuel Baskin, "Quest for Quality," *New Dimensions in Higher Education,* no. 7, U.S. Office of Education, Washington, D.C., 1960.

The results of these studies are reviewed in a later section of this chapter. While there is a good deal that yet needs to be done before one can assess fully the impact and meaning of these independent study programs, there is good evidence from these studies that students are able to learn and achieve particular course objectives, through independent work, with much less class time than heretofore has been required of them.

Interterm plans

One of the most frequently attempted of the emerging experimental patterns in independent study is the "intersemester," "January term," or "winter term," as it has come variously to be known. The winter term at Florida Presbyterian College, the January term at Macalester and Colby Colleges, and the winter half semester at Bard College are representative of this innovation. The purposes appear to be similar in all these undertakings. The familiar "lame-duck period" of the standard fall semester, i.e., the time between the Christmas holidays and the beginning of the spring semester, has been sacrificed to make way for a more stimulating experience for faculty and students alike. Many of the faculty are freed for periods of research, travel, or vacation, and the students participating are occupied with projects and activities different in kind from their normal class undertakings.

The program at Florida Presbyterian has been commented on in Chapter 1. This program is designed to provide the student with an early exposure to independent inquiry, i.e., beginning with his first year, and to provide the opportunity for independent study to all students. It is insisted that this period is an adjunct to, and not a substitute for, standard courses, and it is recognized that a nucleus of committed faculty is required to assure success in such a venture.

At Colby College, as at Florida Presbyterian, the program appears to be directed primarily toward freshmen and sophomores, with a focus upon general education; upperclassmen may elect such studies or projects under the aegis of the departments in which they are majoring. Conversely, at Macalester College the January term is designed primarily for juniors and seniors, and freshmen may undertake an independent project by special permission.

At Bard College, the winter half semester is an outgrowth of the well-known "field period" and runs concurrently with it during the months of January and February. A student may thus elect either a period of work experience or a program of independent study off campus.

In all these interterm plans, the importance of initial structure and preparation for independent study has been emphasized by early experience. With too much autonomy or with an ill-defined project, students tended to flounder ineffectually. In some other institutions, the interterm is devoted to an effort to provide a common experience outside the standard curriculum, with emphasis upon community of interest rather than originality or individuality. For example, Colorado College devoted its 1964 interterm to the re-creation of World War II through lectures, films, and discussions. There are doubtless many other such efforts to provide the necessary framework, information, and conceptual systems to permit further excursions of individual students adventuring from a base.

Seminars for initiative

C. L. Barber's highly literate *More Power to Them*[7] presents a sober and critical account of an imaginative experiment by faculty members of Amherst, Smith, and Mount Holyoke Colleges and the University of Massachusetts in 1959–1960. A series of special courses presented under the aegis of the Committee for New College produced somewhat mixed results and served the intended purpose of pointing up successes, failures, problems, and opportunities in independent study approaches. The most unmistakable result was the illustration of the extraordinary hold that the standard course system had on the minds of students and faculty and the remarkable lack of sophistication of the normal college student when faced by an unstructured learning situation. Participating teachers, by their own accounts, experienced some exhilaration and much despair in viewing their handiwork after a year of hard work.

This cooperative project, which the participants preferred to

[7] C. L. Barber, *More Power to Them: A Report of Faculty and Student Experience in the Encouragement of Student Initiative,* the Committee for New College, Amherst, Mass., 1962.

think of as an exploration rather than a rigorous experiment, centered upon two features of a larger New College plan: the offering of "freshman seminars" and "student seminars." The former were aimed at introducing the college student at the beginning of his academic career to the methods of the scholar in exploring a limited subject in depth as an adjunct to, and corrective for, the usual broad survey courses. In experimental sections replacing the usual introductory courses in freshman English, philosophy, and political science, four groups of ten to fifteen students, selected as representative of the range of the student body rather than handpicked for talent or initiative, made up the experimental group. When the students evaluated their experience in the political science course, they reported that their first impression was one of bewilderment and disorganization, followed by growing confidence and excitement; they regretted both the slow start and the too early conclusion of the semester's work. In a two-semester philosophy course, it appeared that the application of the techniques of the graduate seminar to freshmen was only partially successful. "What often fails with graduate students worked only fitfully with freshmen";[8] papers and oral reports were often superficial and tedious to the relatively uninvolved listeners. In English literature, "results indicate what appears also in a number of the other experiments: that, once given the initiative, the students tend to make good use of it in proportion to the clarity of the outlines of the situation they are given to work in—the intellectual or academic stimulation established for them by the instructor."[9] It is apparent that the freshman seminars were a qualified success; they required a greater expenditure in faculty time per student than a conventional course, and they revealed sometimes surprising inadequacies in organization and perception of relevance in even highly qualified freshmen. However, this revelation arises from the fact that anonymity was impossible in the small groups, and students perforce demonstrated more of their strengths and weaknesses as students to themselves, to one another, and to their seminar instructors. Indeed, the crucial factor for success seemed to have been individual attention in a framework of painstaking organization and definition. The report concludes: *"By itself,*

[8] *Ibid.,* p. 18.
[9] *Ibid.,* p. 19.

individual attention can be of very little use indeed. . . . The attention that educates is that which we give to a student when he is performing, and in a defined situation."[10]

In the second part of the experiment, student seminars were offered as an adjunct to lectures in nine upper-class courses in the humanities and social sciences. It is perhaps worth noting that experiments in independent study rarely are centered in mathematics and the natural sciences. This may be because the laboratory method is considered to be itself an exercise in independent study, but it may also suggest that scientists are characteristically and paradoxically less interested in the application of the experimental method to teaching than their colleagues in less scientific disciplines.

Findings in the upper-class student seminars paralleled those in the freshman seminars for the most part. The primary innovation was the introduction of *student-led seminars* as an addition to, or substitution for, conventional classroom instruction. Generally the experience was found to have been fruitful by both students and faculty. However, difficulties included the inhibiting effect of disaffected or uncommitted students and the tendency of a discussion to degenerate into a "bull session" in the absence of the instructor's guiding, correcting, and arbitrating hand. A virtue of this defect was a new realization by instructors of the gap in communication between what an instructor presents in a lecture and what is actually absorbed by the listeners and a new awareness on the part of the students given initiative of their normal failure to avail themselves of it.

The essence of the four-institution cooperative venture was the application to undergraduates, including freshmen, of instructional techniques normally reserved for graduate students and the provision to students representing the full range of undergraduate ability and motivation of educational experiences normally reserved for the unusually talented and highly motivated. Along with the heartening evidence of the zest, the fresh insights, and the desirably increased autonomy provided by such experiments, the participants in this undertaking soberly and usefully point out the expense in faculty time, the initial and pervasive skepticism of many faculty members and students (including most of those not directly involved in the experimentation), and the well-established

[10] *Ibid.,* p. 25.

and frequently reinforced professionalism of the faculty and the amateurism of the student in scholarly matters.

Individual study in the laboratory

Among the most serious bottlenecks in efforts to accommodate dramatically increased enrollments are the limitation in size of laboratories and the difficulty of scheduling and staffing for fullest utilization of even the present facilities. A promising experiment in laboratory instruction in botany at Purdue University[11] is therefore attracting a great deal of eager attention. In the experiment the laboratory is open on a "library basis" from 7:30 A.M. to 10:30 P.M. each weekday for supervised study. Instructions are provided by audio tape, and a single student assistant is on duty as monitor. A student is expected to spend approximately four hours per week in supervised study with laboratory material and audio-tape directions, but he may fit this time into his schedule at his own convenience and can either use his skill to accelerate his laboratory work or repeat experimental procedure as often as he feels is required for mastery. This laboratory experience is one of four phases of instruction; a student also attends each week one hour of large-lecture instruction and one hour of small-group assembly (approximately thirty students) and is expected to conduct independent home study of texts and notes. The advantages sought through the library approach to the laboratory include the accommodation of larger numbers of students with the same facilities and smaller numbers of staff, flexibility of pace, flexibility of scheduling both initial instruction and makeup and review, minimizing distractions, and focusing of attention upon learning rather than teaching and upon the student's responsibility for his own learning. The results of this and comparable experiments will be followed with great interest, since it already appears that only by the application of technological innovation through electronic and programing devices can the values of direct laboratory experience for every student be preserved. Already many science courses have been reduced to lecture-demonstration sessions, and the feasibility, though rarely the desirability, of direct laboratory experience is being widely questioned.

[11] S. N. Postlethwait, "A Systems Approach to Botany," *Audiovisual Instruction,* pp. 243–244, April, 1963.

RESEARCH ON INDEPENDENT STUDY

Experimentation with independent study, as with class sizes, television presentations, and programed learning, demonstrates clearly that students in the experimental group will normally learn as much and retain it as long as students instructed in the standard classroom situation. This familiar result may be explained away by the skeptic as being merely the result of the Hawthorne effect, in which the experimental group, knowing they are in some way special, will compensate for any deficiency in the experimental system by increased awareness, motivation, and effort. There is little doubt that the results may in some instances be at least to a degree contaminated by this factor. However, who is to say that the effects of increased awareness, motivation, and application are anything but desirable in an educational setting?

In his chapter entitled Procedures and Techniques of Teaching: A Survey of Experimental Studies in *The American College: A Psychological and Social Interpretation of the Higher Learning,*[12] W. J. McKeachie gives a comprehensive account of the research related to the efficacy of independent study procedures. He demonstrates eloquently that research in this area is as yet meager and ambiguous, that strong biases of faculty and students together with the familiar Hawthorne effect contaminate the findings of even the most careful studies, and that only with the recent availability of computer techniques does the multivariate analysis required for reliable investigations in these areas become feasible. Nevertheless, a combination of professional experience, educated insights and intuitions, and controlled experiments provides some tentative conclusions regarding the strengths and weaknesses of the independent study approach to learning in higher education.

These tentative conclusions may be summarized as follows: "Student-centered" methods of learning, including various methods of independent study, tend to produce greater gains in insight and problem-solving capacities and to promote more attitudinal changes than comparable "instructor-centered" methods. However, instructor-centered methods, such as the lecture and the "authoritarian" leadership of discussion groups, tend to produce greater

[12] Nevitt Sanford (ed.), *The American College: A Psychological and Social Interpretation of the Higher Learning,* John Wiley & Sons, Inc., New York, 1962, chap. 8, pp. 312–364.

gains in information and better performance on conventional tests of subject mastery. Thus it is apparent that the goals and objectives of a particular learning experience must be taken into account when a decision is being reached as to which method of study is most promising. As Professor McKeachie suggests:

From the standpoint of theory, student-centered teaching in its more extreme forms might be expected to have some serious weaknesses at least in achieving lower-level cognitive goals. With the instructor's role as information-giver reduced, his role as source of feedback virtually eliminated, his opportunity to provide organization and structure curtailed, it is apparent that a heavy burden falls upon [the individual or the group] to carry out any of these functions that are necessary.[13]

Although the evidence is not conclusive, particularly concerning the expectation of a loss in lower-order cognitive objectives (where students have in fact appeared to be able to acquire information as well from textbooks as from instructors), there is support for the hypothesis that student-centered teaching is effective in improving problem solving and the ability to apply concepts to fresh situations and in promoting noncognitive changes. In the few experimental studies available to date, notably at Antioch and Oberlin, the results are not as significant as proponents of the independent study approach might hope. To quote Dr. McKeachie again: "As with other comparisons of teaching methods, few differences have been found between achievement of students working independently and that of those taught in conventional classes. Moreover, the expected gains in independence have also often failed to materialize. Students taught by independent study do not always seem to develop greater ability or motivation for learning independently."[14]

These ambiguous results and the predominance of "no significant difference" in research findings are, of course, subject to a variety of interpretations. It may be, as suggested in Prof. C. L. Barber's report, that the extraordinary power of the conventional classroom conception of college instruction is a definitive factor. It may be that the kind of learning taking place in other contexts is so different as not to be accessible to measurement by the devices

[13] *Ibid.*, p. 328.
[14] *Ibid.*, p. 340.

employed. Or it may be that the critical factors are the motivations and perceptions of the particular students and instructors concerned and not the methods employed. A still unanswered question is: Do the preferences of many students for lecture-discussion approaches over independent study approaches derive from mere familiarity, from a preference for anonymity and passivity, or from some objective but unmeasured superiority of one method to the other? Continuing experimentation, particularly at Antioch, with the efforts to use a measure of "learning resourcefulness" may provide further clues to this and other perplexing questions that have hitherto been largely inaccessible to research.

It may be useful at this point to cite and comment on the findings of the Fund for the Advancement of Education studies. These findings are reported by Prof. Samuel Baskin, of Antioch College:

Students can learn as well by the independent study method as they can by the regular methods of instruction. While there were occasional differences, sometimes favoring the independent study group, and sometimes favoring the regular lecture-discussion group, an analysis of the over-all results of test scores on a wide variety of examinations reveals few significant differences favoring one group over the other. These results held true whether multiple-choice examinations, short-answer tests, or tests of critical thinking were employed as the evaluative criteria; they held true for beginning as well as advanced courses of study, they held true whether group or individual methods of independent study or combinations thereof were employed as the independent study procedure, and they held true for each year of the experiment.[15]

This result could perhaps have been predicted for several reasons. Those versatile, imaginative, and energetic enough to undertake rigorous experimentation in instructional methods are highly likely to communicate their own intellectual excitement and zeal for the acquisition of knowledge to the students with whom they come in contact. Further, the shock or arresting quality of an unconventional approach is likely to awaken awareness and readiness in students who would probably drift comfortably along in

[15] Samuel Baskin, "Independent Study: Methods, Programs and for Whom," paper presented at the meetings of the Association for Higher Education, March, 1962; see also *Current Issues in Higher Education,* Association for Higher Education, Washington, D.C., 1962, pp. 65ff.

the stream of a conventional lecture-discussion course without putting forth any special effort. And finally, long and melancholy experience has demonstrated that it is not necessary for any new mode of instruction to be startlingly successful to equal the success of whatever system has been conventionally employed. What may be demonstrated is not that the new system has so much to recommend it but that the conventional system has little to recommend its continuance.

While students at first tended to express some dissatisfaction with these methods of independent study, in that they felt they were being somewhat unfairly deprived of the instructional function, the study data reflect a growing satisfaction with the independent study method. This was true, for example, at the University of Colorado, where after some initial resistance, students, by a margin of three to one, indicated that they would prefer that the independent study methods be retained; at Antioch where the data show a decided shift of student attitudes from general dissatisfaction with the independent study methods when first introduced, to a point of general acceptance and satisfaction with these methods after they had been employed over a period of two to three years; and in the final report of the Vanderbilt University study group where some eighty-two per cent of the students indicated a desire for more experience with independent study, though they would not want to take all their courses on that basis.

The most common objection made was that the independent study method required more of the students' time than did the conventional method. This was especially the case in those institutions that employed group procedures in independent study and attempted to provide students with specific training in group methods for their work in the autonomous groups.[16]

The initial dissatisfaction with the withdrawal of familiar supports, a firm time schedule, and guaranteed feedback afforded by the conventional classroom instruction is also to be expected. It is quite evident that one of the effects of reducing the number of class meetings in an experimental section of a course for which other sections are meeting according to a regular schedule is an unwonted interest on the part of the students freed of class attendance in what has been discussed in other classes during the "missed"

[16] *Ibid.*

sessions. On the other hand, students permitted optional attendance at lectures from which they are formally excused seem rarely to exercise this option.

Without much doubt, students in the American educational system have been thoroughly conditioned to expect presentation in one or another form by their instructors of the "approved" information, attitudes, analyses, and procedures that make up a course and to reproduce on tests and examinations facsimiles of these classroom presentations. It should hardly be surprising that students are initially uneasy and uncertain about what will be expected of them if they are attempting to glean the same details without benefit of frequent contact with the instructor who is to examine them. It requires a significant shift of goals and expectations on the part of both student and examiner to rationalize the approach to higher education through genuinely independent study. And if the student simply perceives himself not so much as independent but as dependent upon other students no better informed than he or upon infrequent and fleeting contacts with an instructor-examiner whose views and expectations he must somehow divine despite this handicap, independent study emerges as more a threat than a promise, more a deprivation than an enfranchisement. To prosper under a system of independent study, a student must somehow come to experience the thrill of discovery and the delights of tough-minded debate; he must develop habits of self-discipline that are by no means uniform among college students; he must learn to read swiftly, thoroughly, and analytically, for most independent study requires the substitution of original books or manuscripts for cursory textbooks and bland digests and the substitution of textbooks for oral dissertations by an instructor.

While data on retention of learning is meagre, in that few institutions have been able to conduct control group follow-up studies in this area, study results, at least at this point, reveal few significant differences in learning-retention between the independent study and the conventionally taught groups.[17]

Although the data available indicate little difference in learning retention, it would seem intuitively plausible that the learning acquired by a student participating actively in the process should outlast that acquired by a student passively taking in the same informa-

[17] *Ibid.*

tion. This is a complicated matter on which we need many more psychological data. For example, does anyone ever learn anything entirely passively, or is learning of any kind an active process? What are the effects of individual differences in perceptual habits and capacities upon learning from hearing an oral presentation as against reading a written one? In most learning, whether conventionally taught or presented through independent study, some conbination of sense modalities is normally employed. What is the optimum combination, and will it differ widely from one individual student to another? While there are many cues and conjectures on these matters, there are as yet no definitive data to guide us.

There is no evidence that these independent study methods need to be reserved for the superior student only. Students at different levels of ability and at different year levels did well (or poorly) with these teaching methods. Academic potential does not appear to be a sole or determining criterion in the success or failure of these methods; and there are some indications that attitudinal and personality factors may be as important, if not more important, in learning by these methods as level of ability.[18]

This seems a highly significant finding. Although the impetus of many independent study programs was a desire to free the superior student from the academic lockstep and permit him to proceed at a faster pace and with greater depth and latitude than his less gifted classmate, it now appears clear that the slower student is equally galled by the chains of conventional classroom procedures and equally disadvantaged by a Procrustean bed. Students who have been helped to see that they have an appropriate pace for learning and that they can, given the opportunity to proceed at that pace, experience success and achieve goals rather than meet with continual reproof and frustration are emancipated souls. In this, as in other learning experiences, success is apparently a positive reinforcement and can do much to motivate and encourage students who have been frustrated by their minimal achievement with conventional instruction.

Freshmen appear to be able to learn as well this way as the more "advanced" upperclass student. Two factors may be important here:

(a) freshmen expect college to be different and may be more ready to accept these methods of independent learning, and
[18] *Ibid.*

(b)   *following on this first point, freshment have not as yet been exposed to an additional two or three years of our own habits of teacher-direction in learning at the college level.*[19]

Despite the assumption by most faculties that independent study must be reserved, if not for the superior student, at least for the upper-class student, there is much reason to suppose that freshmen and sophomores can manage as well as, or better than, advanced undergraduates with independent study techniques. In addition to the reasons cited by Dr. Baskin (i.e., that freshmen are ready for a new approach and have fewer years of conditioning to conventional approaches), it may be that freshmen respond favorably to independent instruction because of the shabby alternatives. Too often freshman courses are poorly taught because they are entrusted to inexperienced graduate assistants or to regular staff members who undertake this function as an unwelcome duty. When a fully trained and highly competent professional teacher undertakes to program a course for independent study, the resultant structure is likely to be tighter, more logical, more adventurous, and more demanding. Also, when grading must depend upon bases other than accumulated impressions from classroom performance, the examinations are likely to be more searching and more penetrating and to be read with less prejudice and more attention.

Teaching by the independent study method should not be thought of as a method that eliminates the teacher from the teaching process. Students come to college largely unprepared for learning on their own and need help in learning how to learn this way. While the teacher's job is different, it is no less difficult, for he must play a crucial role in preparing students for working on their own. As here conceived, the teacher is viewed as the designer and manager of learning opportunities for the students, rather than as the provider and dispenser of what is to be learned.[20]

Nothing could be more apparent than that the specter of technological unemployment for college professors is entirely hallucinatory. A congeries of forces is imposing on the short supply of fully qualified teachers demands that simply cannot be met within our conventional framework. The increasing number of college-age

[19] *Ibid.*
[20] *Ibid.*

citizens, the increasing proportion of them who will be seeking higher education, and the increasing proportion of the population at large that will be seeking continuing education support projections that stagger the imagination. Further, the continuing accumulation and production of knowledge that results from, and in turn stimulates, a research orientation on the part of college teachers impose demands that compete for the time once assignable to the classroom. To operate effectively under these new conditions, it may be necessary to abandon the practice of providing the same information through both texts and lectures. By analogy, the college teacher may be abandoning his former role as retailer and restaurateur for that of wholesaler, engineer, production and distribution manager, coach, and counselor. Such analogies fall harshly on the ear of many dedicated teachers who fear that the teacher-student relationship will thus be depersonalized or destroyed. It may be plausibly answered that the kind of intimate relationship deemed so desirable can be won in some areas only at the expense of sacrificing it in others. To insist on small classes taught uniformly by the lecture-discussion method is to doom students to inferior instruction and teachers to frustration and exhaustion. One of our priority tasks in higher education is to determine what can best be learned from programed materials, by independent reading, by laboratory experimentation, by television demonstration, by live lectures, from tapes and films, from classroom discussions, from seminar papers, and from private tutorials and then to adapt our system in such a way as to optimize learning. In this process there should be ample room for every shade and variety of pedagogical skill and for the efficient employment of all the personnel who can legitimately claim to belong in the teaching profession.

THE PRESENT AND THE FUTURE
Technological developments

A major direction of experimentation in a form of independent study is the use of programed learning devices as either adjuncts to, or substitutes for, standard lecture-discussion courses. This attempt has at base the purpose of most independent study: to permit each student to proceed at his own pace and to avoid any lockstep that, if geared to the average student, is almost certain to bore the able and mystify the slow. It also serves the purpose of freeing the qualified instructor from repetitive routines and reserves his time and energy for productive research and for vital exchanges with students on matters that do not lend themselves to routine treatment or to presentation through step-by-step linear programing. A good deal is said elsewhere in this book about the techniques and approaches of programed learning. However, it is evident from the experiments at Hamilton College in philosophy, psychology, mathematics, and modern languages that this approach to freeing both student and instructor from classroom routines is extraordinarily promising. It must be recognized that the preparation and validation of adequate programs are immensely time-consuming, taxing to the ingenuity and intellectual power of the teacher, and by nature devoid of the spark that is communicated by the physical confrontation of teacher and students caught up in infectious enthusiasm for a given line of inquiry. However, this is a limitation to which most forms of independent study are subject. And for this reason, it seems likely that independent study, however conceived, will continue to be only one of the modes of instruction at the most effective institutions. Lecture and discussion in groups of various sizes and composition appear to have special capacities and effects that are different from, and unobtainable through, the solitary engagement of student with textbook, scrambled book, tape recorder, or other distillation or surrogate of the teacher.

Facilities for independent study

One of the obvious implications of any large-scale shift from classroom-centered instruction to independent study is that in new circumstances each student has an increased need for a space of his own. One of the early discoveries in postwar Britain was that the traditional long vacation is but ill adapted to the circumstances of the new national scholarship students from the middle and lower classes. While the son of a peer could travel or hole up in a baronial library to continue the most important part of his education on his own, a less fortunate student sharing a room with two younger brothers in a Birmingham tenement was infinitely worse off in freedom than within the structure of the university program, with the university resources at his disposal. Similarly, if students are to spend more of their learning time outside the classroom and lecture hall, thought needs to be given to a new set of needs. At the University of Delaware, for example, all new dormitory rooms are designed in nesting, irregular shapes, so that the desks can be separated from the beds, or one tenant's space from his room-mate's. The new Delaware library has a vastly increased number of individual carrels as well as multiplied, rather than merely enlarged, reading rooms and lounges. Spaces are provided for listening to tapes and viewing films as well as for listening to musical record-ings and reading microfilm. Elsewhere, the most radical proposal for accommodating space to the needs of independent study tech-niques is the construction of an "independent study center," in which each student is provided a personal office in lieu of a seat in each of a series of classrooms. This may be too extreme a solu-tion, but it is evident that the design of new classroom and seminar spaces, new libraries, and new living quarters in institutions with a significant commitment to independent study will require new departures in campus architecture. Many of these new develop-ments in "building for learning" are described in Chapter 7.

Experiments in the use of autonomous study groups like those conducted by Professor Leuba, of Antioch College,[21] indicate the need not only for special preparations by the supervising and coordinating instructor but also for special equipment. Professor Leuba employed a system of communications by which he could remain in a central office and monitor a group discussion by sound only and could be called upon for information or advice by a buzzer and voice-channel intercommunication system. He observed that, helpful as this was, it was impossible to recognize student discussants by their voices alone and thus to give praise or criticism, as would have been desirable. This limitation would be in large part obviated by a system of television monitoring, which might be economically feasible if one professor were monitoring ten groups of ten discussants each. A comparable installation is already in operation at the U.S. Air Force Academy, where a group of class-rooms can be effectively monitored from a central office by tele-vision. The overtones of *1984* and the totalitarian methods of "Big Brother" will doubtless be hard to dissociate from these techniques, but a system supplied for the purpose of combining the learning

[21] Clarence Leuba, "Using Groups in Independent Study," *Antioch Col-lege Reports,* no. 5, June, 1963.

resources of the individual student, his peer group, and a trained specialist can hardly be construed as an invasion of privacy.

New institutions

It is significant that many of the entirely new colleges and universities have developed plans for breaking with tradition and emphasizing organization for independent study. Dr. Lewis B. Mayhew describes a number of these programs in Chapter 1, The New Colleges. The programs at Monteith College, the New College at Hofstra, Florida Presbyterian, Grand Valley State College, and Florida Atlantic University are of particular interest in this regard. The hope in each of these institutions is that independent study will play a very major role in the student's educational experience. It will be interesting to observe whether the forces that militate so effectually against the engraftment of new techniques and procedures upon a traditional curriculum and conventional patterns of instruction in even the most vital of established institutions can be effectively countered in the development of these institutions. It is surely a hopeful prospect. And if means can be devised to enable students to develop habits and skills of self-learning, then all higher education will be in debt to these new institutions.

Implications for university relations

Widespread introduction of independent study on a large scale is certain to elicit from parents and students the question: Why should I pay a high tuition for an arrangement where students are learning from one another or by themselves rather than from qualified instructors, as suggested by the root meaning of "tuition"? Indeed, there is a rising dissatisfaction with the present situation, in which, at many of the best institutions, students receive most of their initial instruction at the feet of graduate assistants or other subinstructors and find it difficult to make even the remotest contact with the distinguished professorial staff whose reputations initially attracted them to the institution. Often these senior faculty members are in Washington, Karachi, or an inaccessible study or are limiting themselves to offering one or two advanced graduate courses. Surely the answer must be that for many reasons the student must rely more heavily on books, articles, programs, records, films, tapes, and other surrogates for the immediately present instructor. If he is thus compelled to master techniques and to acquire habits of independent learning, the necessity will have been turned to advantage. As Professor Cooper observes in Chapter 9, Improving College Teaching and Administration: ". . . the good professor today is becoming a senior partner working with the student in searching out resources for the solution of problems." In his new role, the teacher may need to serve not so much as a dispenser of information but rather as a designer and manager of the student's learning.

Questions for the future

If there is so much to recommend the widespread use of the techniques of independent study, why are there such small beginnings and so much skepticism and opposition? First, of course, there is the compulsion of habit. It is a rare professional person in any field who will lightly give up principles or practices honored by tradition and ingrained by generations of recapitulation. In higher education, much more than in the elementary and secondary schools, there is a powerful and persistent tradition that harks back to the medieval university. That institution is still perceived vividly, if not entirely accurately, as a community of scholars to whose individual members those who wish to learn apprentice themselves. The focus is upon the teacher and upon students who are patterning themselves in his image. This archaic ideal is one that will have to be supplanted by another more relevant to contemporary society. Modes of disseminating knowledge will have somehow to keep pace with the rate of production of new knowledge and the pressing requirements for the application of complex knowledge. Although independent study offers a promising lead in closing this widening gap, new ways are always embraced with reluctance.

At the same time that we stand in awe of the discoveries of the physical sciences, we must lament the gaps in our knowledge of the psychology of learning. Epistemologists and learning theorists present no such solid front as, say, nuclear physicists. The respective roles of contiguity, reinforcement, retroactive inhibition, closure, intuition, and motivated perception in learning are far from being established by consensus. Who can tell us surely the extent to which the acquisition of a given set of desired attitudes, skills, perceptions, and modes of behavior depends upon conditioning or upon active integration or reintegration? Can a student really be taught, or can he only learn? How can he best be taught to learn? Why do some personalities seek and embrace freedom, while others avoid or flee freedom? How can one confidently distinguish between the two tendencies among students?

A group at the University of Michigan under the leadership of Wilbert McKeachie has been exploring questions of the personality patterns and needs of students and instructors and of the relation of these factors to the processes of teaching and learning. Samuel Baskin and his associates at Antioch have sought to test the applicability of independent study for all students and to develop instruments for measuring the student's ability to work on his own. Much, however, remains to be done in these areas. A body of knowledge on the effectiveness of several kinds of active learning experience is being assembled by institutions conducting essays and experiments in independent study, but as yet only a few books and brochures provide a comprehensive summary of these findings. The strength of the pressures toward continuing experimentation with the development and application of techniques for independent learning will ensure that the next few years will produce many fresh approaches and analytical studies. And to whatever extent some segments of the profession of higher education greet these ventures with dismay and opposition, other segments will welcome them with gratitude and hope.

SOURCES FOR FURTHER INFORMATION

Aydelotte, Frank: *Breaking the Academic Lockstep,* Harper & Row, Publishers, Incorporated, New York, 1944.

Barber, C. L.: *More Power to Them: A Report of Faculty and Student Experience in the Encouragement of Student Initiative,* the Committee for New College, Amherst, Mass., 1962.

Baskin, Samuel: "Quest for Quality," *New Dimensions in Higher Education,* no. 7, U.S. Office of Education, Washington, D.C., 1960.

Better Utilization of College Teaching Resources: A Report by the Committee on Utilization of College Teaching Resources,

Fund for the Advancement of Education, New York, May, 1959.

Bonthius, Robert H., James F. Davis, and J. Garber Drushal in collaboration with Francis V. Guille and Warren P. Spencer: *The Independent Study Program in the United States,* Columbia University Press, New York, 1957.

Churchill, Ruth: "Evaluation of Independent Study in College Courses," unpublished doctoral dissertation, University of Minnesota, Minneapolis, Minn., 1960.

Cohen, Joseph: "On Independent Study," *The Superior Student,* vol. 3, no. 8, December, 1960.

"Experiment in Independent Study (1956–1960)," *Antioch College Reports,* no. 2, March, 1961.

Faust, Clarence: "The Years ahead for Higher Education," *Transactions of the Ohio College Association,* Columbus, Ohio, April, 1957.

Hatch, Winslow, and Ann Bennet: "Independent Study," *New Dimensions in Higher Education,* no. 1, U.S. Office of Education, Washington, D.C., 1960.

Sanford, Nevitt (ed.): *The American College: A Psychological and Social Interpretation of the Higher Learning,* John Wiley & Sons, Inc., New York, 1962.

"Using Groups in Independent Study," *Antioch College Reports,* no. 5, June, 1963.

IRWIN ABRAMS

4

the student abroad

*There is little question that the student abroad has already be-
come an established part of the American educational landscape.
The growth of this movement has been spectacular. In 1950 there
were only six programs through which undergraduates could
earn credit abroad during the academic year. In 1960 over fifty
institutions offered such programs, with an enrollment of over
fifteen hundred students. In 1963–1964 there were over 120
programs of many different types, with more than twice as
many students enrolled as in 1960. These figures do not include
over one hundred summer programs for academic credit
organized by colleges and universities, in which over two thousand
students participated. By 1964 over half of our liberal arts
colleges were either administering their own programs or else*

allowing their students to earn credit in programs organized by others. But the movement is still young. The problems are many, the potentialities are barely realized, and the full implications for campus education have hardly been grasped.

This chapter presents an overview of developments in programs of study abroad. It deals with the objectives these programs seek to achieve, the kinds of programs that have evolved, problems that need to be faced, and the potential these programs hold for improving the quality of the total educational experience. Particular attention is given to the problem and to the need for maintaining standards in these programs if we are to develop programs of quality and strength.

PURPOSES OF FOREIGN–STUDY PROGRAMS

There is fundamental agreement that the first criterion of a program of quality is a precise statement of purposes. Not only should the aims and objectives be clearly stated, so that the participants will have no question about how their personal goals can be served by the program they enter, but they should also be formulated in terms that will permit evaluation of the program itself. Moreover, an institution should plan the program as an integral part of its general plan of education, never as an extra frill or as a device for securing prestige or financial profit. Finally, the educational aims should be clearly related to the special opportunities of the particular foreign culture in which the program is located.[1]

The general objectives of foreign-study programs can be classified

[1] The rapid expansion of programs has given rise to serious concern among educators over the proper maintenance of standards. This problem led to the convening of the first National Conference on Undergraduate Study Abroad (which met in Chicago in 1960), to a series of statements on standards by various educational bodies, and finally to the establishment in 1963 by the Institute of International Education of the Consultative Service on U.S. Undergraduate Study Abroad. The report of this consultative service, published by the IIE in 1964, is now the basic work in this field. It includes a complete directory of programs and an excellent analysis of the situation by Dr. Stephen A. Freeman, who directs this program. For specific references to these developments, see Sources for Further Information.

as follows: (*1*) the general education of the student, (*2*) the intellectual and professional development of the student in his specialized field of study, and (*3*) the furthering of international understanding.

General education

It is usually agreed that for the great majority of undergraduates, the proper aim of study abroad should be general rather than specialized education. The values commonly offered to prospective participants include the increase in understanding of their own culture through exposure to another, the growth in knowledge and understanding of world affairs and our cultural heritage, and the acquisition of a foreign language, both as an intellectual achievement in itself and as a means of exploring new cultural horizons. Frequently the objective of furthering the student's "personal development" or "maturity" appears in the prospectus. If this means that the student may gain a new understanding not only of the world and of man but also of himself, this is surely a valid aim. But if what is meant is mainly that the student is given some experience in handling his own affairs and is made more self-reliant, as some program announcements suggest, then it may be questioned whether it is justified to transport the student across the sea in order to help him grow up.

Specialized objectives

In American higher education, specialized studies are generally left for graduate years. There are, however, certain special academic and vocational objectives that are valid for an undergraduate to pursue abroad. The first junior year programs were designed for French and German majors, and a large number of today's programs are similarly built around intensive study of a particular language and civilization. The oldest of all, now conducted by Sweet Briar, offers students a ". . . full academic year at the University of Paris where, with French classmates, they may broaden and deepen their comprehension of the language, customs, history and culture of France, and specialize to great advantage in such international subjects as art, government, history, international affairs, philosophy or political science."[2] It should be clear that the students are specializing only in the sense that they are furthering well-defined academic aims, not in the sense that they are following advanced studies. The extent to which most American juniors follow courses on the same level as their foreign classmates is a question to which we must return later. But while for most of the participants in such programs the values achieved are those associated with general education, it is true that mastery of the French language, for example, may represent a major stride toward a career in the French department of a college or in the foreign service. And there have been certain valid preprofessional undergraduate programs abroad, such as the Rome center of the Rhode Island School of Design, which arranges for its seniors to study under Italian masters.

International understanding

The goal of furthering international understanding needs much more careful definition than is usually supplied in the promotional literature. If it is the student's understanding of international affairs or his world-mindedness that is sought, then this is properly an objective of his general education. If what is meant is goodwill toward the United States on the part of nationals of the host country, this may be a legitimate purpose of the institution that is conducting the program, but it is something different from the education of the student, which should remain the primary goal of the whole enterprise. It is a purpose, incidentally, which involves the maintenance of high academic standards. It has been the experience of the Fulbright program that students who assume the role of traveling salesmen of American culture can do more harm than good, whereas young scholars whose main purpose is to achieve proficiency in their chosen field of study may earn a respect through their performance that in the long run well serves the interest of their country.

In the interests of international understanding, the principles of mutuality and reciprocity should govern institutional arrangements overseas. Cooperation with the nationals of the host country should be sought at every turn when planning and operating the program.

2 "Sweet Briar College, Junior Year in France, 1963–1964," *Bulletin of Sweet Briar College,* vol. 45, no. 6, November, 1962.

Many programs do nothing to reciprocate for the government subsidies their students receive in the form of low academic fees and inexpensive costs for board and room. For schools whose foreign programs enable them to enroll more students without expanding campus facilities, measures of reciprocity are absolutely essential, lest it appear that these institutions are seeking to deal with overcrowded conditions at home by increasing such problems overseas. One solution is to provide special facilities abroad, as Stanford does for its own students. As a small return for favors received abroad, Antioch has instituted work-study programs in this country for young foreigners, designed to provide an introduction to American life. There are many possibilities of reciprocating by offering special opportunities for foreign scholars and students to come to American campuses as well as by contributing resources and physical facilities to foreign institutions.

PATTERNS AND PROBLEMS

The programs through which these purposes are pursued are as varied as the institutions that administer them. They vary in time spent abroad, from the traditional academic year at one end of the spectrum to the summer program at the other, and in between there are various configurations of semester, summer plus, or quarter abroad. Some programs are restricted to students of the administering institution; others are open to students of all institutions and may even, like Sweet Briar's Junior Year in France, enroll very few of their own. Programs also range widely in locale. Paris has continued to be a favored site, but the movement has spread first to other cities, such as Munich, Geneva, Madrid, Florence, and Rome; then to university centers, such as Heidelberg, Bonn, Caen, Neuchâtel, and Bordeaux; and then to other provincial universities in most Western European countries.

More recently programs have been sprouting on other continents, first in Mexico, then elsewhere in Latin America, and now in Asia and Africa. In Latin America, the Syracuse Semester in Guatemala joined such programs as those of Fordham in Chile, Indiana University in Peru, and the University of Kansas in Costa Rica. In Lebanon, Princeton broke new ground by establishing the National Undergraduate Program for Overseas Study of Arabic. Wisconsin sponsors an Undergraduate Year in India, and the University of

Southern California sends students to Tunis University. There is a welcome move toward interinstitutional cooperation in these newer regions. In Latin America, Columbia administers a summer anthropological program in cooperation with Cornell, Harvard, and the University of Illinois; in Taipei and Tokyo, Stanford administers interuniversity programs that accept undergraduates. The Great Lakes Colleges Association sponsors programs at the American University of Beirut, Waseda University in Japan, and in Bogotá. The association's Colombia project makes use of the Guanajuato study center of its member college Antioch as a staging area for Spanish-language study.

Cross-cultural experience: how intense?

There are important differences in the types of relationship established by the American institution with the foreign university. In more ways than one, each represents a different world. The American student comes from a system of higher education for the many; he is girded about by all manner of aids to learning, course syllabi, prescribed assignments, periodic examinations, reserve-book shelves, and even occasionally some individual attention from the professor. The European university, on the other hand, is an operation for the elite, where in a rarefied intellectual atmosphere, there is fierce competition for books, for library and laboratory space, and even for seats in the vast lecture hall, where the professor may condescend to give of his learning more or less regularly.

The junior year abroad: misconceptions

Relatively few of our undergraduates are able to follow courses as regular students in Continental universities. The junior year pattern was conceived as a means of providing a shelter in the midst of the hostile environment, from which the American student could make occasional forays into the foreign world of learning. Professor Helen W. Randall, who served for many years as the chairman of the Junior Year Abroad committee of Smith College, describes the arrangements like this:

In Paris, Florence and Madrid, Smith College hires foreign professors, lecturers and teachers to give in their own language

American-style courses with all the paraphernalia of quizzes, papers and examinations. Each of these three Junior Years has its own rented classroom, library of reference books, its own program of courses with appropriate credit hours from which each girl who is not prepared for the competition of a university course can accumulate the necessary thirty hours for the year's work. It is an essential part of the director's job to indoctrinate newly engaged teachers, who are often the junior members of the foreign university, in the conventions of American pedagogy so that the students will be operating in the familiar context and the registrar's office back home can record the results in the familiar pattern. . . . To a much greater degree than one would wish, the Junior Year is a Smith College in miniature operating in its own splendid isolation in France, Spain, and Italy, and with a large complement of safeguards in Switzerland.[3]

Some of Professor Randall's Smith colleagues would dissent from her final judgment, but her description of a classic junior year program has been cited at length because it may serve to correct a common misconception. It is a prevailing opinion, unfortunately furthered by descriptions in college catalogs, that a junior year abroad means study as a regular student in a foreign university and that anything less than that is not properly foreign study at all. There is a tendency to decry any arrangements that do not put the American student cheek by jowl with his opposite numbers abroad in courses that have been designed for a totally different kind of academic creature. But there is nothing wrong in taking advantage of courses organized for foreigners by French universities, for example, or even in placing students in preuniversity courses. The student who works with a *sympathique* young scholar from a *lycée* near Paris may receive a much more effective introduction to French culture than he would get by listening to lectures of renowned but remote scholars. What is to be avoided is advertising this as studying at the Sorbonne.

The American "campus abroad"—pros and cons

The problem for the American college is not how to provide for its students a university experience abroad, but rather how to draw maximum profit from all the available resources for education,

[3] Helen W. Randall, "Smith's Junior Year Abroad," *Institute of International Education Newsletter,* pp. 13ff., February, 1961.

whether they are universities or not. The cutting edge of Professor Randall's criticism is not whether her institution has set up "miniature Smith Colleges" abroad, but whether what has been set up is really in "splendid isolation." Consider the case of Stanford, which has made no bones about establishing miniature Stanfords overseas. In branch campuses in France, Italy, and Germany, Stanford students live and learn in English under Stanford professors, with no formal relationship with a foreign university. The Stanford purpose reads:

Overseas classwork, while partaking deeply of the human and cultural riches of Europe, is fully coordinated with Stanford's regular curriculum so that it is available to students not only of the humanities and social sciences but also of natural sciences, engineering, and other professions. The program furthers Stanford's philosophy that her men and women shall achieve a broad comprehension of the society in which they live in addition to preparing a specialty.[4]

By one measure Stanford clearly achieves its purpose: under this program, one-third of all its undergraduates are able to study abroad. Stanford's detractors shrug off this remarkable figure and point to the isolation of the living and studying arrangements. But a foreign base of this sort is not in itself necessarily good or bad; what counts is how it is used. The Stanford officials claim that the academic courses ". . . derive extra dimension and value from being taught in the European environment," that classes ". . . are enlightened and enriched by direct contact with source material, that professors must tailor their instruction to the opportunities of the setting." To what extent? One would like to hear from the professors whether the setting is restrictive or inspiring. To what extent does the foreign setting infiltrate the classroom, as by a process of osmosis, and to what extent do the Stanford professors seek their teaching materials outside the classroom and design their courses differently from the way they design those at home? This is the test that should be applied to a branch campus abroad. The question to ask is the one we raised in discussing purposes: How clearly is the program related to the special opportunities of the particular culture where it is located?

The student need not enroll in a foreign university to have a

[4] *Standard Overseas Campuses,* Stanford University, Stanford, Calif., December, 1962.

significant educational experience abroad, but there is solid agreement that the more he is enabled to participate in the life of a
foreign people, the richer his experience is likely to be. The better
programs seek to multiply such opportunities and to encourage
their students to discuss differences in values and institutions with
members of their own age group and others. Young Americans at
foreign universities have the advantage of being exposed to a new
educational system, and they have opportunities to take part in
student activities and even to live in student dormitories with room-
mates from the host culture. At the same time, it must be remembered that the student community abroad is a distinctive sub-
culture; in large universities it is likely to be an international
one, and an American program does not necessarily achieve a deep
immersion in a national culture for its students when it arranges
for merely an academic dip.

Planning cross-cultural encounters

Many programs seek a fuller exposure by lodging their students
with families, where they may participate in a basic group. The
difficulties of finding the right families cannot be minimized. In
many cases the relationship remains formal, and the student is
never more than a paying guest. On the other hand, he may become
so much one of the family that he resists its possessiveness and
yearns for more freedom. Paradoxically, each successful placement
makes the family a little more cosmopolitan and a little less typical.
But whatever its problems, the home stay is one of the most valuable experiences the student can have abroad, and it is worth the
trouble involved. In arranging for it, colleges have had the help of
the Experiment in International Living, with its years of experience
in this type of activity.

There are other ways of providing exposure in depth to the
foreign culture. After the study period, some colleges plan for their
students' participation in youth activities, such as work camps. A
period of study at Bryn Mawr's academically challenging French
Institute at Avignon was followed by a period during which students could join a French archaeological expedition nearby. Job
experiences are just as much a part of the Keuka and Antioch
programs overseas as they are at home. More unusual is the
Princeton noncredit summer work program, under which college

men from a number of American institutions have worked in factories, banks, and business firms in various countries of Europe and Latin America: "Working side by side on the job with people of another nation, speaking their language and sharing their burdens, they can penetrate deeply into the life of the country."[5] Each student investigated some study project while on the job and submitted a report at the end of the summer. This is the kind of experience that might well be exploited by educational programs abroad. With a wide range of opportunities available for Americans in work camps, in trainee programs in German business, in children's summer camps in France, and as interns in international agencies, it is a pity that the major noncurricular activity of so many American programs is more travel.

Of course, even a travel program may manage to contrive more than a slight brush with the foreign society for its students if planning is not dominated by the number of countries the participants can collect. Youth centers may be used instead of hotels, and public transportation instead of chartered buses; intergroup activities may be stressed instead of lectures by a succession of local dignitaries. Every opportunity should be taken to encourage the properly prepared student to do some exploring on his own. That such independence is actually the nightmare of the typical tour leader is commentary enough on the conventional program of this sort.

How much language preparation?

Closely allied with the question of the intensity of the cross-cultural experience is the question of how much language preparation the student should have before departure. Many educators insist upon the strictest language requirements. The advisory statement of the National Committee of the Regional Accrediting Agencies declares, for example, that students ". . . must be sufficiently prepared in the language of instruction to be able to take courses as taught by nationals." This is a counsel of perfection. Even high-quality junior year programs commonly give their already well-prepared students an intensive language course on

[5] Edward D. Sullivan, *Princeton Program for Summer Work Abroad: Report for the Summer of 1962,* Department of Romance Languages, Princeton University, Princeton, N.J., 1962. (Mimeographed.)

arrival overseas to try to bring them up to this level. Moreover, the statement seems directed entirely toward programs of study in universities. A more moderate statement, but with similar emphasis, is that of the Carnegie Corporation:

To the extent that it is possible and reasonable to expect, full use of the relevant language should be the central feature of study abroad. In areas where French, German and Spanish are spoken, it is fair to expect that Americans enrolling for study will already have had a considerable amount of instruction in the language, and that they will use it intensively during their experience abroad, with additional instruction if necessary. The more exotic the language the less reasonable it is to expect such mastery.[6]

There can be no question about the desirability of as much language preparation as possible. To gain the most significant experience of a foreign society clearly demands knowledge of its language. Returning students report that perhaps their greatest intellectual satisfactions abroad came from the competence they acquired in living and moving and having their being in another tongue. But there are valid programs in non-English-speaking areas that do not have such entrance requirements. Syracuse has intentionally designed its semester in Florence for the great majority of American undergraduates who lack language proficiency. Students with no previous language are accepted in this program, and the courses are conducted in English. But immediately upon arrival the students are placed with non-English-speaking families, and there is intensive Italian course work. The Syracuse administrators report that under such conditions both a high-caliber academic achievement and a meaningful cultural experience can be attained in a period of fifteen or sixteen weeks.[7] Hollins College similarly includes students without language study among the participants in its French program and reports that at the end of a year, they have shown remarkable progress in the language. For the Stanford program, "language prerequisites are kept at a moderate, easily met level so that it is possible for students in virtually all academic fields to attend." As in the Syracuse semester in Florence, they receive

[6] *Carnegie Corporation of New York Quarterly*, vol. 9, no. 1, p. 2, January, 1961.
[7] John Clarke Adams, *A Report on the Semester in Italy*, Syracuse University, Syracuse, N.Y., 1960.

intensive language instruction, although the compelling incentive of the family stay is lacking.

The insistence upon language preparation is in general a sound one and can help upgrade standards. Stiff language requirements may well be the hallmark of a program of quality, while complete neglect of the local language will raise questions about a program's isolation. Even a summer program in general studies can make some effort along this line. The Hope College Summer Session in Vienna, for example, is conducted in English, but students live with Viennese families, and German study is required of all participants, the lowest level being a noncredit introduction to the *Umgangsprache,* "German for Visitors." Yet language study can be overemphasized. In countries where an exotic language is spoken, a program might well settle for a rudimentary conversational ability and plan academic work in English, either in classes or in field projects which require no great competence in the local tongue. Otherwise, far too much of the world would be off limits to our wandering students, including those very regions that will be of the greatest importance in their future. Language qualifications must depend upon the general purpose of the particular program; there can be no universally set standards.

Who should go?

Language ability is only one of the student qualifications about which there is debate. A fundamental question is whether the average student should be allowed to go. Such educators as Harlan Cleveland and Samuel Gould have urged that every undergraduate should have the chance. There are colleges where this is attempted. Lake Erie, for example, sends its whole junior class abroad for the winter semester, and the Oberlin Conservatory formerly had a similar policy. Kalamazoo, with a well-endowed program, seeks ". . . to provide as an integral part of a Kalamazoo undergraduate education a period of foreign study for as many of our students (hopefully almost all) as can profit from it." To implement this aim, the Kalamazoo planners have had to arrange three different types of programs for students with differing levels of foreign-language ability.[8] Most colleges are more selective in their require-

[8] *Kalamazoo College Foreign Study Program,* Kalamazoo College, Kalamazoo, Mich., January, 1962. (Mimeographed.)

ments and insist on an academic average of at least C+, while several institutions restrict the foreign opportunities to honors students. There is general agreement that participants should be mature and stable, and some colleges specify that they should be qualified to be good ambassadors for their country. The programs that provide the greatest cultural immersion need to be most careful about personal qualifications other than academic prowess. The basic problem is that a student's success on the home campus by no means ensures success abroad, and tests have not yet been devised that can confidently predict good performance under conditions of cross-cultural impact. Moreover, individual failure abroad can have serious consequences, and not only for the student. As President Murray of Elmira College has pointed out in a letter to the author: "Some kinds of aberrations at home would be ignored and considered par for the course, but the same actions by students abroad could cause something just short of an international incident."

When to go?

Another consideration in student selection has to do with the moment in his college career when a student should study abroad. The traditional junior year has recently come in for questioning. It has became clearer that an American junior is usually not really in the same class as his European fellows when it comes to advanced work in his field and that in any case the major values of foreign study for the undergraduate lie in the realm of general education, which is usually the main emphasis of his course work during the first two years of college. Moreover, the student returning for his senior year has too short a time to reintegrate himself in both academics and social relationships. Newer programs have consequently been experimenting with the timing of the foreign study. Hollins students leave campus at the end of the first semester of their sophomore year and return for the second semester of their junior year. Smith has begun to include a few sophomores in the junior year. Stanford can readily permit qualified sophomores to participate in the general education programs of its branch campuses, while a well-supervised "nearby" program, such as Goddard's in French Canada or Antioch's center at Guanajuato in Mexico can accept well-qualified freshmen after a period on campus. The

most daring innovation is the program at Lewis and Clark College
in Oregon, which includes a large number of freshmen in groups
sent on independent study programs to Latin America and Japan
after only a few days on campus, with the hope that their whole
subsequent education will be illuminated by this early experience.

One inventive solution to the problem of "when?" is to use the
summer before the senior year for a seminar abroad for superior
students, which is the basis of the European program in international relations administered by Princeton on behalf of ten cooperating colleges. For colleges with a well-organized honors program, like that of Swarthmore, one of the participating institutions,
this program represents the only opportunity for abler students to
take part of their college work overseas.

IMPROVING THE EDUCATIONAL RESULTS

The fundamental objection to foreign study involves its relationship
to the conventional college curriculum. Summer study abroad may
supplement the curriculum; an academic term abroad replaces part
of it. What can the foreign experience do for the student to make
up for his loss of a rigorous intellectual experience on campus?
The faculty members who raise this question are not to be dis-
missed as benighted provincials. They believe in what they are
doing in their classrooms. They have, to the best of their ability,
worked out a program that they feel adds up to a liberal education,
and they are loath to surrender a major part of it. They deplore the
estrangement from campus which an extended absence abroad can
produce. Thomas Jefferson opposed foreign study on the very
grounds that it alienated youths from the national community.
"They return as strangers," he wrote.[9] In the eyes of many of their
professors, this is generally true.

What evidence do we have that the returning student has made
educational gains as significant as or more significant than, those he
would have made on campus? It is surprising how few researchers
have tried to measure the impact of foreign study upon the American student. But the classic study of Pace on the alumni of the

[9] Letter to J. Bannister, Jr., Paris, Oct. 15, 1785, in Andrews A. Lips-
comb and Albert E. Bergh (eds.), *The Writings of Thomas Jefferson*,
library ed., Washington, D.C., 1903, vol. 5, pp. 185–188.

Delaware–Sweet Briar program has found many echoes in the anec-
dotal data gathered by Garraty and Adams and others. In the
better programs, foreign study appears to have had a "strong and
pervasive" influence upon the lives of the participants, especially
in regard to general cultural values and political and international
attitudes.[10]

For purposes of analysis, four types of educational outcome of
foreign study may be identified: (*1*) language skill; (*2*) content
learning knowledge about the arts, international affairs, and a
foreign civilization; (*3*) cross-cultural understanding; and (*4*)
development of personal values—a clearer sense of what one believes about the good, the true, and the beautiful and of what one
knows of oneself. These educational results may all be furthered on
campus, but a well-designed encounter with the world abroad is
more certain to produce most of them.

Nothing on campus, of course, can match the ideal conditions for
language learning abroad. As for factual learning, the incentive
can be similarly heightened by the practical needs of the student
not only to communicate but also to find out about his new environment. It must be admitted that such knowledge is likely to be
more selective and less systematic than that acquired on campus
and that many programs fail to take full advantage of this incentive
and actually set academic standards lower abroad than at home.

Cross-cultural understanding, like linguistic skill, is obviously
more likely to be achieved abroad, where the textbook concept of
cultural relativity becomes real through actual encounter and where
a student may gain a real appreciation of a foreign people and an
understanding of how they live, what they take for granted, and
how their values differ from his own. Such an understanding goes
far deeper than intellectual comprehension and can even force the
student to reconsider his own values and assumptions.

[10] C. Robert Pace, *The Junior Year in France,* Syracuse University
Press, Syracuse, N.Y., 1959; John A. Garraty and Walter Adams, *From
Main Street to the Left Bank: Students and Scholars Abroad,* Michigan
State University Press, East Lansing, Mich., 1959; Edward W. Weidner,
The World Role of Universities, McGraw-Hill Book Company, New
York, 1962, pp. 71–76.
For some interesting summaries of recent research in this field, see
George C. Coelho (ed.), "Impacts of Studying Abroad," *Journal of
Social Issues,* vol. 18, no. 1, January, 1962; and Sven Lundstedt (ed.),
"Human Factors in Cross-cultural Adjustment," *Journal of Social Is-
sues,* vol. 19, no. 3, July, 1963.

Exploring the extracurricular experience

It may be argued that cross-cultural understanding and the self-examination to which it can give rise constitute the most significant educational result of foreign study, an outcome rarely produced by the conventional curriculum on campus. For that matter, it is no automatic consequence of exposure to a foreign environment or of a classroom-centered experience abroad. These values are most likely to be attained when there is in the educational design itself a plan for interaction between the curricular and the extracurricular, between life and study.

We know that it is the nonacademic experiences that leave the deepest impression upon our students abroad. It is these which lead him to spend less time with formal studies than he would at home. After all, the student hardly would be normal if he preferred a bout with the books to the stimulating discussion awaiting him at the sidewalk cafe—if he stayed in his room studying when history was being made under his window. He should be encouraged to make the most of such opportunities to explore the foreign community, and as much on his own as possible. But his discoveries are not an end in themselves. They are the raw stuff out of which an appreciation of life and a new understanding of man and his cultural heritage can be fashioned. It is up to the college to make sure that the student subjects these experiences to thoroughgoing intellectual examination. Not life abroad, but the *examined* life, is to be chiefly valued.

Weakest link: integration with campus education

The best way to answer the objection that the student abroad is missing a rigorous intellectual experience on campus is to give him one, to plan the sojourn overseas as the laboratory period of an intellectual adventure begun before his departure and carried forward on his return. As matters stand, integration with campus education is the weakest point in most programs. Orientation sessions are frequently hurried affairs, tucked into some corner of the student's busy schedule and generally confined to travel tips and a dash of current affairs. At best there may be come solid area study. Rarely is orientation a full-dress course, offered for academic credit and specifically intended to prepare the student for cross-cultural exploration.[11] There are a few exceptions. Goddard's course in comparative cultures introduces the student on campus to methods of social analysis, which he is later to use in Quebec. Antioch provides the student with some experience in techniques of social observation, which can be tested both on campus and during the job period before departure for foreign shores. Adelphi students who studied in Japan, Hong Kong, and elsewhere in the Pacific began with a summer Across the U.S.A. course, exploring America from coast to coast.

The language preparation for foreign study offers an excellent opportunity to introduce the student to the cultural behavior of the society he is to encounter. But most language teachers have not had room for cultural anthropology in their graduate programs, and very few are equipped to teach language as an aspect of cultural behavior. Some of the best of them, it is true, have an intuitive grasp of the culture whose language they teach and manage to communicate it to their students through study of literary works and through their very handling of the language in the classroom. But for most language teachers, what is needed is an assortment of cultural readers—not the anthologies so widely in use today, which represent a hodgepodge of information about a civilization and which are mainly intended to increase vocabulary, but carefully arranged selections of materials from both literary and everyday sources, which would provide the basis for some logical analysis.[12] Language teaching overseas could profit even more effectively from such methods. There, the whole waking day outside the classroom serves as a living language laboratory, and the results of language study are spectacular. There appears to be little effort to arrange for this purposefully, with laboratory exercises and experiments designed to be performed outside class and the results brought back for inspection. But who can expect language teachers abroad to tamper with the time-honored methods that they credit for their successes?

---

[11] The question of orientation is discussed in Irwin Abrams, "Preface to Study Abroad," *Journal of General Education,* vol. 14, no. 4, pp. 220–229, January, 1963.

[12] Cf. the contributions of Dan Desberg to the volume edited by Tatiana Fotitch, *Teaching Foreign Languages in the Modern World,* Catholic University of America, Washington, D.C., 1961, especially pp. 64–65.

The foreign classroom and the world outside

Programs overseas that move beyond the classroom to make imaginative use of the world outside are few and far between. The typical study tour, which so often is no more than sightseeing with a syllabus, could actually do better *with* a classroom. In the usual program of this sort, one exciting experience follows so rapidly on the heels of another that there is neither time nor incentive for reflection, let alone intellectual analysis. The advisory statement of the accrediting agencies does well to discourage granting academic credit for study tours. There are residential programs that leave the classroom for group visits, but this pattern often gives more exercise to the feet than to the intellect. It is best if it is not the class that moves en masse, but the individual student who ventures forth, following his natural bent for exploring the world around him—not unguided but as part of an educational design that leads him to submit his findings to intellectual scrutiny and ultimately to classroom or professional examination. The conventional course in art history abroad might make more use of the classroom; the professor could prepare his students for individual sorties to the crowded art galleries or even for purposeful strolls through the streets, observing the city itself as a work of art and noting architectural monuments and the skyline as social documents. There are drama courses, especially in the Paris programs, that use such methods, planning the curriculum according to the season's theatrical fare. The student prepares for the performance by reading the play and listening to lectures; then he spends the evening at the theater, and afterward he writes his critique.

This takes no great imagination to arrange, but it suggests a pattern that could be used in other courses. A lecture in geography would introduce the student to a landscape. Then he would explore it for himself on a hosteling trip, asking questions at marketplace, farm, and railroad station; perhaps taking photographs or making sketches; noting his observations in his journal; and on his return, putting his findings together in a formal report.

There are a few programs that send students on well-planned independent study projects. The Princeton International Relations Program, already referred to, is an excellent example of how this can be done as part of a total experience that integrates campus and overseas. As part of their application, superior students from the cooperating colleges propose individual subjects for investigation that fall within an announced general topic, such as "Nationalism" or "The Impact of the Non-European World upon Western Europe." In the spring period on campus, they receive academic credit for preparatory work on the project. Soon after the end of the school year, the director and the students assemble at the Institute for Social Studies at The Hague, where in a two-week seminar they criticize one another's projects and make arrangements for the research period. Then the students move individually to the scene of their research, where they spend the next two months. During this period each is on his own, although during the first month each is placed in a family by the Experiment in International Living and may be visited by the director. At the end of the summer the group reassembles at Oxford University to report findings at a two-week seminar. After his return to campus, each student works his data into a thesis submitted to his professor. The thesis represents the equivalent of at least one year-long course.

Another pattern that holds promise is for the American institution to establish a field station overseas, where its professors would be engaged in research, assisted by superior students who might at the same time carry on individual study projects. The anthropology program administered by Columbia has been organized along these lines. Designed not for fledgling anthropologists but to yield cross-cultural understanding, the program has placed Spanish-speaking students at work on individual research projects in field stations of these universities in Ecuador, Mexico, Brazil, and Peru. Some of the students have worked individually in small villages. Such project-centered programs are likely to increase in the future, not only in Europe, but (especially as foreign study moves into new parts of the world, like Africa) also where the traditional patterns devised for Europe are less appropriate. It is worthy of note that both the Columbia anthropology program and the Princeton international relations program draw support from the Carnegie Foundation, which has a special concern that overseas programs be constructed that can appeal to the ablest students.[13]

Educational experimentation is also fostered in the study centers abroad in which American faculty live with their students. There may be drawbacks in such an arrangement, but it has all the advantages of the very small college, and new teaching methods, some

[13] *Carnegie Corporation of New York Quarterly,* pp. 1–4, January, 1961.

of them quite impromptu, may be tried. What Stanford says of faculty-student relationships is true of many another American faculty abroad: "the professors . . . literally live with their students, teaching in and out of the classroom." Redlands reports similar advantages in its Salzburg program, where faculty and students lived together in a hotel and where the dining room was transformed at breakfast time into a classroom, with each table taking a special topic for discussion. The Redlands professors found that in such informal settings students could take far more responsibility for planning and leading discussions, and they came to know the students so well that they were able to dispense with formal examinations.

Debriefing: planned or unplanned?

In such a discussion setting or through some other device, the student should be called upon not only to demonstrate the factual knowledge and the linguistic skill he has acquired abroad but also to try to transmute some of the intangibles of his foreign experience into data for intellectual examination. The results of his "extra-curricular" exploration are too often left unexamined on the student's return. The college has the responsibility, not so much to pry into his inner life, but to see to it that he gives careful scrutiny to the values of which his foreign experience has helped him become aware. This is all the more essential because the returning student, often the very one who has most successfully come to grips with the demands of living in an alien society, suffers a cultural shock on reentry that is all the more severe because it is so unexpected. He knew he would find things very different abroad, but he is ill prepared on his return for the realization not only that he himself has changed but also that the old familiar surroundings are no longer the same and that he "can't go home again." It is at this very moment, when the student is seeking to relocate himself and his world, that the college should provide academic arrangements through which potentially disruptive and negative feelings can become the stimuli for one of the most crucial educational experiences of his college years. At the very least there should be occasions when he discusses with his mentors what he is learning about cultural differences; at most his professors can help him refine the questions that he is asking himself as he develops a philosophy for his life. Unfortunately, there is little indication that colleges have been very imaginative in aiding the returned student to consolidate such gains of study abroad.

Academic crediting

In the evaluation of the results of a student's study abroad, the problem of academic crediting is a major concern. Here is an area where something positive can be done to raise standards, and the statements of the various educational bodies are emphatic about the point that academic credit for foreign work should be granted using the same criteria for quality that are used for work on campus. Prevailing methods of handling crediting differ considerably. Institutions that set up their own programs alongside those of the foreign university have no problem in duplicating stateside practices, although they must acquaint the local teachers whom they employ with American expectations of quality and quantity of accomplishment. Programs that encourage participation in regular university courses overseas run into difficulties. Course examinations are not common, and when the American director arranges for special ones to be given or seeks to take advantage of such available examinations as those for scholarship students in Germany, he often finds that the European professor does not take these occasions very seriously. Frequently our student will receive as a grade the equivalent of the "foreign-student B" in America. In any case it is up to the American director to translate the local evaluation into the appropriate symbols for the registrar at home. Some colleges simplify this procedure by granting a "satisfactory" for the whole program abroad, when deserved, instead of a distinctive grade for each course. Colleges follow different policies when their student returns from a program administered by another institution. His grades may be automatically registered as transfer credit, or he may also have to submit for inspection tangible evidence of his accomplishment, such as his class notes, papers, and examinations, and then be tested once more. The final examination at home is viewed in different ways. There are those who are indignant about the fact that credits earned in reputable institutions abroad need any review whatsoever. On the other hand, there are professors who are disposed to hold foreign evaluations as suspect. Such matters of principle apart, many faculty members agree in regarding the examining of the returning students as simply an unwanted chore. Under proper circumstances, however, a formal occasion for the evaluation of the results of study abroad could mean for the professor not a burden, but rather the privilege of participating in the most educationally exciting part of the student's whole adventure.

The performance of the student abroad must be evaluated quantitatively as well as qualitatively. How many credits should he receive? Here again practices differ. The most common policy is to attempt to arrange a program that will give the student the same number of credits that he would have earned at home, and this generally means giving him the same number of courses. If he is attending regular university courses, which ordinarily do not meet as frequently as in America, this may necessitate some mathematical calculation concerning the number of hours spent in the lecture hall in order to arrive at the proper number of credit hours. Institutions that make use of the world outside may devise a formula to account for the nonclassroom experiences. In the study tours of the State University of New York, for example, it takes fifteen clock hours to equal one hour of semester credit. While one hour of lecture or discussion is reckoned at par value, it takes two hours of attendance at performances or visits to museums, preceded by adequate preparation, to equal one such hour; for such activities engaged in without preparation but with the approval of the instructor, three hours are credited as one.

Such efforts give rise to mixed feelings. On one hand, one can only applaud the attempts to maintain high standards. On the other hand, the transplantation of the American credit system to the foreign scene only sets off more sharply the mechanistic approach to education that it represents. We are accustomed to dividing the undergraduate's education into segments called "credits," which he collects systematically as though he were stringing beads and which are reckoned by the number of sitting hours he passes reading a book or listening to a lecture.[14] But overseas, where much of what the student learns is not acquired through sitting hours at all, this kind of calculation is even less relevant to what is in his mind.

[14] There are some indications that American higher education may be beginning to question this "class-hours-attended formula" for determining the number of academic credits a student may earn. Chapter 3 deals with some of the new programs of independent study and presents a fuller discussion of the issues involved here.

HOW REVOLUTIONARY?

What has happened is that in the commendable attempt to make
foreign study respectable, there has been an understandable but
deplorable deference to traditionalism that ill becomes a revolution-
ary new vehicle for education. The foreign laboratory should serve
to test the conventional way that we tend to take so much for
granted. The apocryphal professor who planned to take his students through the Louvre in his usual class period of fifty minutes
was lecturing to the sound of a distant bell indeed. Study abroad
will achieve its promise only when we break through the old patterns and strike out for something new.

A challenge to the college teacher

The key to such educational experimentation is of course the
American faculty. Too many programs have been initiated by the
administration, by one department, or by a professor with a special
interest and have not been brought to the general faculty for considered approval. Sometimes the initiative has even come from
travel bureaus, whose blandishments are hardly to be resisted by
the professor who is promised a free trip abroad in return for signing up the required number of customers and inducing his college
to grant academic credit. The college that allows itself to be used
in this way has a serious responsibility. It forgets that any project
that bears its name overseas involves its whole faculty, who must be
regarded as standing behind any grant of credit by their institution. At least the project should be first approved by them and then
overseen by the appropriate dean and committee. But this is the
very minimum. What is needed is somehow to turn the imaginative
and creative minds of American college teachers to the vast potentialities that are waiting for us overseas, and this cannot be done by
committee report alone. The campus faculty must take part in the
entire educational process of foreign study, from the preparation
on campus to the final debriefing. To this end, means must be found
to give the faculty some experience in the foreign program, not
through junkets for deserving professors, but by sending them on
well-defined educational missions. Many institutions, as we have
seen, send their professors abroad to teach in the program. Others,

such as a number of junior year programs, rotate their professors in administrative posts abroad, although this generally reaches only one department and has the further disadvantage that the position abroad, especially if it is that of the director, requires a totally different set of qualifications from the teaching job at home. The best arrangement would seem to be to send the professor abroad as part of an ongoing program for faculty improvement, with an assignment as consultant, part-time student adviser, or simply observer abroad, without administrative responsibilities. This can be financed in part through the financial savings from group travel. As programs expand beyond the Atlantic Community, it is imperative that professors have opportunities for travel and training in the new areas, not only so that they can actively participate in developing the very different educational patterns that will be called for, but also so that they will have enough expertise to enter intelligently into the dialogue with the returning student.

Implications for campus education

In improving the educational results of foreign programs, then, we must be prepared to take not only the student but also the professor out of the classroom. And when we take the student from the campus classroom, shall we rest content if we merely transport him to its equivalent abroad? When we observe something of the impact upon him of his life abroad, can we make the traditional division and say, "This much for the registrar; this other is 'non-academic'?" Are we not rather compelled to consider more carefully this vital interaction between life and study, to seek teaching methods that exploit the environment, and to submit the experience outside the classroom to intellectual examination? Will we not be more willing, perhaps, to trust the student more on his own, to develop ways for him to take more responsibility for his own learning? Will we begin to look askance at that academic lockstep, the credit system, when we see students returning from abroad with something more valuable than a collection of assembled credit hours, and will we seek new methods of transmuting their experience into academic coin of the realm through seminars, theses defended, oral examinations, or whatever? Might we even come to conceive of college education not so much as a rigidly prescribed pattern of courses with specific titles (so that courses abroad must bear the same appellations, no matter what the student actually does), but rather as a series of experiences to be examined in the light of the knowledge and methodology of the several disciplines?

If we strike out along these lines, not only may the impact of the foreign-study movement internationalize the student and his campus, but it may also lead us to reexamine some of the fundamental premises of how we assure our students a liberal education.

SOURCES FOR FURTHER INFORMATION
Sources of Information

Academic Programs Abroad: An Exploration of Their Assets and Liabilities, Report of a Special Conference at Mt. Holyoke, January 14–16, 1960, Institute of International Education, 809 United Nations Plaza, New York, May, 1960.

Guide to the Evaluation of Overseas Programs, Council of Student Travel, 777 United Nations Plaza, New York. (In preparation.)

Report of National Workshop on Overseas Programs for Students, Council of Student Travel, 777 United Nations Plaza, New York, Dec. 5–7, 1962.

Transplanted Students: A Report of the National Conference on Undergraduate Study Abroad, October, 1960, Institute of International Education, 809 United Nations Plaza, New York, June, 1961.

Undergraduate Study Abroad: Report of the Consultative Service on U.S. Undergraduate Study Abroad, Stephen A. Freeman, consultant, Institute of International Education, New York, 1964. (Good bibliography; one of the most basic and up-to-date references on programs of study abroad.)

Interpretation and Discussion

Abrams, Irwin: "Study Abroad," *New Dimensions in Higher Education,* no. 6, U.S. Office of Education, Washington, D.C., 1960.

———: "Preface to Study Abroad," *Journal of General Education,* vol. 14, no. 4, pp. 220–229, Jan., 1963.

Garraty, John A., and Walter Adams: *From Main Street to the Left Bank,* Michigan State University Press, East Lansing, Mich., 1959.

———— and ————: *A Guide to Study Abroad: University, Summer School, Tour and Work-Study Programs,* Channel Press, Inc., Manhasset, N.Y., 1962.

Journal of General Education, articles by M. Battsek, Lewis Hoskins, Paul Weaver, and John A. Wallace, Jan., 1962.

Shank, Donald J.: "The American Goes Abroad," *Annals of the American Academy of Political and Social Science,* vol. 335, pp. 99–111, May, 1961.

Weidner, Edward W.: *The World Role of Universities,* McGraw-Hill Book Company, New York, 1962, chaps. 4–6.

Statement of Standards for Foreign Programs

Carnegie Corporation of New York Quarterly, p. 2, Jan., 1961.

Kurtz, John W.: *Summer Study Programs Abroad for American Students: A Statement of Principles Adopted at a Conference at Oberlin College in February, 1961,* Department of German and Russian, Oberlin College, Oberlin, Ohio.

Programs of Foreign Study: An Advisory Statement by the National Committee of Regional Accrediting Agencies, Council on Student Travel Membership meeting, New York, Nov. 17, 1961. (Mimeographed.)

Research

Coelho, George V. (ed.): "Impacts of Studying Abroad," *Journal of Social Issues,* vol. 18, no. 1, Jan., 1962.

Lundstedt, Sven (ed.): "Human Factors in Cross-cultural Adjustment," *Journal of Social Issues,* vol. 19, no. 3, July, 1963.

Pace, Robert C.: *The Junior Year in France,* Syracuse University Press, Syracuse, N.Y., 1959.

MAXWELL H. GOLDBERG
NORMAN D. KURLAND

5

the abler student

*T*he present surge of concern for the abler student is no novelty
in American education. While Sputnik may have been the immediate stimulus, the impulse had already been set in motion before
October 4, 1957. As far back as 1963, observers such as Ralph W.
Gerard were alerting Americans to Russia's zeal for its abler
students in the sciences. Time, in its issue for January 14, 1957,
referred to talented youth as "our perishable resource." Although
the tide was already changing when Sputnik went into orbit, as
Elizabeth Paschal has observed, "few changes in education have
come with more dramatic rapidity than the change of attitude
toward special programs for the more able or gifted students . . .
the vast majority of the programs in existence today and the great
preponderance of research were initiated within the past decade."[1]
This chapter reviews developments in programs for abler students.

[1] *Encouraging the Excellent,* Fund for the Advancement of Education,
New York, 1960, p. 7.

BACKGROUND

The new honors movement, launched and advanced by the Inter-University Committee on the Superior Student, graphically illustrates the extraordinary speed and vigor with which the tempo of concern and action for the abler student has been accelerating and gaining in breadth and impact. More than half the current honors programs have been inaugurated since 1960. In its last count of programs (October, 1962), ICSS figures showed a total of 334 institutions as having some kind of honors offering, with over forty thousand students participating in these programs. Since that time, many more programs have come into being.[2]

While competition with the Russians has given great impetus to the concern for the abler student, the fact that this concern antedates Sputnik shows that other forces were at work. A maturing culture was beginning to see more value in intelligence, and a maturing economy was providing greater scope for its exercise. A rapidly advancing technology was calling for a large increase in highly trained manpower, concurrent with rapidly decreasing opportunity for those with low ability and little education. The pressure on everyone to get more education, coupled with a postwar birth boom that was soon to send the size of the college-age group spiraling upward, posed a threat to the quality of higher education and to its ability to provide educational opportunities suited to the needs of the ablest.

These factors set thoughtful educators and laymen to considering ways to ensure, first, that more of our abler youth would go to college and, second, that they would receive the best possible education once they got there. Since the actions required to find, motivate, and enable talented students to go to college are different from those required to provide for their educational needs, different groups and different kinds of programs have been involved in

[2] While honors programs have witnessed their largest growth in the decades since World War II, mention should be made of some of the very early programs, such as that pioneered by Frank Aydelotte at Swarthmore in the early 1920s. For a review of many of the earlier honors programs, see Robert H. Bonthius, James F. Davis, J. Garber Drushal, in collaboration with Francis V. Guille and Warren P. Spencer, *The Independent Study Program in the United States,* Columbia University Press, New York, 1957.

these two activities. This distinction provides a natural division for the review of developments that is the subject of this chapter.

Identification, Recruitment, and Support

The need for action to increase the number of abler students going on to college is evident from the estimate made in 1954 by the Commission on Human Resources and Advanced Training that "fewer than half of the upper twenty-five per cent of all high school graduates ever earn college degrees, [and] only six out of ten of the top five per cent do."[3]

When the nation was alerted to this situation, action followed swiftly. There was a concerted attack on all the factors that influence the decision to go to college: high school programs, teaching, counseling, and climate; public and parental attitudes toward going to college; financial ability; familiarity with colleges and their expectations; and college recruitment and selection policies.

In recent years, high schools have made great strides in upgrading their curricula and in instituting programs for able students. Everything from formal honors programs to informal Saturday seminars has been introduced. Valuable guidance has been provided by the National Education Association's Project on the Academically Talented Students, whose many publications contain descriptions of programs, bibliographies, and recommendations for action.

Although the high schools have done much on their own, programs of college–high school cooperation have been increasing. Their net effect for the abler student is to blur the traditional sharp line between high school and college. Early-admission programs have permitted able high school students to begin all or part of their college work before graduation from high school. While the practice of complete omission of the senior high school year has not been widely adopted,[4] a number of colleges now encourage abler high school students to take a course or two on campus while completing the regular work of the senior year in high school. The University of California and the California junior colleges have

[3] Dael Woefle, *America's Resources of Specialized Talent*, Harper & Row, Publishers, Incorporated, New York, 1954, p. 8.
[4] See *They Went to College Early: A Report on the Early Admission to College Program*, Fund for the Advancement of Education, New York, 1957.

extended this practice quite widely. The summer college program for abler high school students is another way the colleges reach down to give the youngsters a taste of college and influence their attitudes while they are still in high school.

Moving in the other direction, the College Entrance Examination Board's Advanced Placement Program moves portions of the college curriculum down into the high school. Its influence is reflected in its growth. In 1956, 1,229 students from 104 high schools took 2,199 examinations and entered 130 colleges; the corresponding 1964 figures were 28,874 students, 2,086 high schools, 37,829 examinations, and over 888 colleges.

The curriculum revisions, carried out in cooperative efforts between school and university faculties, so far largely limited to the sciences, under the sponsorship of the National Science Foundation, are helping prepare all students for more advanced work in college.

These developments are creating new expectations among entering students and are forcing the colleges to reexamine their freshman offerings, especially for their abler students.

Although ostensibly a program to provide financial aid for talented students, the National Merit Scholarship Corporation program has had an impact on public and parental attitudes far out of proportion to the relatively small number of students (about nine thousand) who have received scholarships in its nine years of existence. When many thousand students (800,000 in 1964) compete annually in a program awarding less than seventeen hundred scholarships, when high schools brag as much about their NMSC winners as about their star basketball players, and when colleges proudly announce their annual "bag" of winners, it is clear that the program is having a profound impact on the popular image of the talented student. Although this development has its detractors, there can be little doubt that the public, parents, and students are today more aware than ever before of the importance of high ability and achievement and of the financial opportunities available to those who qualify.

While the NMSC program is the most widely publicized scholarship program and involves the largest number of competitors, it is by no means the largest scholarship effort if the total amount awarded and number of recipients are taken into account. The New York State Regents Scholarship Program in 1964 awarded new scholarships to 17,400 students, which was about 8.5 per cent of all high school graduates in the state, and it is providing a total of 24 million dollars in scholarship aid to over seventy thousand students. The free-tuition policies of the highly selective University of California and City University of New York are another form of large-scale assistance to able students.

The financial-aid programs of the colleges themselves taken together probably constitute the largest single source of support. A report of January 9, 1964, in the *New York Times,* however, notes that at seventeen high-tuition institutions, tuition is rising faster than scholarship aid. At these institutions the scholarship budgets were 15.6 per cent of potential income from tuition, as opposed to more than 17 per cent two years before. Nonetheless, some colleges are acting to ensure that no qualified student will be denied admission for financial reasons. For example, in 1963 Yale announced a policy of admission without regard to financial ability, a policy that if widely followed by private colleges could go a long way toward eliminating economic condition as a factor in college attendance.

Yet the picture is not entirely rosy. A recent report by Donald L. Thistlethwaite notes that over half of the stipends from scholarship foundations and over 40 per cent of those from private colleges and Federal governmental agencies went to relatively well-to-do students and that available scholarship funds are not being administered so as to maximize their effects upon the recruitment of qualified students who are undecided about going to college. "A conservative estimate of talent loss among National Merit Scholarship examinees who have shown an interest in college," Dr. Thistlethwaite says, "is that one out of every six ranging in the upper thirty per cent of ability fails to enroll in college immediately."[5]

In March, 1963, U.S. Department of Health, Education, and Welfare secretary, Anthony J. Celebrezze, said: "Estimates indicate that between twenty-five and forty per cent of our most capable students—those with IQ's of 120 and above who want to go to college—do not now go beyond high school, largely because of financial need."[6]

Serious as the financial obstacle is, 1963 may be looked back upon as the year that saw the colleges and the public become aware that financial need is only one of the obstacles to the full development of the talents of those who suffer also from cultural deprivation. Even before the nation had found ways of ensuring that every

[5] *Recruitment and Retention of Talented College Youth,* unpublished final report to Cooperative Research Program, U.S. Office of Education, Washington, D.C., 1963.
[6] *Higher Education,* vol. 19, p. 13, March, 1963.

talented youngster from favored backgrounds went on to college, it had to take on the even more difficult challenge of finding, preparing, and motivating the hidden talents within the large disadvantaged minorities of the country, a task that had only just begun at the writing of this chapter.

This effort is tied closely to college recruitment programs that have been extending their nets ever wider in recent years. Whereas only a few years ago the more select institutions sent their admissions officers to only a small number of high schools, today these officers range widely over the country. The results are reflected in the extended geographical distributions and number of feeder high schools represented in the freshman classes of these institutions. What they have found is that as they broaden the base from which they select, the ability of those selected mounts ever upward. Thus, year after year, admissions officers are able to report to their faculties that "this year's freshman class is better than ever." At the same time, rising admissions standards are excluding students who would easily have gained admission a few years ago. And the students so excluded may in large part be coming from those groups and locations that have been subjected to severe educational deprivation. Thus an educational system that promoted the movement of previous minority groups into the mainstream of American culture may now be restricting that flow for contemporary minorities. There is grave concern lest the results be a stratification of institutions by ability and socioeconomic levels, a decline in the heterogeneity of student bodies, and a reduction of educational opportunity.

Colleges have been greatly aided in getting the kinds of students they want by increasingly effective selection devices. The high school record, a good but imperfect indication of ability and predictor of college performance, has been increasingly supplemented by standardized, nationally administered admissions tests. While these tests have come in for considerable criticism, they have, as Dean K. Whitla of Harvard notes, ". . . served us far better than we could have hoped when the conservative, slightly reluctant but persuadable members of the College Board almost forty years ago agreed to underwrite the Scholastic Aptitude Test, and later, the series of achievement tests. We would not, at the present time, be the same Harvard College without them."[7]

Colleges and testing agencies are experimenting with tests

[7] Leo Bramson (ed.), *Examining in Harvard College,* Harvard University, Cambridge, Mass., 1963, p. 59.

measuring a wider range of abilities as well as personality factors relevant to high achievement and creativity. They and the high schools are working on the introduction of electronic data processing for student records. These two developments should provide the colleges with far richer information on the basis of which both to select their students and to evaluate their programs. With due sophistication in the use of new measurement instruments and information analysis, each college can have greater control than in the past over the kind and variety of students it selects and, hence, over the kind of institution it will be.

Although there are well-known hazards in excessive testing and record making, when properly used, increased information available at the right time to the right person in a form that can be readily interpreted will work to enhance, not diminish, attention to the needs of the individual student. And it is just such concern that the needs of the individual talented student not be neglected amidst mounting enrollments that led to many of the programs to be described in the next section.

PROGRAMING FOR THE ABLER STUDENT

While not all college programing for the abler student is officially called "honors" or even organized explicitly in a "program," honors programs have in recent years come to be characteristic of the organized efforts to provide for the abler student. For this reason we can conveniently describe developments within the context of the honors movement.

This movement has derived its general impetus from all those factors cited earlier in this chapter for the increased attention to the abler student; the more specific impulse has come from the work of the Inter-University Committee on the Superior Student and its dynamic founder and first director, Joseph W. Cohen.

The ICSS itself was the product of a conference convened at the University of Colorado in June, 1957, to consider the problem of maintaining quality education in the face of rising enrollment, particularly in large publicly supported institutions.

The conference recommended that honors programs of the kind pioneered at the University of Colorado be established. It urged the creation of a central clearinghouse to facilitate the sharing of experiences among institutions and to stimulate discussion of new ideas, new techniques, and new understanding of the needs of the talented. The Carnegie Corporation supplied funds, and the ICSS in April, 1958, began publication of its newsletter, *The Superior Student,* which has since become the single most valuable source for information on all aspects of honors developments.

It has contained reports on honors activities in over two hundred colleges and universities. It has treated every aspect of honors programing, from the appointment of directors and the content of honors courses to the role of women in honors and the kind of rewards appropriate for honors students. It has listed the brochures published by many honors programs to inform prospective participants. These can be quite helpful to colleges considering the initiation or expansion of programs.[8]

A perusal of this wealth of material makes clear that there is no single pattern characteristic of all honors programs. Yet out of the experience of a great variety of programs and approaches, the ICSS has distilled a set of "major features" that have served as helpful guidelines to innumerable faculty committees as they sought a pattern appropriate to their own needs.

These major features are:

1. *Identify and select students of high ability as early as possible. This involves far closer cooperation than has hitherto been the case with high schools and preparatory schools. New experience has accumulated on the proper uses of predictive techniques, past records, entrance tests and interviews, as well as in studies of aptitude, motivation, readiness, and achievement.*

2. *Start programs for these students immediately upon admission to the college or university and admit other superior students into these programs whenever they are later identified by their teachers.*

3. *Make such programs continuous and cumulative through all four years with honors counseling especially organized and equally continuous.*

[8] Indexes published in the February, 1961, and May–June, 1962, issues provide useful guides both to the materials and to the institutions with programs. Brief descriptions of honors offerings at over 280 institutions are in the honors inventories published in the issues for January, 1961; November–December, 1961; and January–February, 1963.

4. *Formulate such programs so that they will relate effectively both to all the college work for the degree and to the area of concentration, departmental specialization, pre-professional or professional training.*

5. *Make the programs varied and flexible by establishing special courses, ability sections, honors seminars, colloquia, and independent study. Course credit for these is important to the students. Advanced placement and acceleration will serve in a contributory role.*

6. *Make the honors program increasingly visible throughout the institution so that it will provide standards and models of excellence for all students and faculty, and contribute to the substitution of an "honors outlook" for the "grade outlook." For the latter purpose gradelessness in some honors offerings is a frequent advantage, i.e., a "pass," "fail" approach.*

7. *Employ methods and materials appropriate to superior students. Experience has shown that this involves:*
   a. *Bringing the abler students together in small groups or classes of from five to twenty students.*
   b. *Using primary sources and original documents rather than textbooks where possible.*
   c. *Less lecturing and predigesting by the faculty of content to be covered; approaching selectively the subject matter to be covered; discouraging passive note taking; encouraging student adventure with ideas in open discussion—the colloquium method with appropriate modification of this method in science and professional schools.*
   d. *Supplementing the above with increased independent study, research and summer projects, honors study abroad and imaginatively conceived summer institutes.*
   e. *Continuous counseling in the light of the individual student's development, by teaching personnel rather than by full-time nonteaching counselors, but the professional counseling staff should include specialists in honors.*
   f. *Making a special effort toward differential counseling as between men and women in the program in the light of the steeper erosion of talents after graduation among the latter.*
   g. *Embodying in the program the required differentia between the creative and the formally cognitive approach.*
   h. *Giving terminal examinations to test the honors results.*

8. *Select faculty qualified to give the best intellectual leadership to able students and fully identified with the aims of the program.*

9. *Set aside, where possible, such requirements as are restrictive of a good student's progress, thus increasing his freedom among the alternative facets of the honors and regular curriculum.*

10. *Build in devices of evaluation to test both the means used and the ends sought by an honors program.*

11. *Establish a committee of honors students to serve as liaison with the Honors Committee or Council. Keep them fully informed on the program and elicit their cooperation in evaluation and development.*

12. *Use good students wherever feasible as apprentices in teaching and as assistants to the best men on the faculty. It is often possible to achieve this for them even as freshmen. There is increasing use both of available research institutes and laboratories in the area for a semester or a summer. Foundation funds in support of such undergraduate research and independent study are increasingly available.*

13. *Employ honors students for counseling, orientation, and other appropriate honors purposes within the general student body.*

14. *Establish, where possible, an honors center with honors library, lounge, reading rooms, and other appropriate decor.*

15. *Work towards closer liaison between the undergraduate honors program and the graduate school.*

16. *Assure that such programs will be permanent features of the curriculum and not dependent on temporary or spasmodic dedication of particular faculty men or administrators—in other words, institutionalize such programs, budget them, and build, thereby, a tradition of excellence.*

The inauguration of an honors program need not await full implementation of all the above features but should be started where feasible and move in the direction of a full program.[9]

Although programs involve many administrative, scheduling, financial, and staffing arrangements, everything comes to focus on the point where the honors student engages with the program. This

[9] *The Superior Student*, vol. 5, no. 4, pp. 10–11, March–April, 1963.

he does first in his encounter with the honors adviser. Because honors programs generally provide for fewer students per adviser than the normal campus ratio, for careful selection of advisers, and for flexibility in the application of academic regulations, honors advising is often given much of the credit for the impact of the program.

The honors faculty is the next most crucial factor. No program is better than its staff, though any staff can be helped to do a better job by a carefully conceived program. Most programs claim that they involve the leading teacher-scholars on the faculty. Indeed, some programs have been instituted with the notion that they would help in the attraction and retention of able faculty.

The teaching arrangements that are at the heart of the program include special sections and courses, tutorials, theme groups, seminars and colloquia, research and independent study, summer and off-campus projects, and interdisciplinary as well as departmental offerings. Only a study of the varied and imaginative ways in which each of these forms has been developed on individual campuses can give a full appreciation of the extent to which honors programs have brought a spirit of experimentalism to the college curriculum.

Reports on new approaches to content in the various subject areas are scattered throughout *The Superior Student*. The entire September–October, 1963, issue was devoted to honors in science; the May–June, 1963, issue to honors in the performing arts; and the entire March, 1961, issue to the extensively utilized colloquium method.

The honors opportunities are offered to students at various points in their careers. In some institutions they are available only to seniors or upperclassmen, a situation almost universally characteristic of the honors programs of the 1920s and 1930s. Increasingly, however, they are available from the freshman year on. It is this change that is one of the most significant ways in which the newer honors programs differ from their predecessors. The need to provide for able students at the point when they are most ready for engagement—the importance of preventing the erosion of talents when able students are subjected to the routine freshman and sophomore offerings designed for the average—has been a central theme of the ICSS.

The honors program in the University of Michigan's College of Literature, Science, and the Arts was one of the first to recognize the importance of beginning with freshmen. During the 1963–

1964 school year, 280 freshmen and 520 upper-class students participated in the program. The following description of the Michigan program is indicative of the kind of programs that have been developed.

The Michigan program began with departmental honors for juniors and seniors. In 1957 the program was revised and extended to include honors work for freshmen and sophomores.

The program is controlled by the Honors Council, which determines policies and reports to the faculty on the progress of the program. The council is appointed by the executive committee of the college and includes representatives of all departments and additional members chosen by the dean. The actual administration of the program is delegated to an appointed director and an executive subcommittee of five elected members.

A separate honors office is maintained as a part of the college administration. The director of the Honors Council holds a half-time appointment, and his administrative assistant is full time.

The director has been granted the authority to make exceptions to existing college rules and to establish special courses for the program.

Selection of under-class students is the responsibility of the director. Approximately 8 per cent of each incoming freshman class is invited to join the program on the basis of (1) high school rank, (2) CEEB and National Merit Scholarship Corporation Qualifying Test scores, (3) a local test battery, (4) recommendation of high school principals and counselors, (5) autobiographical material on the application form, and (6) an interview with the director. Students who make half A and half B or better on college work and who seem otherwise qualified are invited to participate at the end of the first and second college semesters. Students who have fallen below a B average at the close of the second or third college semester are dropped from the program.

Selection of upper-class students is delegated to the departments of concentration under general standards set by the Honors Council: a B average overall and a B+ average in courses previously elected in the field of concentration.

Upper-class counselors are chosen from the membership of the Honors Council. Each counselor is responsible for approximately fifteen students for the first two years. Students are encouraged to talk over their program plans thoroughly. When the student reaches junior standing, he moves on to a concentration counselor in the degree program of his choice.

Among the instructional opportunities provided are special sections for honors students in all large courses, departmental and interdisciplinary honors courses, summer reading for credit in selected courses, faculty-student discussion groups, and independent study. Separate living facilities are also available in the dormitory for honors students.

Participation in the honors program is noted on the student's transcript.

After successful completion of a department's honors program, the student is nominated for an honors degree by the department in accordance with standards set by the Honors Council.

Honors opportunities are also available in the Schools of Music, Medicine, and Engineering.[10]

Honors offerings may be provided through a variety of administrative structures. In some colleges, each department organizes its own program with little relation to what other departments are doing. In others there is an all-college program in which departments participate and to which they may add their own programs. In some universities, the units each develop their own programs; in others there is an all-university honors program in which students from all schools may participate.

Just as significant as the trend toward freshman honors has been the development of the all-university honors program, particularly in large public institutions such as the Universities of Illinois, Oregon, and Michigan State.

This approach does produce problems of structural and functional interrelationships among the various schools. There is the matter of appropriate relations between honors in the college of liberal arts and honors in other schools and colleges of the university. There is the matter of place in the honors program of the first two years for students who will later move into professional honors curricula. In working out these relationships, interesting honors programs have been established in professional schools, such as schools of agriculture, home economics, business, engineering, nursing, medicine, music and fine arts, and education.

Developments in the latter are particularly worthy of note. To explore ways that honors might be developed in professional edu-

[10] Various features of the Michigan program are covered in articles and notes in many issues of *The Superior Student*.

cation programs, the ICSS in April, 1962, convened a conference at the University of Wisconsin. In the introduction to the U.S. Office of Education report on the conference, Sterling M. McMurrin, then Commissioner of Education, said: "Quite certainly the key to the quality of our entire educational enterprise is the intellectual strength of our teachers, their grasp of the aims and purposes of education, the quality of their own liberal education, and their competence in the subjects they teach. Without question the establishment of effective honors programs for selected potential teachers can have far-reaching consequences for our schools." [11]

In several ways, honors programs in teacher education serve to provide the "key to quality." They help to attract superior students to careers in education and give them opportunities to acquire the kinds of effective learning experiences on which they themselves may later capitalize in their own work with students. Also, development of effective honors programs calls for cooperative planning by the faculty of subject disciplines and professional education. Not only does this promote greater understanding of education on the part of all concerned, but it also helps to bring together on the campus two groups that are often too far apart for the good of either themselves or the students they are helping to prepare.

This bringing together of two often contending groups is an illustration of the way in which the honors movement has become a valuable agency for integration in American higher education. This integrative role serves the abler students too. For one thing, it is an antidote to that fragmentation that is the foe of the essential wholeness on which the health of a college or university depends and which should be a cardinal experience of the abler students. This comes about because the honors task, as William Anderson, of the State College of Iowa, has pointed out, ". . . is a subtle one of establishing a pervasive intellectual climate on a given campus."

Climate, of course, is not something that can be directly produced. It is a by-product of the many things that go to make up an effective honors program. It comes about when there are effective administrative linkages between the various units involved in honors programs. It comes from the working together of faculty,

[11] Lanora G. Lewis, "Talent and Tomorrow's Teachers: The Honors Approach," *New Dimensions in Higher Education,* no. 11, U.S. Office of Education, Washington, D.C., 1963, p. 1.

administration, and students in building an effective program; it comes from the intense effort often required to convince doubting faculty, administrators, students, alumni, and boards of control; it comes from the exciting teaching in honors classes; and it comes from the informal interaction of honor student with honor student, honor student with faculty, and honor student with other students. This effect of the honors program on the campus climate, which is the hardest outcome to document, is nonetheless one of the most persuasive arguments for acceptance even by those who are least enthusiastic about providing special treatment for a selected segment of the student body. As Mr. Cohen has said: "What one is after is the 'critical mass' of students to be given special attention, and visibly so, in such a way as to produce what we have called a 'spilled-over effect' on the rest of the students. Students visibly benefiting from a visible honors program have as much and more influence on the latently strong among the student body as will faculty people working without a program."[12]

To make an educational innovation such as honors programs self-sustaining seems also to require a "critical mass" of programs. The ICSS executive committee has decided that the critical mass of the faculty members and administrators committed to honors is being approached and that the momentum of the honors movement will soon be irreversible. They have therefore announced that the ICSS will be terminated as of June 30, 1965. This result will have been achieved not only because of the sheer spread by contagious enthusiasm and emulative power of the honors movement, but also because of the continually multiplying evidence of the quality and effectiveness of the honors programs themselves.

This evidence is found in the increasing number of honor students whose names appear on the rolls of those selected for graduate scholarships and other awards. It is shown in the increasing recognition by graduate schools of the quality of the product of the good honors programs. It is coming from the several research projects that have developed out of ICSS encouragement to the behavioral scientists to make honors programs a subject of intensive study.[13] It shows up in results of research studies under-

[12] *The Superior Student,* vol. 5, no. 3, p. 2, January–February, 1963.
[13] A conference on research and evaluation of honors programs was held from Nov. 25 to Nov. 28, 1963. For a brief report, see *The Superior Student,* vol. 5, no. 1, p. 22, September–October, 1962. For reports on research leading up to this conference, see the issues for October, November, and December, 1960, and October, 1961.

taken for other purposes, such as those by Donald L. Thistlethwaite, of the National Merit Scholarship Corporation.[14] And it will undoubtedly emerge as the studies undertaken by Project Talent continue.

While the honors program has been one of the most widely adopted innovations in higher education in recent years, there are questions about it that must give pause to any institution contemplating the adoption of a program or considering the continuation or expansion of one. First of all there is the matter of costs. As Dean James H. Robertson, of the University of Michigan, has said: "Education of this quality does not come mass produced; it is expensive. But if the cost is considered against the likely outcomes on the investment, the educational yield from an honors scholar will be unquestionably great. Essentially for colleges, universities, and society in general, it is a question of values."[15]

There is the question: Honors for whom? At one extreme, there is the austere answer given, for example, by Chancellor Edward W. Strong, of the University of California, that honors programs should be only "for the best of the best."[16] At the other extreme, there are those who would like to have "honors programs" for the average student. Honors programs, generally, have sought to avoid either of these extremes. Depending upon local conditions, anywhere from the top 5 to 15 per cent of the student body is selected for honors work. In large state institutions like the Universities of Michigan and Illinois, this means honors programs that number participants in the many hundreds.

Institutions, too, must be wary of instituting or continuing honors programs merely because "it is the thing to do." It is too easy to establish mere paper programs, which cater to the institution's self-image but which are not grounded in a sound commitment to the promotion of quality.

To be vital contributors to excellence on a campus, honors must, as Mr. Cohen has urged, ". . . remain vigilant against organizational 'business,' against mere reiteration of claims of excellence accompanied by mere or narrow elitist programs. Claims of achievement must be subjected to rigorous analysis to forestall mere affectation and mannerisms of excellence."[17]

One of the honors programs' greatest problems, one they share

[14] *The Superior Student,* vol. 4, no. 3, p. 16, April, 1961.
[15] *The Superior Student,* vol. 4, no. 8, p. 5, March–April, 1962.
[16] Lewis, *op. cit.,* p. 53.
[17] *Ibid.,* p. 21.

with any institutional program, is that institutionalization is essential for ongoing continuity, and yet such institutionalization is the most severe threat to that *élan* essential to success. Whether "second-generation" honors faculties can carry on programs with the same enthusiasm and quality as their predecessors remains to be confirmed. It is a matter to which every administration must be alert if it is not to allow its honors program to live off the reputation established in the years of its enthusiastic generation.

The word "elitist," used by Mr. Cohen, suggests another set of issues. Are honors programs creating an intellectual elite? Does the selection of honors students generate antidemocratic attitudes among those selected? To explore these questions fully would get us into a debate on the large question of selection and distinction in a democratic society. It is sufficient to note that honors students seem to integrate well with the rest of the student body. This impression has been confirmed by careful studies of the attitudes of nonhonors to honors students at the Universities of Michigan and Illinois.[18]

Finally there is the question that faced the conference in 1957 that gave birth to the ICSS: Can we continue to maintain quality in our education and give attention to the needs of individual students in the face of rising enrollments and growing faculty shortages? The period of greatest challenge lies ahead. The existence of strong honors programs may help make the answer affirmative.

As Mr. Cohen wrote in the introduction to the 1960–1961 "Inventory of Honors Programs":

It is, however, much too early to indulge in any complacent assumption of a fait accompli. It is all a becoming rather than a being. Many of the programs described are so new that few have completed their first four years. Some are in their very first year of honors offerings. Only a handful of the many new ones have graduated more than one or two groups of honors students. But the scene everywhere is one of intense critical concern about the past and present; of probings and tentative innovations; of change, variety, growth and evolution. It is not, as some might think, a mere rapid replacing of new dogmas for old. There is skepticism of panaceas, distrust of mere post-Sputnik fashions and insecurely based plans. There is avid exploration of possibilities

[18] *The Superior Student*, vol. 4, no. 7, pp. 8 (Michigan), 11 (Illinois), January–February, 1962.

*and the will to assess all that is tried out. There is constant travel
by deans and honors directors, conferences and consultations between institutions. We have recorded much of this in our
newsletter. These are the signs of a healthy movement whose core
is an affirmation of faith that we have the students and the
faculties to do an infinitely better job of higher education. It is
well to bear in mind that the issues at stake are profound ones,
both intellectual and moral, and that a window-dressing approach
to them is futile. The need is to carry on, to make a searching
evaluation and assessment of the objectives of programs and
of the means used for their attainment. The test of honors lies not
in the hopeful rhetoric of brochures and catalogue descriptions,
but in the impact upon the students themselves in the calibre of
faculties and their dedication to excellence.*[19]

FLEXIBILITY IN EXISTING ARRANGEMENTS

In the preceding section we dealt with arrangements designed
specifically for the abler student. There are, in addition, a number
of arrangements for increasing academic flexibility that, though
not designed solely for the abler, redound greatly to their benefit.
In a useful study of these arrangements, Charles C. Cole, Jr., has
defined flexibility as ". . . those practices and combinations of practices by which each student is permitted to progress in his college
program at the rate and depth of which he is capable."[20] While
some types of academic flexibility are as old as good teaching, these
have lately been given new emphasis, and to them have been added
some new practices.

A useful distinction that can be made is between (*1*) flexibility
in the rate of academic progress, typified by such practices as advanced placement, early admissions, placement examinations, credit
by examination, heavier than normal programs, waiver of all specific course requirements for graduation, auditing privileges, and
year-round study, and (*2*) flexibility in teaching-learning arrangements such as independent study, both in conjunction with regular

[19] *The Superior Student,* vol. 3, no. 9, p. 3, January, 1961.
[20] "Flexibility in the Undergraduate Curriculum," *New Dimensions in
Higher Education,* no. 10, U.S. Office of Education, Washington, D.C.,
1962, p. 1.

courses and as alternatives to them; undergraduate research;[21] utilization of combinations of very large and very small classes; wholly reorganized curricular arrangements; off-campus study; work-study programs; use of new instructional media; and just plain imaginative teaching tactics. Some of these, such as placement examinations and heavier than normal schedules, are part of the traditional procedures in higher education; some, such as advanced placement, have become integral parts of honors programs; and others, such as independent study, changes in the academic calendar, and new media, are treated fully in other chapters of this book. Here we shall indicate only how some of the latter are serving the needs of the abler student and shall discuss one of the newest developments in an old practice, credit by examination.

Independent study

As a means of flexibility, independent study has gained great popularity in recent years. Although not restricted to abler students, nearly every honors program has provisions for independent study. Yet the ICSS has taken a very strong stand on the limitations of independent study when relied upon too exclusively as the means for meeting the needs of abler students. An editorial in the December, 1960, issue of *The Superior Student* declared:

An undergraduate program of independent study is not an honors program. It is a single device. In itself, without the power of a continuous and varied honors program, it cannot provide the needed climate for motivation, the required range of flexibility. In our large public institutions it has been meager indeed in a number of good students attracted and engaged. Equally meager has been its impact upon other students and faculty. . . .

Independent study simply has not proved satisfactory or effective as the sole reliant in meeting the requirements of superior undergraduates. It can be demonstrated that its effect has really been the restriction of honors to a mere handful of students, the

[21] The National Science Foundation, through its undergraduate research and independent study programs, has played a very large role in promoting these practices. A report on a special study of these programs made by the ICSS is in *The Superior Student,* vol. 5, no. 6, pp. 3–14, September–October, 1963.

survivors of the predominantly routine treatment of the first two years. . . . Within the setting of such [honors] programs, independent study finds its appropriate place and can serve some of the functions originally anticipated for it. [22]

Acceleration

Acceleration has obvious advantages and attractions for the abler student. Yet there are those who are worried about the effects of excessive acceleration on liberal education for the brighter students. Dr. Rosemary Park, of Barnard College has expressed her concern about what she calls the "inflation" or "devaluation" of the bachelor's degree, caused by advanced placement and early entrance into graduate study. Like many others today, she is concerned lest the functions of the liberal arts college be taken over by the high schools at the one end and truncated by growing pressures toward professionalism and graduate study at the other. She suggests that enrichment replace pressure toward acceleration, perhaps by encouraging abler students to take a fourth year of college and work toward an "honors B.A.," which would represent a more liberally oriented curriculum than the three-year master's degree that is becoming increasingly popular.

These latter programs deserve special mention. Thirty-nine universities, aided by funds from the Ford Foundation, are experimenting with three-year master's programs designed to prepare college teachers.[23] They begin in the junior year and seek in a unified program to ready a student either for entry directly into college teaching or for expeditious completion of the doctorate.

In another related development, Yale announced in January, 1964, the inauguration of a program that would permit abler students to earn the bachelor's and master's degrees simultaneously in four years. Students who enter Yale with enough advanced-placement credits for sophomore standing could do the required work for both degrees in three years.

[22] Ten of these programs are described in *The Superior Student*, vol. 5, no. 4, pp. 14–46, March–April, 1963; Chap. 3 describes other developments in the use of independent study.
[23] See Chap. 9 for a fuller description of these programs. Also see Ray P. Cuzzort, "The MA-3 in 1964," *The Superior Student*, vol. 6, no. 3, pp. 3–10, March–April, 1964.

New media

If imaginatively used, the newer media may have a profound impact on the education of the abler student. The newer media combined with sophisticated programing techniques will make it possible for each student to regulate his own progress through the curriculum and will assure mastery at every stage before advancement to the next level. Ready access to a wide variety of learning materials will be of great value to the imaginative teacher. Freed from routine instructional tasks, he will be able to devote more of his time to the needs of individual students and, particularly, to the intense interaction that is so vital to effective honors work. Whether the newer media will tend to reduce all higher education to a common level of mediocrity or will be used to enrich learning for all will very much depend on the attitude toward, and use made of, them by faculty leaders, most of whom see in the honors student the image of the kind of student with whom they would always prefer to deal. Chapter 6, which deals with the new media, describes this issue in greater detail.

Credit by examination

As with most other methods for achieving flexibility, credit by examination is not restricted to abler students. Because the development of good examinations for this purpose is a difficult undertaking, not many colleges have made extensive use of this practice in the past. In 1963, however, two new programs, one national and one limited to New York State, were organized to provide "proficiency examinations" for the purpose of determining whether individuals met the requirements of college courses and therefore could be awarded credit for them.

The Educational Testing Service is developing comprehensive and course examinations for use by colleges throughout the country.

The New York State Education Department's College Proficiency Examination Program is developing course-oriented examinations designed to reveal the extent of mastery of the objectives of regular undergraduate courses. The department hopes that colleges will agree to give credit for satisfactory performance on these examinations, and already over 130 institutions in New York have agreed to consider granting credit on the basis of the examination.[24]

Proficiency examinations can be used in programs for abler students as (*1*) a basis for the evaluation of students who have undertaken independent coverage of regular courses or whose educational careers have not followed a typical pattern, (*2*) a means of determining whether students undertaking independent research projects have satisfied any course requirements from which they have been excused, (*3*) a means for awarding credit for off-campus study, (*4*) diagnostic instruments to help devise programs more nearly suited to the needs of each student, and (*5*) general evaluation instruments to help determine the effectiveness of honors programs or other curricular innovations.[25]

As James B. Conant observed in his recent book, *The Education of American Teachers,* the option of meeting requirements by examination, rather than by course taking, places the emphasis where it should be: ". . . on the subject itself rather than on the arbitrarily defined segment of it." This is the emphasis that honors programs also seek to give.

Conclusion

Writing in 1956, John Gardner contrasted our still casual and sporadic concern for our academically talented with the zeal of the Soviet Russians for theirs. He pointed up this contrast by several references. On one hand, he referred to William Benton's *Encyclopedia Britannica* article on Soviet education, which pictured the great strides taken in the last generation and which made one realize ". . . the crucial relationship between the Soviet scientific, technological, and ideological revolutions and the assiduous cultivation of the U.S.S.R.'s best young minds." On the other hand, he referred to the figures of Arthur S. Adams, then president of the American Council on Education, to the effect that there are over one hundred thousand young people each year who are highly qualified for college, yet who never matriculate. He likewise referred, in this connection, to Byron S. Hollinshead, who, in his

[24] Information on these programs may be obtained from the Educational Testing Service, Princeton, N.J., and the College Proficiency Examination Program, New York State Education Department, Albany, N.Y.

[25] See *The Superior Student,* vol. 5, no. 4, pp. 7–9, March–April, 1963.

book *Who Should Go to College* (1952), suggested that only about 40 per cent of the top quarter in ability of our college-age population are in college and who noted, also, that nearly one-fifth of the top quarter never graduate from high school.[26]

More than three years later, Chancellor Franklin D. Murphy, of the University of Kansas, was still writing of "our dangerous complacency." He reminded us that: "This is not the America of the 1850's where the national need was the development of an underdeveloped continent. This is America of the mid-twentieth century, technologically sophisticated, with the subtleties of history, political science, fundamental physical science, and an understanding of foreign cultures and languages, as the primary and urgent needs."[27] Dr. Murphy then put this question: "How much longer can we afford the intellectual wastage involved in either unwillingness or inability to drive our young people to the outer limits of their native ability?"

At the 1962 AHE Conference on Higher Education, Dean Robertson gave a partial answer, and in this answer we have a striking indication of the great change that has come over the climate of concern and motivation on behalf of the abler student and his needs, as these are related to the national needs:

The existence and growth of many first-rate honors programs in a wide variety of educational institutions is tangible evidence of the deep-rooted reality of this salutary change in educational philosophy. It is my own conviction that the most significant development in American higher education since World War II has been this awakened and constructive concern for challenging our students to use their full intellectual power. This interest, properly motivated and directed, really means that American education for the first time is becoming fully democratic. In effect, it is now willing to pay the price for providing equal opportunity for all levels of our young men and women, to give the promising young man as much attention as we have been lavishing on our remedial student and on those with special athletic prowess.[28]

[26] *Carnegie Corporation New York Quarterly,* January, 1956.
[27] Franklin D. Murphy, "Our Dangerous Complacency," *NEA Journal,* vol. 48, p. 9, November, 1959.
[28] *Current Issues in Higher Education,* Association for Higher Education, Washington, D.C., 1962, pp. 193–194.

SOURCES FOR FURTHER INFORMATION

The following organizations have been active in the area of programs for the abler student and have publications and services of great value to all concerned with the abler student in higher education:

The Inter-University Committee on the Superior Student, University of Colorado, Boulder, Col. Publishes *The Superior Student*—current and back issues available on request, free of charge.

The National Merit Scholarship Corporation, 1580 Sherman Avenue, Evanston, Ill. Publishes information on its scholarship program and research studies.

National Education Association Project on the Academically Talented Student, 1201 Sixteenth Street, N.W., Washington, D.C. Numerous publications, primarily for secondary schools but some useful at the college level.

Project Talent, 1808 Adams Mill Road, N.W., Washington 9, D.C. Reports on its extensive longitudinal studies will have increasing value for colleges as the 400,000 high school students tested in 1960 move through college.

The College Entrance Examination Board Advanced Placement Program, 475 Riverside Drive, New York. Has various useful reports on the program.

U.S. Office of Education, Washington, D.C. See particularly the following publications in its series *New Dimensions in Higher Education:* Winslow R. Hatch and Ann Bennett, "Independent Study," 1960; Samuel Baskin, "Quest for Quality," 1960; Charles C. Cole, Jr., and Lanora G. Lewis, "Flexibility in the Undergraduate Curriculum," 1962; and Lanora G. Lewis, in cooperation with J. Ned Bryan and Robert Poppendieck, "Talent and Tomorrow's Teachers: The Honors Approach."

C. R. CARPENTER
L. P. GREENHILL

6

providing the conditions
for learning:
the "new" media

We live today in the midst of an electronic revolution. Rapid
advances in communication equipment and data processing since
World War II have had a profound effect on education. The
effect is most noticeable in the development and new applications
of teaching instruments used singly or in combination as "systems
of instructional instrumentation."

This chapter reviews some of the ways that the new media can
be employed in teaching and learning. The media considered are
those which have a wide range of sound and visual capabilities.
Although printed materials are properly included in the
definition of "media," these are not emphasized here.

The chapter is concerned primarily with ways of using the
media to offer a better education to more students. It outlines de-

velopments in the use of televised instruction, programed learning, language laboratories, and instructional films. A variety of new media formats are discussed, and attention is given to some of the newer facilities for instructional instrumentation. Final sections of the chapter discuss how to introduce the new media into existing educational organizations, suggest limitations in their use, and outline the need for additional research and development.

THE REVOLUTION IN COMMUNICATIONS AND INFORMATION PROCESSING

During the fifteen years from 1950 to 1965, developments in the use of the media of communications have taken place at an almost unbelievable rate. These developments have been of several kinds: the improvement and application of apparatus and equipment, the invention and development of new kinds of instrumentation, and the extension of the use of communication- and information-processing technologies from other fields to education.

Television, for example, was an infant industry just after World War II. It has grown, until today 95 per cent of American homes have television receivers. Audiences have grown from a few thousand in 1947 and 1948, until today as many as 50 million people may view some special programs. There are three nation-wide commercial networks, and a national educational television network using films and video tapes as a means of distributing cultural and educational programs has been established with more than eighty affiliated stations. Similar expansions and developments have occurred in other media. In the publishing industries technological developments have made it possible to use black-and-white and color pictures in far more extensive ways and to increase vastly the amounts and kinds of electronically disseminated pictorial-graphic information. In the field of electronics, new developments in the use of electronic computers have opened up wide new possibilities for dealing with problems of classifying, recording, storing, retrieving, and displaying information.

Three specific developments dramatize the significance that this revolution in communication technology has for education.

Since 1958 the nation has been blanketed by the Continental Classroom, televised courses of excellent quality available in millions of homes for the price of rising early and turning the dials. The Continental Classroom programs have initiated new concepts, not only in the wide diffusion of instruction, but also in cooperation between commercial broadcasters, industry, foundations, and educational institutions. A second development was the Midwest Project of Airborne Television Instruction. Prior to World War II, few could have imagined that courses of instruction would one day be transmitted from a single source—a plane flying at 23,000 feet—and be made available to the schools and colleges of all or part of five Middle Western states. The third highly significant technological achievement was the launching of communication satellites, such as the historic Telstar. The communications satellites, using television, may eventually provide for global origination and dissemination of information and increase significantly the interactions of nations and cultures.

These scientific and engineering accomplishments exemplify the enormous amount of new communication power that has been put into the hands of industry, commerce, and education. How this power is to be used and for what purposes and effects is a story that has hardly begun to unfold.

MEDIA CHARACTERISTICS: POTENTIALS FOR INSTRUCTION AND LEARNING

The media are devices for recording, storing, retrieving, or reproducing information in a manner that encourages learning. Thus defined, the functions of the media are similar to those of many other educational facilities. Therefore, the media should be viewed as of great significance to education.

Many media are capable of reproducing faithfully a wide range of visual and auditory stimuli. The problem is to select those media which, when used singly or in combination with other teaching and learning procedures, will stimulate in students the desired kinds of learning responses. The approach may include lectures, discussions, laboratory experiments, projects, field observations, community work, foreign study, or other procedures, as described elsewhere in this book.

One of the main functions of the new media is to make instruction available to those who need to learn but who otherwise would not have the opportunity to do so. Instruction can be made available not only in remote areas but also in rare subjects. Uncommonly taught languages and special science and mathematics instruction can be provided for students in colleges where such instruction is not presently available.

Another advantage of the pictorial-graphic media is that they may represent reality more effectively than numbers or words alone. Therefore, they can be used with such symbols in two major ways: (1) to develop understanding progressively from the levels of perception of the objects to a more abstract, symbolic, and conceptual level and (2) to relate abstract subject matter to concrete reality. The first may be one means of motivating students for accomplishing effective learning; the second may be desirable as a means of adding a full body to abstract intellectual learning.

The media also enable the teacher to vary the patterns of instruction, and they can be used to preserve the realism of historic events and present these to students with full force. Motion pictures of Churchill speaking during the dark hours of World War II and of Roosevelt's inaugural address during the great Depression of the early 1930s have a fullness and strength of impact that cannot be equaled by even the most eloquent written descriptions. The pictorial-graphic-sound media add dimensions to written history and serve, as other historical records do, a time-binding function.

The pictorial media, usually supplemented by language, can also serve space-spanning functions. Film and photographic records can be made of the lives and behavior of peoples in remote countries and very different cultures.

The use of media for ordering and presenting stimulus materials for learning often requires that the teacher modify the traditional teaching relationship, wherein the principal interaction is between the students and the teacher. It is suggested that this relationship may be in error and that the principal interactions (or transactions) should be between the learner and the materials to be learned.

In brief, the media can be used to provide many of the basic, necessary, and favorable conditions for learning. When properly developed and used, they provide a means for emphasizing the primary interactions between the stimulus materials and learners and vastly extend the reach of our instructional facilities.

Modern technology has thus opened up for education a wide variety of new opportunities. What remains to be solved are the problems of logistics, strategies, and tactics of their production, distribution, and use over a full range of curricular possibilities.

THE SYSTEMS APPROACH TO PLANNING FOR AND USING MEDIA

The "systems" approach to learning involves a rational and objective analysis of the uses of media in college and university instruction. The approach raises the more general question of what media, or combination of media, should be used with specific subject matter and students of given characteristics in order to provide the most favorable conditions for desired kinds of learning to occur. The media are viewed as some ways among many for providing some of the essential conditions for learning.

An initial systems analysis can be made in terms of three general functions: *instructing, mediating,* and *learning.* In any teaching-learning situation, learning or performance objectives must first be specified, and then appropriate content must be selected and organized. Alternative ways of transmitting what is to be learned must be considered; clearly the full range of possibilities must be assessed. Judgments should be free of the biases of tradition and should be based to the greatest extent possible on objective information. Finally, the learning functions, which are essentially the learning activities of students, are specified.

All teaching and the methods used to accomplish it are only means designed to encourage student learning. Any function that either does not make an adequate contribution (relative to "cost") to learning or interferes with this result should be eliminated from the system. This requirement should apply equally to teachers and teaching and to media. The focus of the whole system is on student learning activities and the effects on the student's development.

In the employment of media, decisions must be made as to the specific medium or combination of media, how they should be used, and in what form. In the context of a systems approach, it is illogical to conceive of a specific medium or class of media as serving instructional functions by themselves. These media must have organized content, designed to serve specific learning functions and produce the right responses. The stimulus value of any medium for learning depends basically upon its content, the way it is produced, its format, the instructional methods and techniques used within the medium, and the ways in which the instructional materials are used. More particularly, the effectiveness of an instructional medium will depend on the appropriateness of its structure and content to what students have previously learned and to how the instruction fits into the total pattern and sequence of instruction.

Extensive research, including that of the Instructional Film Research Program at Pennsylvania State University and similar research at Yale and elsewhere, shows that the effect of a film on learning is highly specific to the film, to the subject matter, and to the students. It is this fact that is often overlooked by both the proponents and the opponents of the media in education. The importance of the media for learning lies in the stimulus materials that are incorporated in them and not in the media per se. The debates should be over how to select, organize, and present content or how to stimulate and advance desired learning on the part of students. The point at issue is not media qua media, but how to stimulate learning.

RESULTS OF SOME RESEARCH AND DEVELOPMENT WORK WITH MEDIA

During the past fifteen or twenty years there has been a considerable increase in both the volume and the quality of research on teaching and learning. Much of this has involved experimentation with the "newer" media, to develop means of improving the learning of students in large groups and to find better methods for stimulating the self-instruction of learners.

Televised instruction

During the ten-year period from 1954 to 1964, instructional television has been the subject of considerable research. Much of the research was conducted at the college level and was aimed at determining the extent to which television could be used to extend the reach of experienced faculty members to a larger number of students without diminishing the quality of learning.

This research may be classified under four headings: relative effectiveness, acceptability, feasibility, and appropriateness.[1] Many of the earlier research studies compared the effects on learning through television with learning from the conventional classroom manner. The vast majority of these studies reported no significant differences when the same teachers taught by both methods. These studies demonstrated that the influence of outstanding teachers could, in fact, be extended to large numbers of students with no measurable loss in learning.

Many studies also were conducted on students and faculty attitudes. These may be summarized as follows: Students tended to be somewhat negative in their initial attitudes toward instructional television. After experience with televised instruction, attitudes became more favorable. For example, in one study involving eight different courses at the university level, almost 80 per cent of the students rated televised instruction as either very good or fairly good.

Faculty attitudes have varied greatly but tend to be less favorable than those of students. Surveys generally have showed that there is a small group with negative attitudes, another small group that is favorable toward the use of television for teaching (television teachers are usually drawn from this group), and a large group that appears to be indifferent toward it.

Studies of cost have indicated that television can be economically feasible if the type of equipment chosen is appropriate to the task and if the system is used for several courses each involving 300 to 400 students.

Most of the current experimentation is focusing on trying to improve the effectiveness of learning by television and on developing new ways of using the medium for solving problems faced by education. The experiments include the use of television in laboratory

[1] For an overview of research and developments in the use of television, the reader is referred to the following: Wilbur Schramm, "Learning from Instructional Television," *Review of Educational Research,* vol. 32, no. 2, pp. 156–167, American Educational Research Association, Washington, D.C., April, 1962; A. A. Lumsdaine, "Instruments and Media of Instruction," in N. L. Gage (ed.), *Handbook of Research on Teaching: A Project of the American Educational Research Association,* Rand McNally & Company, Chicago, 1963; and Lee E. Campion and Clarice Y. Kelley, *Studies in the Growth of Instructional Technology. II. A Directory of Closed-circuit Television Installations in American Education,* Occasional Paper no. 10, Technological Development Project, National Education Association, Washington, D.C., 1963.

instruction, for observation of teaching demonstrations, for presentation of lifelike test situations, and for bringing a wide variety of learning situations into the classroom. Several of these developments are discussed further in the section of this chapter titled New Media Formats and Methods of Presentation.

Programed learning

Through the use of a wide variety of visual and auditory materials, films and television can do a rather effective job of stimulating the learners' interest and attention and of helping them to perceive and organize what they are to learn. However, these media do not give students a chance to practice what they are learning, nor are students informed of their progress. Indeed, this problem of response and reinforcement often is not well handled in the regular college classroom. For example, not all students in a class participate in discussions, relatively few questions are raised and answered, and immediate and detailed knowledge of results on tests is frequently not provided.

Programed instructional materials, however, do provide many opportunities for all students to make appropriate responses, and they do provide them with immediate knowledge of results. Programing emphasizes specific instructional objectives. The facts and principles to be learned then are analyzed in detail and broken down into carefully ordered, sequential steps. After each step *every* student is required to respond by answering a question or solving a problem. After each response has been made, the learners are given the correct answer. In this way each knows what progress he is making. A program is generally tested empirically and refined as it is developed, and the steps are so designed that a high proportion of students get the right answer each time; thus their efforts are rewarded by success.

There has been much experimentation with different formats for the presentation of programed instruction. Among these are linear programs, in which all learners follow the same sequence of steps, and "branching" programs, which permit learners to jump ahead if they readily grasp the material or to go through remedial "loops" if they need additional instruction.

Research on programed instruction has centered on an analysis of the programed material itself (e.g., analysis of different response modes, desirable sizes of steps, problems of sequencing and comparisons of different prompting and confirmation methods, comparisons between branching and linear programs, comparisons between machines and programed texts, etc.) and comparisons of the results of field tests using programed and conventional instruction. Most studies of comparisons of groups using programed material and those taught by conventional instruction show that students learn at least as well from the program as they do from conventional methods. In a number of instances the studies favor the programed groups (in relation to level and amount of learning achieved). The experiments also show that the programed groups usually take less time to learn the material than conventionally taught groups.[2]

The most comprehensive directory of programs presently available, *Programs, '63,*[3] provides information on a total of 352 programs. The great majority of these programs have been developed for use at the secondary and elementary school levels.

Programs for college-level instruction began with subject areas that obviously lent themselves to a step-by-step development, such as mathematics or statistics. The technique is now being applied to a wide variety of subjects, including law, certain aspects of medicine, and even the appreciation of poetry. Some college teachers are finding a short program to be an excellent way of teaching a complex concept with which students have difficulty.

Most programs tend to emphasize the symbols of print and are often presented in textbook form. However, a few years ago there was a flurry of interest in the use of various mechanical devices (teaching machines) for the presentation of programed material a frame at a time. Research is also being conducted on the use of computers to control the sequences of program frames for individual students.

Recently Pennsylvania State University and the American Insti-

[2] For a review of research and developments in this area, see Harry F. Silberman, "Self-teaching Devices and Programmed Materials," *Review of Educational Research,* vol. 32, no. 2, pp. 179–193, American Educational Research Association, Washington, D.C., April, 1962; Lumsdaine, *op. cit.;* J. L. Hughes (ed.), *Programmed Learning: A Critical Evaluation,* The Foundation for Research on Human Behavior, Educational Methods, Inc., Chicago, 1963; and W. Schramm (ed.), *The Research on Programmed Instruction,* U.S. Office of Education, Washington, D.C., 1964.

[3] *Programs, '63: A Guide to Programed Instructional Materials Available to Educators by September, 1963,* compiled by The Center for Programed Instruction, Inc., in cooperation with the U.S. Department of Health, Education, and Welfare, Washington, D.C., 1963.

tute for Research have been experimenting with the use of television as a medium for the presentation of programed materials. Not only does such a procedure provide opportunities for student response and reinforcement during a television presentation, but it also makes possible the inclusion of nonprint materials such as films, pictures, demonstrations, and resource people in programed sequences. It is confidently believed that motion pictures, video tapes, audio tapes, television broadcasts, and radio can be so managed as to mediate programed instruction. It is also believed that when the general requirements of producing and pretesting programed materials are followed and adaptations are made for the new media, the results on learning will be greater than for the same content taught in conventional ways. It is suggested, finally, that the most important contributions of the teaching-machine movement will be the effects on methods and techniques of producing instructional materials for the new media.

Instructional films

Research on the use of instructional films demonstrates conclusively that such films can be used effectively to teach performance skills of many kinds and of varying complexity.

Other studies showed that films could be used effectively for the communication of facts and principles or for the formation of concepts and indeed that a series of films (or slides plus audio tapes), together with printed study guides, could be used to teach an entire course or segment of a technical training program. The research pointed the way toward the development of recorded courses such as those now available on video tape or film.

The studies also demonstrated that appropriate films could be used to modify attitudes and that the role of the communicator in the film and the credibility of the film as perceived by the viewers are important factors in the successful restructuring of attitudes.

A number of these film research studies showed that the way in which the content of a film is organized and the way in which it is used could influence greatly its instructional effectiveness.[4]

[4] For a review of research and developments in instructional films, see Paul R. Wendt and Gordon K. Butts, "Audiovisual Materials," *Review of Educational Research,* vol. 32, no. 2, pp. 141–155, American Educational Research Association, Washington, D.C., April, 1962; Lumsdaine, *op. cit.;* and Loran C. Twyford, "Operations Research on Instructional Films," *AV Communication Review,* vol. 8, no. 156, May–June, 1960. (Abstract.)

Recent developments have been concerned with the applications of films to college-level teaching. These are discussed under New Media Formats and Methods of Presentation.

Language laboratories

Language laboratories have shown a remarkable growth, especially on the school level, since Federal funds for them became available through the 1958 National Defense Education Act. Colleges and universities are also installing them at a rapid rate. Many of the concepts presented in this chapter apply to these laboratories because prepared audio tapes are used in them.

In spite of the fact that much research must be done to learn what formats, patterns, drills, etc., are most effective, sufficient experience has been gathered to show the practical values of the language laboratory.[5] The uses are many and varied and range from simple pattern drills, designed to build up skill in sound discrimination, to the teaching of complex scientific language. There is great variety in the types of equipment that have been designed to serve language-learning requirements. These include simple recorders; systems that permit the student to listen and then record his own response, which he can then compare with the master tape; telephone dialing systems for tapes; combinations of tapes, printed materials, still pictures, or films; and, finally, a wireless language laboratory in which each student wears a headset that contains a small transistorized receiver that receives its audio signal from an antenna in the classroom. Thus, the need for wiring is obviated, and any classroom can become a language laboratory.

It is predicted that early and important advances in language-laboratory strategies and tactics could be made if established principles of learning were systematically applied to their operations. Also, it can be expected that audio tapes accessible directly or over

---

[5] For studies and developments in this area, see Gustave Mathieu, "Language Laboratories," *Review of Educational Research,* vol. 32, no. 2, pp. 168–178, American Educational Research Association, Washington, D.C., April, 1962; Lumsdaine, *op. cit.;* Alfred S. Hayes, *Language Laboratory Facilities,* U.S. Office of Education Bulletin 37, 1963; and F. R. Morton, *Recent Developments in Language Laboratory Equipment for Teaching and Research,* Language Laboratory Publication 5, University of Michigan, Ann Arbor, Mich., 1961.

telephone lines from automatically selected tape cartridges will be programed. Prototypes of these developments have been made at the University of Michigan. Language laboratories that combine the use of print, audio tape, and pictorial materials are developing combined uses of media. But the questions of what are the optimum conditions and sequences and, especially, what are the most appropriate pictorial components remain to be answered.

It is surprising to observe that the so-called language laboratories are generally limited in their use to the foreign-language curricula. It would seem that similar apparatus could be applicable in instruction in English, speech, the performing arts, and even mathematics and some phases of science, e.g., concept formation and the learning of scientific terminology. Some developments along these lines are already under way, as at the University of Michigan.

NEW MEDIA FORMATS AND METHODS OF PRESENTATION

Within recent years a number of new media formats and modes of presenting instructional materials have been developed. These developments are reviewed briefly here.[6]

Course developments, recorded courses, and the use of combinations of media

Efforts to solve the problems of designing, developing, pretesting, producing, and using instructional materials of the best possible quality have led recently to new kinds of cooperative actions. There are three important examples: the Physics Study Group,[7] the Committee on Mathematics,[8] and the American Institute of Biological

---

[6] For a fuller discussion and more detailed case examples of these developments, see J. W. Brown and J. W. Thornton (eds.), *New Media in Higher Education,* National Education Association, Washington, D.C., 1963,

For the most recent and complete directory of educational media, see Educational Media Council, Inc., *The Educational Media Index,* McGraw-Hill Book Company, New York, 1964.

[7] Headquarters for the commission is the Physics and Astronomy Building, University of Michigan, Ann Arbor, Mich.

[8] Headquarters for the committee is P.O. Box 124, Berkeley 11, Calif.

Sciences.[9] These efforts reflect the important fact that the quality
of the instructional materials is of primary importance and that
instructional materials need to be expertly organized (structured)
and pretested in order to achieve desirable levels of effective learning. The projects cited have involved concentrated cooperation of
highly selected and competent men in the subject-matter areas and
in the methodologies of selecting, preparing, producing, and pretesting the instructional materials.

The physics, mathematics, and biology courses have in the main
been planned and produced by leaders in these subject-matter fields
from colleges and universities, but the materials are designed principally for secondary schools. Similar efforts are now under way to
produce comparable high quality instructional materials for college
and university courses. It is likely that future developments in this
area will stress the production of core units of courses (e.g., materials considered to be the backbone or essential skeleton of the
course), as contrasted with the production of full courses. Developments in the use of single-concept films, described below, reflect one aspect of this approach. As was done in the American
Institute of Biological Sciences project, variations of the main
course structure are also likely to be developed, thus allowing for
local selection and adaptation. Parts of the course that are not recorded would be filled in by local teachers, by laboratory or project
work, and by the independent efforts of students.

The single-concept film

At the opposite end of the spectrum from the complete film or
video-tape course is the concept film. This is a short film, clearly
and cohesively organized, to present a single concept or event. The
film may show a limited situation, a set of objects, or a process,
frequently leaving the expository commentary to the instructor.
Irrelevant elements are scrupulously excluded; frequently there are
no titles or credits. The concept film might show a brief excerpt
from a scientific or other film dealing with a particular process or
event. It might present a laboratory demonstration in chemistry or
a single physiological phenomenon in the biological sciences. It

[9] Headquarters for the institute is 1105 Truman Road, Kansas City 6,
Mo.

may demonstrate an elementary concept or deal with examples of behavior or phenomena primarily of interest to the scientist or graduate student. In effect, such concept films are like building blocks and can be used in various combinations in conjunction with regular or televised instruction.

One outstanding effort in this direction is the Encyclopaedia Cinematographica, which was established a few years ago in Germany. This is a growing collection of concept films that eventually will constitute an encyclopaedia in film form. At present it includes principally films in microbiology, botany, zoology, and cultural anthropology, but other disciplines will be included as the availability of films grows. Another major effort in this area is that recently completed at Ohio State University, where a series of nineteen short physics demonstration films have been produced. The project, under contract from Kenyon College, was developed by Prof. Franklin Miller, Jr., of Kenyon, under the auspicies of the National Science Foundation and the National Association of Physics Teachers.

Recent technological advances in the development of magazine-type film cartridges and small automatic projectors add greatly to the potential uses of short concept films in instruction, particularly as they may be employed in independent study. The manipulations required for the operation of the projectors are simply the insertion of the film enclosed in the plastic cartridge and the flipping of a single switch. Using these films and projectors, the student can now, by assignment or choice, consult a film as he would a book.

8-mm films and film loops

Learning often requires repetition, reiteration, reviews, and progressive condensation and abstraction. Developments in the production of film and audio-tape loops now make it possible to repeat instructional units as many times as is required to achieve desired levels of learning. These film and audio loops hold many useful applications, particularly in the teaching of languages and scientific nomenclature, where factors of repetition and review tend to be of special importance. These films and audio loops are also being produced in cartridge-type form, thus greatly increasing their uses for classroom instruction and individual study.

Research films

Another media format that is ready for more extensive application in American higher education is the use of the film as an instrument for research. Technical developments in apparatus for high-speed cinematography permit the photographing of fast-acting phenomena at rates of speed up to 1 million or more pictures per second. This permits the analysis of action that cannot be observed by the unaided human eye. Conversely, time-lapse photography, in which slow-acting phenomena can be photographed at intervals of one picture every few seconds or minutes, enables researchers to speed up motion. New developments in fiber optics and the use of X-rays and other special kinds of radiation permit human vision to be extended into areas otherwise denied it.

The film is also an excellent medium for recording research activities in the field and the laboratory and for communicating the results of such research to other scientists or advanced students.

Media tests and examinations

The media have been conceived of, and used principally as, means of presenting instructional materials. Slowly, however, it is being realized that tests and examinations can be constructed and administered by and through the media. This procedure is being used to a limited extent by Midwest Airborne Research and has shown that printed tests can be administered satisfactorily by television. However (and more significantly), it is being realized that pictorial tests, both still and action, and with sound, permit new kinds of tests. Such tests have potential for sampling an extended range of information and proficiencies. Successful efforts are being made, particularly in the sciences, to present lifelike problem situations on film or video tape for students to diagnose and solve.

Audio tape

Many applications of this medium, besides foreign-language instruction, are now under way in the instruction of college students. Tape recorders are being used in speech and literature courses, for teaching nomenclature in the sciences, and as resource material for independent study. Recent applications have been made in laboratory work in the biological sciences to guide students through laboratory experiments with an efficient degree of pacing and some saving of the time of laboratory assistants.

Moderate-cost video tape recorders

Video tape machines are now in the moderate price range ($12,000), with even less expensive equipment likely.[10] Consequently, it is now possible to use video tape for instructor evaluation, repetition of course presentations, language instruction, guiding students through complex laboratory operations, off-campus instruction, and exchange of course materials among institutions.

Large-screen television

Efficient projectors capable of projecting television pictures, ranging in size from 6 by 8 feet to 16 by 20 feet, are now available and make possible the utilization of auditoriums for televised instruction. Experiments in several courses at Pennsylvania State University showed that students learned as well from large-screen television presentations in auditoriums as from televised instruction in small classrooms with regular receivers. Furthermore, student reactions were favorable to large-screen television.

FACILITIES FOR INSTRUCTIONAL INSTRUMENTATION

As media and technology have assumed an increasingly important role in the instructional process, they have had an important bearing on the development of facilities for their use. These developments are discussed below.

[10] A *New York Times* story of Apr. 4, 1964 (p. 1), indicates that such equipment may be available for as little as $500 within the next few years.

Presentation and feedback systems

As has been stressed previously, it is advisable to think in terms of systems of instructional instrumentation rather than in terms of a single medium. These systems combine a variety of audio and visual aids and equipment for presentation of stimulus materials for learning: facilities for daylight and rear-screen projection; large-screen and regular television receivers; video-tape and audio-tape facilities; and various types of film, slide, and other graphic materials. The stimulus materials in these systems are frequently programed and controlled by punched tape or some other method of automation. The program at the University of Miami is illustrative of such a presentation system. This program is described in more detail in Chapter 7, Facilities and Learning: An Overview of Developments.[11]

Much effort has been put into developing instrumentation for performing the teaching or mediating functions. Equal effort now needs to be given to the development of methods of obtaining, recording, and analyzing student responses and of providing reinforcement to the learners through immediate knowledge of results. The Classroom Communicator, designed and built in the early 1950s at Pennsylvania State University and used in film research studies, was an early prototype of these response systems. Systems are now needed which are usable by large numbers of students simultaneously (400 or more) and which have simple, rugged student-response stations. These systems would be useful for obtaining responses to questions or problems in programed instructional presentations and for large-scale testing. Computer control of programed learning sequences is a possibility with such systems, as is being demonstrated by the Plato Project of the University of Illinois, the Systems Development Corporation, and the project under way at the New York Institute of Technology.[12]

[11] Also see Charles Doren Tharp, "The Learning and Instructional Resources Center at the University of Miami," *Current Issues in Higher Education,* Association for Higher Education, Washington, D.C., 1963; H. D. Hauf, W. F. Koppes, Alan C. Green, and M. C. Gassman, *New Spaces for Learning: Designing College Facilities to Utilize Instructional Aids and Media,* Rensselaer Polytechnic Institute, Troy, N.Y., 1961; and *Planning for Schools with Television,* Educational Facilities Laboratories, New York, 1960.
[12] See Donald D. Bushnell, "The Role of the Computer in Future Instructional Systems," *AV Communication Review,* vol. 11, no. 2,

Designs for teaching auditoriums

The recent development of teaching auditoriums for relatively large classes has emphasized improvements in visual display systems, good acoustics, control of external light, internal illumination that is also controllable, good ventilation, seats so arranged that every student obtains an unobstructed view of the chalkboard, demonstration areas, television receivers or screens, good projection facilities with provision for rear- and multiple-screen projection, electrical connections for the remote control of equipment, and arrangements which allow for the installation of student-response equipment. Design projects undertaken in recent years at Rensselaer Polytechnic Institute, the University of Miami, the University of Wisconsin, and Pennsylvania State University offer useful guidance on these problems.[13]

Learning resource centers

Michigan State University has plans in the advanced stages of development for what are being called "learning resource centers." The new Florida Atlantic University was planned with learning resources as a core for the institution. The new James M. Wood Learning Center at Stephens College is made up of a complex of five buildings centered around a four-story resources library and a Television-Radio-Film and Audiovisual Center. Such centers are being planned to help solve the logistical, strategic, and tactical problems involved in making available whatever instructional means and materials are needed to accomplish the instructional goals. The proposed learning resource centers include and emphasize library materials, but in addition they include all other new media that are appropriate to the instructional functions of colleges and universities. Generally it is planned that these centers, which may serve one or more institutions and their branches, would not only procure but also produce instructional materials to specifications. Excepting most books, which would be purchased, special printed

March–April, 1963; and J. A. Easley, Jr., "Plato: A Computer Controlled Teaching System," paper presented at the nineteenth National Conference on Higher Education, sponsored by the Association for Higher Education, Chicago, 1964.
[13] See Hauf, Koppes, Green, and Gassman, *op. cit.*

materials would be produced. Units of instruction and full courses would be developed, using methods previously outlined and including the cooperative efforts of content, methods, and media specialists. Current thinking about learning resource centers tends to emphasize "new" media like films of all kinds, audio and video tapes, graphics, models, simulation mechanisms, and, prospectively, programed instruction. Emphasis is also put on facilities for distributing high-quality pretested stimulus materials and on presenting them to students in a wide range of study situations both on and off campus. The emphasis is on achieving enough flexibility so as to make instructional materials available to students when and where desired.

An important concept is that there can be a reduction of the demands made on and for teachers as the the quantity, kind, and accessibility of instructional materials are increased. However, the human factors in the system are considered of special importance. It is considered mandatory to have academic people of the highest competencies to plan and produce the materials and engineer their distribution and use. Skilled supporting personnel such as writers, programers, media producers, engineers, and technicians are required in numbers and kinds not now found on the academic scene. Not only will the training of people in new skills be necessary, but also the continuous training of regular faculty members will be necessary if the learning resource center systems are to serve effectively in educational institutions.[14]

GUIDELINES FOR INTRODUCING THE NEW MEDIA

The problem of introducing the newer media into education is a special case of the more general problem of the introduction, acceptance, and use of innovations by society. The opening question is: What are the main conditions that favor the successful introduction of the newer media into educational institutions?

The right people must sponsor the introduction of the media. In

[14] For an excellent model of such a facility, see Ralph C. Leyden and Neal Balanoff, *The Planning of Educational Media for a New Learning Center: A Report by Stephens College, Columbia, Missouri,* U.S. Office of Education, Washington, D.C., 1963.

colleges and universities this means that respected members of the teaching faculty should have the major role and the responsibility.

Two time factors are important. First, when the media are introduced to a significant degree may determine their success or failure. The question of "when?" however, is closely related to what the prevailing conditions are. Second, the amount of time provided for the introduction is important. More time is usually required than is planned for. Time must be allowed for familiarization, for accommodation, for changes in attitudes, for changes of roles and habits of teachers, and for learning how to use and learn from the newer media. Furthermore, much time is required for institutional adjustments in class scheduling, space assignments, and library procedures and also for developing new instructional services that are necessary to support the use of the media.

The real merits of what is being introduced have an important effect on the acceptance of the newer media. It can be assumed that many faculty members are skeptical and critical. They should be, and therefore the evidence of relative merit and observable demonstrations must be convincing to them.

The introduction of the media must have clear relations to needs as perceived by faculty members. Faculty members need relief from heavy work loads; they want to teach what they like to teach, and many prefer to teach advanced specialized courses rather than the large introductory general courses. Some have opposing preferences. When the new media actually help meet critical needs as perceived by faculty members, the introduction of the media is advanced, although not assured.

Many of the newer media require the services of competent specialists. If these needed skills exist in the "in group" of the faculty, the introduction is made easier; if the specialists do not exist in the family and "outsiders" must be engaged, the introduction is made more difficult.

It is a great advantage if the use of the newer media can be shown to be economically sound and if the savings in funds and effort can be returned as rewards to those men or departments who helped effect them. Furthermore, the costs of the newer media should be provided as supplements to regular budgets and should not come from resources and funds that are usually in short supply for supporting regular instruction.

Finally, it is not only advantageous but also essential to have media equipment systems that are reliable and work well, when and where needed. It is surprising how a few equipment failures or aborted programs are sufficient to cause faculty members to avoid and oppose the uses of the newer media.

PROBLEMS AND CAUTIONS IN THE USE OF THE NEW MEDIA

It is important to realize that the newer media *can* make important contributions to the solutions of problems but that they cannot provide complete solutions for most of the instructional problems in higher education. The media are good instruments, but as is the case with all instruments, the results depend most on *what they are used for* and on *how skillfully they are applied*.

Unfortunately the newer media, of which television and language laboratories are examples, have been oversold. The media have been proposed, for example, as solutions to the problems of shortages of teachers, limitations of funds, and absence of adequate teaching space and other facilities and also to the problems of raising the "quality" of instruction and teaching ever-larger numbers of students.

The facts are that the media themselves are not and cannot be complete solutions to any of these problems. They *can* make contributions to the solutions of these and even other problems, but when the media are available, many additional things need to be done to capitalize on their potentials.

For example, when language laboratories are installed, special course-content materials must be provided and often produced on tape and in print. Teachers must be trained to use the equipment and the new instructional materials. Students must be taught to study in new ways and to accept new learning demands and performance requirements.

Likewise, when television is introduced into an institution there are new problems and demands which result even as other problems are solved. New people must be employed to operate and maintain the television equipment, new kinds of instructional programs should be produced, and recordings of core-course materials and their repeated use become possibilities. Scheduling and the management of classes must be modified and adapted for television. And finally, buildings and the economics of instruction need to be changed.

The financing of the newer media has always posed a major problem, as yet unsolved. Too often "outside" funds, rather than regular funds, have been sought and used to finance the initial costs of films, equipment for radio, transparencies, graphics, language laboratories, and television. When this is done, there arises the problem of providing funds for expansion, operations, and supplies from regular budgets. Often special projects financed from government funds and foundation grants are sought and accepted without the responsible financial administrators of the institution knowing or realizing the future budget implications of such projects. The costs of original equipment, especially in the case of television, are high, and the costs of operating the equipment are usually underestimated. Almost universally, not enough funds are provided for using the new media properly.

The advancement from one level of technology to another normally requires training and retraining of personnel. These training requirements in the development of educational technology rarely have been adequately provided.

At an earlier time in the development of the new media, the total requirements for their introduction and effective use were not known. Now we know many of these requirements. Either they should be defined and met, or the introduction of television, language laboratories, multimedia systems, and modern classrooms should await the time when all the necessary conditions can be provided to ensure their effective use and success.

NEEDED RESEARCH

The research most urgently needed now is that designed to develop a *science of learning* and its applications. Too often educational institutions operate on residues of tradition, common sense, and raw experience. A kind of traditional superstition provides answers that work well enought so satisfy minimal requirements, and these answers reduce curiosity about the natural phenomena of learning. These pseudo answers block the development of a science of learning because the needs for such a science are not fully realized.

Research is needed where the most energy, resources, and funds are being spent, namely, in the classrooms, laboratories, seminars, language laboratories, libraries, dormitories, and wherever else conditions are arranged with the expectations that learning and intellectual development will occur. Does it? What kind? How much? How? Why? What are the factors both within and without the person? These questions are simply stated, but the answers are complex, and they are not known in sufficient detail or accurately enough to provide a science of learning that can serve as the basis for the management of colleges and universities.

The need for research is so great that all large universities should have research and development units working on problems of the organic and personal bases of learning, the processes of perception, cognition, and their organization in intellectual performances. Studies should be done on kinds, amounts, and effects of learning responses. Efforts should be made to understand and control reinforcement, rewards, penalties, and the effects on learning and retention or memory. The problems of generalization or transfer of learning, regardless of their basic importance, remain inadequately understood. Research is needed on schedules of intellectual growth and maturity and the changing learning potentialities and possibilities associated with growth. There is much to be done in analyzing basic concepts in many fields to make possible improved learning strategies. There are challenges for designing whole learning environments with variations appropriate to different fields, the characteristics of students, and performance criteria. From this area research could be extended into the effects on academic learning of the characteristics and patterns of student subcultures and peer groups. A science of learning is most important for application in the area of the newer media because the investments are great and the results can be either disastrous or invaluable.

IMPLICATIONS FOR THE FUTURE

The possibilities are that the rate of change in higher education will increase in the future. The rate of change will be affected primarily by the growing needs and demands that cannot be met satisfactorily by traditional facilities and procedures. There will be a growing awareness of the desirability of increasing both the effectiveness and the efficiency of the faculty in teaching and of the students in learning. Concurrently the mounting costs of education will create new emphasis on economies in education.

The recognized requirements for improving the quality of instruction will focus attention on the enormous tasks of selecting, organizing, producing, recording, and distributing instructional materials. Regional production centers will be needed. They could be the focus of interinstitutional efforts in producing and using instructional materials of proved quality. The roles of faculty members will change, and there will be increasing specialization as faculty competencies are matched against the specific requirements of a particular learning situation. As a science of human learning develops, the newer media systems, including special-purpose computers, will be used more extensively and will provide rapid assessment of student learning.

The newer media will be redesigned to make integrated systems for regulating many of the complex aspects of teaching and learning; these integrated systems may replace many of the special pieces of apparatus now in use.

Finally, if the newer media are used to a significant extent in the future, the principal operations and structure of colleges and universities will be changed in important ways. The newer media will find their true roles in higher education when it becomes evident to the decision makers in higher education that innovations are not merely desirable but essential and when it is realized that the continued expansion of what is traditional cannot meet the new and different educational needs of the future.

SOURCES FOR FURTHER INFORMATION

Audiovisual Instruction, vol. 8, no. 2, Department of Audiovisual Instruction, National Education Association, Washington, D.C., February, 1963.

Brown, J. W., and J. W. Thornton (eds.): *New Media in Higher Education,* National Education Association, Washington, D.C., 1963.

De Bernardis, Amo, Victor W. Doherty, Errett Hummel, and

Charles William Brubaker: *Planning Schools for New Media,* U.S. Department of Health, Education, and Welfare, Washington, D.C., 1962.

Educational Media Council, Inc.: *The Educational Media Index,* McGraw-Hill Book Company, New York, 1964.

Elfin, Mel, Bernard Asbell, Alvin Toffler, Margaret Farmer, and James J. Morisseau: *Bricks and Mortarboards: A Report on College Planning and Building,* Educational Facilities Laboratories, Inc., New York, 1964.

Four Case Studies of Programed Instruction, Fund for the Advancement of Education, New York, June, 1964.

Hauf, Harold D., Wayne F. Koppes, Alan C. Green, and Morton C. Gassman: *New Spaces for Learning: Designing College Facilities to Utilize Instructional Aids and Media,* Rensselaer Polytechnic Institute School of Architecture, Troy, N.Y., 1961.

Instructional Television Materials, Instructional Television Library Project, U.S. Department of Health, Education, and Welfare, Washington, D.C., 1964.

Leyden, Ralph C., and Neal Balanoff: *The Planning of Educational Media for a New Learning Center: A Report by Stephens College, Columbia, Missouri,* U.S. Office of Education, Washington, D.C., 1963.

Programs, '63: A Guide to Programed Instructional Methods, compiled by The Center for Programed Instruction, Inc., in cooperation with the U.S. Department of Health, Education, and Welfare, Washington, D.C., 1963.

Review of Educational Research, vol. 32, no. 2, American Educational Research Association, Washington, D.C., April, 1962.

Trow, William Clark: *Teacher and Technology: New Designs for Learning,* Appleton-Century-Crofts, Inc., New York, 1963.

FRANCIS H. HORN
JONATHAN KING
JAMES J. MORISSEAU

7

facilities and learning:
an overview of developments

*D*espite increasing emphasis upon independent study and
self-learning, the essence of the learning process is the relationship of the teacher, the student, and knowledge. The success of
education depends upon people, not buildings. Yet higher education, like all human activities, generates an environment of its own.
Some sort of physical plant has been, and will continue to be,
necessary. Facilities for study and investigation, for confrontation
between the teacher and the taught, and for living and recreation
are part of higher education.

American colleges and universities currently are spending 1.2
billion dollars a year on buildings and campus development. Estimates are that they will need to spend 1.9 billion dollars a year if
they are to keep pace with enrollments and replace obsolete facili-

ties.[1] *These new campus facilities are being erected during an era of upheaval in the educational program. Clearly, new campus buildings must serve not only today's education but also that of the year 2000.*

This chapter outlines the dimensions and complexity of the colleges' physical problems and goes on to describe some of the experimentation under way in an effort to improve the design of campus facilities. In addition, it describes some of the more imaginative buildings that have appeared recently on American campuses. And some broad guidelines are offered to educational administrators as they attempt to plan their campuses for the future.

BACKGROUND

From the American Revolution to the Civil War, the basic pattern of physical facilities in the colleges and universities changed little. Forces were at work, however, that, under the impact of the new university movement, eventually resulted in considerable modification of programs and activities and concurrently of the physical plants. These nineteenth-century developments that affected educational facilities included the expansion of knowledge, especially in the natural sciences; the growth of specialization, with a resulting departmentalization of instruction; and the institution of graduate work and research.

Two external factors had great significance for the expansion of institutions of higher education and the resulting modification of the traditional collegiate approach to educational facilities. The first was the Morrill Act of 1862, establishing the land-grant college system, which stressed instruction in agriculture and the mechanic arts, until then largely absent from the curriculum in higher education. New types of buildings and the enlargement of the campus to accommodate instruction became necessary, and later research in agriculture became essential. Furthermore, the Morrill Act put the

[1] Mel Elfin, Bernard Asbell, Alvin Toffler, Margaret Farmer, and James J. Morisseau, *Bricks and Mortarboards: A Report on College Planning and Building,* Educational Facilities Laboratories, Inc., New York, 1964, p. 10.

Federal government, which had demonstrated its concern for higher education since the Northwest Ordinance of 1787, directly into the financial support of higher education and forced the several states to initiate or expand their support.

The second factor was the growth of private philanthropy on behalf of higher education. Men of great wealth provided funds not only for the construction of single buildings but also for the creation of whole universities *de novo*. Ezra Cornell, Johns Hopkins, and John D. Rockefeller, Jr., were only the first of a group of benefactors whose generosity enabled new institutions to be built. Later, at Harvard and Yale, the funds provided by oil magnate Edward S. Harkness resulted in the development of the Harvard house plan and Yale's college system.

These forces—the proliferation of the curriculum, the growth of research, and the increasing financial support of higher education from both private and public sources—along with an increasing awareness of the importance of higher education for both the individual and the nation, resulting in a growing demand for college opportunities, produced an accelerating expansion of American higher education. In 1900 there were 238,000 students in 977 colleges and universities. By 1920 the figure had grown to 598,000 in 1,041 institutions. Twenty years later, enrollment was 1,494,000, and there were 1,708 institutions, including junior colleges.

The growth curve of higher education rose even higher after World War II, although the number of institutions has not increased proportionately to the increase in enrollment. Enrollment in the nation's colleges and universities in the fall of 1964 was put at 5.3 million,[2] an increase of over 130 per cent since 1950. The net result has been a phenomenal growth in physical facilities.

FINANCING

Financing the rapid growth of physical facilities has strained the resources of even the most affluent institutions.[3] Dollar expenditures for buildings and campus development show an increase from 264

[2] *Opening Fall Enrollment in Higher Education,* U.S. Department of Health, Education, and Welfare, Washington, D.C., 1964.
[3] This topic is discussed in greater detail in Chap. 12, Dollars and Cents: Some Hard Facts.

million dollars in 1951–1952 to 619 million dollars in 1958–1959
and further to an estimated average of 1.5 billion dollars a year for
the period from 1961 to 1965.[4] These expenditures reflect vast expansion projects under way at many public institutions, more
modest efforts by private colleges, the creation of entire new universities in a number of states, and the appearance of a few new
private institutions. Impressive as it sounds, all this apparently is
not enough. Higher education appears to be heading toward a
shortage of as many as 1 million places by 1970.

Colleges draw upon a broad range of sources to support construction programs. Privately supported institutions have been
largely dependent upon gifts and grants, while public institutions
have been largely dependent upon appropriations and general obligation bonds for their construction funds. It is generally acknowl-
edged that increasing Federal assistance for the construction of
physical facilities for higher education is inevitable because of the
tremendous further expansion in enrollments and the cost of providing the facilities necessary to accommodate these students and
the research activities of students and faculty. The argument for
Federal support is based on the conviction that the national welfare
in the last analysis is dependent upon the effectiveness of higher
education and that Federal aid for construction is less controversial
than more direct aid to instruction. Two legislative acts have been
of particular significance for facilities in recent years: the College
Housing Loan Program, which has provided over 2 billion dollars
in loans to institutions of higher education since its enactment in
1950, and the Higher Education Facilities Act of 1963, which was
to provide for an average of 400 million dollars in grants each year
for a three-year period to pay part of the costs of constructing academic buildings and facilities at public and private institutions.

A recent interesting and perhaps very significant development in
the provision of college buildings, especially residential facilities, is
their financing, construction, and management by private corporations. Millions have been invested in the last few years by such
firms on a number of campuses. The facilities range from low-cost
and often minimally equipped dormitory accommodations to more
costly and elaborate student residential facilities, such as those being

[4] Leslie F. Robbins and W. Robert Bokelman, *College and University
Facilities Survey. Part 4. College and University Enrollment and Facilities Survey, 1961–1965,* U.S. Office of Education, Washington, D.C.,
1964, p. 47.

built at Ohio University, which will include an indoor swimming pool, a billiard room, a beauty salon, and ground-floor shops.

In addition to financing housing facilities, some companies are studying the financing and leasing of academic buildings as well. One New York builder expects to invest about 150 million dollars in campus structures over the next two years; another private corporation is considering the establishment of complete privately supported colleges "in certain areas of the U.S. where no private colleges are in existence."

Certainly private financing and operation of college facilities is on the increase and may well prove to be an important additional means of meeting the astronomical needs for college facilities in the years ahead.[5]

Estimates of the cost of future building needs vary. Prof. Seymour Harris of Harvard, who has been studying the financing of higher education for years, estimated that capital expenditures for higher education would average 1.5 billion dollars a year during the ten-year period from 1960 to 1970.[6] In a study made by the U.S. Office of Education, Dr. Leslie F. Robbins and Dr. W. Robert Bokelman reported that new construction, renovation, or campus improvements to be completed between 1960 and 1965 would total 7.5 billion dollars, again an average of 1.5 billion dollars a year. Economist Peter F. Drucker has calculated that to take care of all the additional students expected on the campus by 1975, the colleges will have to construct new facilities equal to twice all the campus buildings that have been erected in the nation since Harvard opened its doors in 1636.

If anything, these figures may be conservative, unless the colleges choose to confront some of their problems in new ways. They do not reflect decreasing dollar value, and announced plans for new construction by individual institutions suggest even higher levels of expenditure. In any case, there seems little question that a fantastic amount of construction will be carried on by colleges and universities in the years ahead. The sound of the bulldozer and the sight of the construction crane will be present on most campuses for many years to come.

[5] For more on this development see the *Wall Street Journal*, October 13, 1964.
[6] Seymour E. Harris, *Financing Higher Education: 1960–1970*, McGraw-Hill Book Company, New York, 1959, chap. 3, p. 36.

SOME FACTORS IN THE DEVELOPING PICTURE

What are the implications of this vast program of building new facilities? What sort of buildings will colleges and universities get for these tremendous expeditures? Will the new buildings be imaginative and creative—indeed beautiful—in addition to being functional? Will we be creating new campuses or adding to existing campuses in such a way that they will be a proud heritage to future generations? Have we come to recognize that architecture contributes in a number of ways to the total institutional environment and thereby may influence learning in its broadest sense?[7]

Unless architecture takes an unpredictable and unlikely turn, most of the campuses will not be built in neohistorical styles. Few attempts will be made to create new Georgian campuses, as was done at Colby and Wake Forest, or new masses of collegiate Gothic, as at Duke and Yale. However imposing these modern adaptations of older architectural styles may be, and regardless of the philosophical arguments about the integrity or falseness of historically eclectic architecture, the cost of building today in these derivative styles will be deterrent enough to prevent their rebirth.

More important than questions of style will be the effects of the many changes that are now occurring in the organization and methodology of higher education. The effects of these changes are dramatically evident in the design and shape of many of the new buildings that are beginning to dot the college campus.

A number of other changes in higher education will bear importantly on the planning and construction of facilities. Consider, for example, the college student. Students are certainly more serious than they were in the past; often they are older, one-fourth are married, and an increasing proportion attend college on a part-time basis. The number of foreign students is increasing. A higher proportion as well as a larger number of students than ever before are going on to graduate or professional school. And many students, taking advantage of adult education and continuing education programs, are reutrning to the college campus after graduation. The result of these sociological changes surely will be modifications of current practices in the design of college buildings.

[7] For a discussion of the architecture and settings as components in the campus climate, see Chap. 13.

Still other factors will be of importance in determining the shape of the campus of the future. Certainly the emphasis on the extension of knowledge through research and the resultant need for expansion of research facilities will continue. Undoubtedly expansion of facilities for creative arts activities will continue. Community services will continue to grow. And finally, changes in the curriculum are inevitable. There will be new disciplines and new fields of specialization now scarcely foreseen. Since buildings are expected to last for many years, they must be planned to meet a variety of uses which can only be anticipated in a general way at the time they are planned.

The great diversity in these more than two thousand institutions that make up higher education in the United States—in their traditions, objectives, and programs, on the one hand, and in their location, size, and wealth on the other—dictates many answers, not just one. But some general principles of design for good facilities and of sound fiscal planning can and must be established.

RECENT DEVELOPMENTS

Stephen Leacock, in his book *Oxford As I See It,* reflected thus: "If I were founding a university I would found first a smoking room; then when I had a little more money in hand I would found a dormitory; then after that, or more probably with it, a decent reading room and a library. After that, if I still had more money that I couldn't use, I would hire a professor and get some textbooks."

Mr. Leacock came close to restating the origins of higher education. The earliest European universities were propertyless; they were simply associations of students and teachers banded together for mutual protection and welfare. But, inevitably, property was acquired. First came residences, and later integrated residential-instructional complexes much like the residential colleges at Oxford and Cambridge today. This British pattern was followed in large part by the founders of Harvard in 1636 and dominated the shape of the American campus for more than two hundred years. The pattern remained substantially unchanged until 1876, when Johns Hopkins, the first American university founded on the German model, was established. The sciences were added to the curriculum as were professional schools of all varieties and, most recently, sponsored research (particularly federally financed research).

What has emerged is a number of campus types. But all of them represent a compromise between the earlier collegiate ideal, with its stress on character, moral, and religious development and later fellowship and well-roundedness as well as intellectual achievement, and the university ideal, with its almost exclusive concern with the advancement and transmission of knowledge.

Nevertheless, there is no single pattern for the 2,000-odd colleges and universities that now dot the American landscape. Clearly, the small rural liberal arts college bears little physical resemblance to the sprawling state universities. And neither of these shares the appearance and problems of an urban college or university. Even among the various institutional types, there is no set pattern.

But certain generalizations are valid. Except in urban institutions, the campus tends to be open in character, with generous expanses between buildings. The campus usually is arranged in zones, with instructional activities relegated to one area, residence facilities to another, and "public" activities, such as athletic and theatrical events, to a third.

The instructional buildings tend to fall under the "ownership" of an academic department or group of related departments. There is a biology building, a psychology building, a social sciences building. Instructional space often is fixed in nature, unalterable in either size or function. There are lecture and seminar spaces, but standard classrooms seating between twenty and fifty students predominate. Laboratories are designed to serve a specific scientific discipline and, because of a fixed pattern of utilities, walls, and furniture, cannot be converted to accommodate other disciplines or functions. The library generally is a functional loft-type structure if it was built in the last thirty years, although a substantial number of the old monumental libraries, with their closed stacks and high-ceilinged reading rooms, still are in use. Most of the seating in the library, whether of the loft type or monumental, is at long tables. There are a few carrels that offer a measure of privacy for the individual library user, but these usually are allocated to faculty and graduate students, not to undergraduates.

Dormitories almost without exception contain a series of two-student cells ranged down both sides of a long corridor. The pattern is interrupted only by the stairwells and by a gang-type toilet and washroom serving all residents of the floor. Except for limited desk and shelf space in each room, there are no physical provisions which are designed because the structure is to serve education. These dormitories resemble nothing so much as a series of stripped-down Hilton hotels.

And the campus, of course, is replete with other types of buildings serving a myriad of purposes. There is a stadium, an auditorium, a theater, a chapel, the president's house, the student union, fraternity houses, a museum, a cyclotron, research facilities, maintenance buildings, and the heating plant or powerhouse.

And that, with few exceptions, is the physical pattern of American higher education today. It is a pattern that in the past did not ill serve the educational process. It is a pattern that, when graced with ivy-covered walls, is built into the American dream. Viewed with nostalgia, it is revered by generations of alumni and would-be alumni, many of whom did not themselves enjoy watching the fall leaves blow across the quadrangles. But is it a pattern that will serve the needs of the colleges and of the nation in the next few years?

By all evidence, the answer must be "no."

The developments outlined elsewhere in this book which are now transforming higher education have prompted dramatic changes on some campuses. These changes have been described as education's "industrial revolution." They attempt to bring industrylike efficiency and technology to bear on the educational process, while preserving or, better, enhancing the role of the professor as an educator. Where properly applied, the new technology is employed to relieve the teacher of the chore of imparting rote fact, freeing him to influence individuals and small groups as a true educator, an arbiter of knowledge. It has, perhaps, been described best by Harvard's B. F. Skinner, who said: "Any teacher who can be replaced by a machine should be."

The revolution demands that students be arranged in different patterns as they move through the educational program and that both teacher and student employ new tools (e.g., television, electronic language laboratories, teaching machines, and others yet to come) in the instructional process. The Board of Education of the city of Chicago runs one community college, an extreme example, which offers an entire two-year course on television. A similar opportunity to study by television will soon be available to New Yorkers. It will be run by the Community College of the Borough of Manhattan.

RESEARCH ON FACILITIES

The most vital research and development work on college and university facilities today revolves around four issues: technology, flexibility, utilization of space, and the sociopsychological aspects of education.

Technology

Education has, of course, been one of the prime stimuli for technology in our society, but ironically it has also proved to be one area of society with a strong resistance to the use of technology for its own purposes. However, stimulated by the growing shortages of faculty members, the increase in students, and problems of cost, and with encouragement from some of the major foundations, the situation is shifting rapidly today.

All over the United States programs are developing which acknowledge and use technology for education. Only a few years ago such programs formed the basis for experimentation; today technology is shaping buildings. Rensselaer Polytechnic Institute,[8] for example, has carried forward a study of the implications of various media on instructional space which has produced not only a report thereon but also a mock-up instructional hall inside a deconsecrated Catholic church that the institution bought recently. The philosophical basis of the experimental facility is that television, slides, movies, overhead projectors, and other hardware are here to stay for instructional purposes and that facilities should be designed to take maximum advantage of all media. This contrasts strongly with the normal habit of adding each device to the instructional space as an afterthought following construction, with each device unrelated to any other device or to the design of the space itself. But RPI has treated projection and television screens, sight lines, lighting, acoustics, and viewing distances and angles

[8] Harold D. Hauf, Wayne F. Koppes, Alan C. Green, and Morton C. Gassman, *New Spaces for Learning: Designing College Facilities to Utilize Instructional Aids and Media,* Rensselaer Polytechnic Institute School of Architecture, Troy, N.Y., 1961.

as part of a systematic solution to the lecture-room problem.[9] Unfortunately, for many years most academic buildings have been planned with the general notion that the only tools of real use for classroom instruction are the jawbone of the teacher and the blackboard.

Within a pink masonry octagon on the Coral Gables campus of the University of Miami, there is evidence of probably the firmest commitment to the use of technology for teaching on the American college campus today. The University College building consists of six 300-seat auditoriums and several smaller spaces which surround a central projection area, where a comparatively small crew of technicians can arrange the projection of televised or filmed programs in any or all of the six auditoriums, each of which is wedge-shaped and comes to a blunt point at a 10- by 10-foot rear projection screen. The building is heavily equipped, even to a video tape recorder, so that repetition of lectures is unnecessary. University College is the place where some forty-five hundred Miami freshmen and sophomores receive their basic instruction in the sciences, humanities, and social sciences. Most of the teaching is done in a studio, not in the auditoriums themselves. Enough money is saved to enable the remainder of the instruction to be personalized.

Similar, if more modest, projects are under way at the University of Texas and at the University of Wisconsin, both using audio-visual systems designed by the Teleprompter Corporation, until recently more concerned with military communications and closed-circuit broadcasting of prizefights than with higher learning.

The language laboratory is by now a commonplace element of the academic world, and it too has made possible certain improvements, not only in instruction, but also in staff utilization. Purdue has made significant strides in this direction with a sixty-student station laboratory developed on the hypotheses that (*1*) first-rate language teachers are hard to find these days; (*2*) they are expensive, and so is language-laboratory equipment; and (*3*) if a sixty-station teaching laboratory is educationally as successful as a thirty-station laboratory, it would obviously be more economical. All three hypotheses have proved to be true.

Technology is not restricted to direct instruction. A quiet revo-

[9] Margaret Farmer, *New Building on Campus: Six Designs for a College Communications Center,* Educational Facilities Laboratories, Inc., New York, Inc., 1964.

lution is under way today in the college library. The stimulus is a simply astonishing proliferation of printed words. Last year roughly fifteen thousand technical journals published 1 million significant papers. The number of books and nontechnical journals is on the increase as well. Microreproduction has offered certain obvious advantages to storing the ever-increasing amounts of information needed by scholars, but so far a convenient low-cost reader has not been developed, despite the efforts and stimulus of the Council on Library Resources. However, Xerox copies of microfilmed materials at a comparatively reasonable price are a step in the direction of making microcopies more usable for library research. But the problem of simplified microstorage remains relatively unsolved. Technology is changing more than the carriers of information in the libraries.

In the areas of administration, purchasing, and cataloging, the computer is moving into the library in a strategic way. Conventionally, university libraries spend on the average of twice the cost of a book to purchase, catalog, and shelve it. Substantial research on the use of data-processing equipment and techniques for library administration is now going forward at the University of Illinois at Chicago, UCLA, the University of Colorado, the National Library of Medicine, and the University of Toronto. This research points toward reduction in administrative costs as well as advantages in cataloging techniques which will be of great benefit to scholars and librarians.

A sophisticated data storage and retrieval system involving microreproduction has been developed by IBM for the Central Intelligence Agency. Called "Walnut," it makes possible a search of substantial amounts of data almost instantly on the basis of certain key words (e.g., "library," "data," "microreproduction"). But it is far beyond the financial resources of education and far too limited for most academic purposes. For the moment, at least, the printed word—in readable size—seems secure, but other informational storage and retrieval systems are being developed which will supplement the book and journal.

Utilization

Certainly the place of technology, and particularly of the computer, has developed into a major factor in the organization of higher educational institutions. Some of the large colleges and universities in the nation—and particularly those in the cities, which tend to teach late into the night—have long enjoyed high-utilization rates for their instructional facilities. High utilization, in this sense, means that classrooms and laboratories are scheduled for most hours of a reasonably long academic week. Some institutions lay justified claim to rates as high as 80 per cent or more. But, in general, higher education makes a rather poor showing, as John Dale Russell notes in Chapter 12. Costly instructional and laboratory facilities stand empty or at least unscheduled much of the time on many campuses. In a survey of sixty small liberal arts colleges in the Middle West several years ago, Dr. John X. Jamrich, of Michigan State University, found that classroom space was in use only 40 per cent of a forty-four hour week, and laboratories only 25 per cent of the time. He concluded that if the problems of residential space and obsolescence were excluded, these colleges could expand their enrollments by 50 per cent without erecting a single new building.[10] It is of course true that most space-utilization studies are based on the fallacious notion that unscheduled rooms are unused. This is not always the case. Laboratories, particularly, are often used for academic purposes during hours when they are not scheduled for group use.

Behind this obviously inefficient pattern lies a whole set of academic traditions, prejudices, and practices. Faculty and students alike tend to shun early-morning, late-afternoon, and Saturday class schedules. Mornings are preferred for lecture sessions, and afternoons for laboratory sessions. Academic departments tend to claim "ownership" of classrooms and laboratories and to bar their use by other departments.

The pressures of enrollment and campus economics have forced many colleges to schedule a longer academic day and week and have caused a substantial number to go to a longer academic year, if not a year-round calendar. This in turn has made air conditioning a necessity on many campuses. Elsewhere, colleges have turned to cooperative programs in an effort to make better use of such facilities as libraries, specialized laboratories, and gymnasiums, avoiding duplication of courses that are sparsely attended and obtaining other economies possible through group effort.

One of the most intriguing attacks on the utilization problem on

[10] John X. Jamrich and Ruth Weinstock, *To Build or Not to Build: A Report on the Utilization and Planning of Instructional Facilities in Small Colleges,* Educational Facilities Laboratories, Inc., New York, 1962.

existing campuses is under way at the Massachusetts Institute of Technology. MIT has put a senior computer to work on the problem of building its schedule and sectioning students.[11] Using a computer to section students into a hand-built schedule is no longer new, but building the schedule by computer is. An IBM 7094 has been used to simulate the Institute—its students, faculty, instructional programs, and available facilities. Among other things, the project is expected to provide, in the long run, a faster, more economical means of class scheduling and more effective use of facilities. This project, known as "GASP," for Generalized Academic Simulation Program, has now been used to simulate a not yet constructed college, the Meramec Community College of the St. Louis Junior College District. The result has been to revise some room sizes and save the building of substantial amounts of space. President Joseph Cosand claims a saving of 3 million dollars on one campus alone and 10 million dollars on all three of his prospective campuses, in contrast to what it would have cost to build the space that would be necessary if conventional utilization patterns were to be followed.

Flexibility

A word of wondrous variety of meanings is "flexibility." But in all its meanings it remains a key element in planning the buildings going up on campuses across America. The recent very rapid changes in education and the obvious implication that the rate of change in education has increased make is a most compelling concept in academic planning.

Perhaps the most obvious and vitally needed kind of flexibility is in the laboratory and research buildings. Science has been changing so rapidly that only the most obtuse scientist thinks he knows the kind of research he will be doing in a decade. This calls for buildings like the recently opened Olin Hall of Science at Colorado College. Olin Hall is essentially a thin slab with no interior structural elements and with all structural, service, and mechanical systems (ventilation, electrical services, piping, etc.) in its thick exterior walls. Like a grasshopper, its skeleton is on

11 Judith Murphy and Robert Sutter, *School Scheduling by Computer: The Story of GASP,* Educational Facilities Laboratories, Inc., New York, 1964.

the outside; hence Caudhill, Rowlett, and Scott, the architects, dubbed it an "exoskeleton" building.

Whatever services or space the future science program in Colorado College requires, the building will not stand in the way of the program, nor will the Pierce and Pierce biology building at Rice University get in the way of scientific or educational change for years to come. Every 28 feet in the center of the 50-foot-wide building, a vertical chase 6 feet square brings utilities up to each floor. To avoid the arbitrary division of the interior produced by the usual central corridor, the corridor has been placed on the outside of the building, on the south side, to serve as sunshade as well as hallway. Almost unlimited spatial arrangements are possible within the building. Services can easily be tapped from the central chases, with minimum need for major remodeling.

These represent but two of a number of well-thought-out buildings designed for flexible use and for minimal remodeling expenses as science and education change.

But there is also the need for instructional space that changes at once and for instructional space that can be changed during a week's vacation to accommodate changing educational programs economically and efficiently.

Chicago Teachers College North,[12] designed by architects Perkins and Will, is based obviously on the assumption that available teaching space must adjust at once to the needs of its users. The major proportion of the space devoted to instruction is divided into a series of hexagons, some sized for groups of thirty, and others for groups of seventy-five. Both sizes are divisible in half at a moment's notice to provide, in the case of the smaller room, two seminar rooms or, in the case of the larger lecture rooms, two medium-sized classrooms. Divided with newer types of operable walls which offer satisfactory sound attenuation between the spaces, these rooms serve double duty for varying types of activities.

Large areas of relatively easy-to-alter academic space provide another approach to flexibility for instructional areas. Southern Illinois's new campus at Edwardsville, designed by Gyo Obata, of Hellmuth, Obata, and Kassabaum, will have much space of this kind. Although not divisible at once as at Chicago Teachers College North, it will be redivisible at minimal expense for the life of the structure. Furthermore, SIU will organize all instructional space

---

[12] See Chap. 1 for a fuller discussion of this program.

by function (lecture, classrooms, laboratories, etc.) rather than by department, to encourage a far higher rate of space utilization than occurs under departmentally controlled buildings.

Spatial flexibility has two main reasons for being. The first is money. College buildings, like other buildings, are bought by the square foot, and flexibility can allow more intensive use of each square foot. The second is change; the truly flexible building can accommodate the new programs which changing educational patterns produce with ever more rapidity and regularity.

Social and psychological factors

How people react to buildings is far from being the subject of an exact science today. Despite a certain amount of research, there remains more mystery than fact. However, there are indications that generalizations are occasionally not only possible but also useful in planning. One recent study of student study habits[13] indicates certain general guides to designers of college facilities. Students prefer a study space inversely to its size. Students study in their dormitory rooms more if there are one or two occupants than if there are more. In short, students like the kind of study space provided by the more intelligently designed modern libraries, particularly individual study carrels and small groups of tables, preferably small tables; they do not like the monumental reading room of yesteryear or its long library tables. Dormitories designed with something other than nocturnal storage in mind should provide students with a reasonable degree of privacy for study.

More basic social issues are also shaping campus structures today. On campus after campus it is possible to detect a dissatisfaction with the growing institutional impersonality, with the separation of students and faculty members, with the separation of the social and the academic, and with the division of the campus into areas for sleep, study, work, and play. Various types of living arrangements and mixtures of living and academic areas are being designed to counter this growing impersonality. Stephens College, for example (see Chapter 1), teaches the five core courses of its curriculum to each of the 100 resident students of West Hall in the libraries and commons rooms of the residence hall itself. The five faculty members who teach these courses have their offices

13 *Student Reaction to Study Facilities,* the Committee for New College, Amherst, Mass., 1960.

within the house as well, and each serves as adviser to 20 of the 100 girls who make up the hall. Stephens is, of course, a student-oriented institution. Such an arrangement would not be appropriate for a more research-oriented college or university.

But Goddard College, Harvard, and Sarah Lawrence all teach within residential buildings, although not in quite such a single-minded fashion as Stephens College. Such programs have the double virtue of eliminating some of the separation between the various aspects of campus life and of serving economy by the multiple use of residential space which often stands empty all day, while instructional buildings stand equally empty all night.

The increasing size and impersonality of colleges have been matters of some concern to many educators. One of the common solutions to the problem has been to subdivide the institution into houses or colleges. Many such programs have a vague resemblance to the Oxbridge colleges or to the Harvard houses or the Yale colleges. In a general way, they all have in common the fact that they attempt to bring together a reasonably small group of students who have a special relationship to certain faculty members, with whom they dine fairly regularly. Perhaps the most English of the new house plans is that announced for New College in Sarasota, Florida. The key concept in New College's planning is individualized instruction in a prestigious institution of the highest quality with intimate faculty-student relationships. Patterned after the tutorial plan Oxford's New College has used for 500 years, Sarasota's New College houses will have a resident faculty member for each thirty-two students. Other faculty members will be expected to join the common table for evening meals as well.

The house plan seems to be a dominant concept in building new institutions as well as in reorganizing older ones. The newest announced campus of the University of California, at Santa Cruz, will be based on a series of decentralized colleges to make up the University campus. Whether new or old, the concept of size limitation or division seems to be taking hold in many colleges and universities across the nation.

Other developments

So far, little mention has been made of elements of the campus other than the four major ones: instructional, laboratory, library, and residential. But much has been happening in the design of

other building types on the campus. Cited earlier was the phenomenon of the research building, with its nearly total flexibility and
controlled environment for research. Nearly as dramatic is the
proliferation of college unions, having a wide range of social and
recreational facilities for students and other members of the campus
community. One of the most striking of these is the student center
of the University of California at Berkeley. Though the buildings
are contemporary, making extensive use of steel, glass, and thin-
shell concrete, an intimate, highly urban arrangement of its elements gives the Berkeley student center a feeling more of an
Italian piazza than of the usual more grassy or suburban American
campus. And because of the usual problem of lack of space, under
it all is a parking garage.

The concern for student welfare also has prompted improvement in college health facilities.[14] Colorado College, for example,
is building a circular infirmary, designed by architects Caudill,
Rowlett, and Scott for efficiency, economy, *and* education. One
nurse will be able to supervise the entire bed-patient area from
a central nurse's station. A study will be located between the
nurse's station and the patient rooms at the perimeter of the
building, and study facilities will be available at bedside to nonambulatory patients. The study area will be convertible to ward
space if the patient load rises.

Meanwhile, drastic new approaches have been tried to the
housing of physical education and athletics. The University of
Illinois at Urbana, for example, boasts a huge new arena re-
sembling nothing so much as a grounded flying saucer. Wrapped
around the perimeter of the reinforced concrete dome are miles
of steel wire, which convert the outward thrust of the roof into
a downward force borne by the forty-eight concrete buttresses
upon which the building rests. Thus, the need for interior supports
was eliminated. The result was a highly adaptable structure, equally
usable for large conventions and athletic events and for small
student assemblies and theatrical performances.

At the Forman School in Litchfield, Connecticut, great economies were obtained through the use of air-supported structures to
house physical education programs. Huge plastic bubbles, held up
by air pressure, cover a tennis court, which is paved with artificial

[14] Bernard Bard, *A College Health Center, with an Architectural Answer by Caudill, Rowlett & Scott,* Case Studies of Educational Facilities no. 6, Educational Facilities Laboratories, Inc., New York, 1963.

turf, and a swimming pool. Both bubbles can be collapsed and stored away during the summer months.

IN SUM

Education, suffering from what was once described in a *Mademoiselle* article (quoting a Princeton undergraduate) as "creeping estheticism," ordinarily tends to underestimate the importance of facilities, with the possible exception of science facilities, stadiums, and parking lots. It is easy to make a case for the fact that instruction and thought do not depend on the physical aspects of the institution, but it is equally easy to find that time and time again the physical aspects of an institution either stand in the way of its educational aims or support them. In extreme cases the physical aspects may be such as to encourage the institution to start all over again. Fifteen have done so recently.[15]

Of late, some additional studies of the physical aspects of education have been supported by Educational Facilities Laboratories, a nonprofit institution established by the Ford Foundation to support research, experimentation, and the dissemination of information regarding facilities for education at all levels. Indeed, a number of the previously mentioned projects have received financial backing from Educational Facilities Laboratories.

One of the obvious dangers in higher education planning is that it is often done without regard to the institution's total educational objectives. Because of the many calls on the time of the college president, the inclination of both president and trustee is to leave technical matters to experts and it is not unusual to find that planning for new buildings will often go on in piecemeal fashion, based on the availability of funds or the whimsy of donors. Each campus is far more than simply the sum of its buildings. To proceed without a basic master plan to govern the organized growth of the institution and to see that its physical environment is indeed a reflection of the philosophy of the institution and its educational objectives is to court disaster

Most colleges get the buildings they deserve; their problem is how to plan in such a way as to deserve the best.

[15] S. B. Zisman and Catherine Powell, *New Campuses for Old: A Case Study of Four Colleges That Moved,* Case Studies of Educational Facilities no. 5, Educational Facilities Laboratories, Inc., New York, 1962.

SOURCES FOR FURTHER INFORMATION

Chapman, Dave, Inc.: *Design for ETV: Planning Schools for Television,* Educational Facilities Laboratories, Inc., New York, 1960.

Dober, Richard P.: *Campus Planning,* Reinhold Publishing Corporation, New York, 1963.

Elfin, Mel, Bernard Asbell, Alvin Toffler, Margaret Farmer, and James J. Morisseau: *Bricks and Mortarboards: A Report on College Planning and Building,* Educational Facilities Laboratories, Inc., New York, 1964.

Farmer, Margaret: *New Building on Campus: Six Designs for a College Communications Center,* Educational Facilities Laboratories, Inc., New York, 1964.

Frame, J. Sutherland: *Buildings and Facilities for the Mathematical Sciences,* Educational Facilities Laboratories, Inc., New York, 1963.

Harris, Seymour E.: *Higher Education: Resources and Finance,* McGraw-Hill Book Company, New York, 1962.

Hauf, Harold D., Wayne F. Koppes, Alan C. Green, and Morton C. Gassman: *New Spaces for Learning: Designing College Facilities to Utilize Instructional Aids and Media,* Rensselaer Polytechnic Institute School of Architecture, Troy, N.Y., 1961.

Jamrich, John X., and Ruth Weinstock: *To Build or Not to Build: A Report on the Utilization and Planning of Instructional Facilities in Small Colleges,* Educational Facilities Laboratories, Inc., New York, 1962.

King, Jonathan: "Campus Cultures and the Cultured Campus," *The Study of Campus Cultures,* papers presented at the fourth annual Institute on College Self Study, July 24 to 27, 1962, University of California, Berkeley, Calif., 1963.

Monograph Series 1960–1961, University Facilities Research Center, Madison, Wis.

Morisseau, James, J.: "Seminar on Campus Planning," reprint from *Journal of the American Institute of Architects,* June, 1963, available from Educational Facilities Laboratories, Inc., 477 Madison Ave., New York.

Mushkin, Selma J. (ed.): *Economics of Higher Education,* U.S. Office of Education, Washington, D.C., 1962.

Palmer, Ronald R., and William Maxwell Rice: *Modern Physics Buildings: Design and Function,* Reinhold Publishing Corporation, New York, 1961.

Riker, Harold C., and Frank G. Lopez: *College Students Live Here: A Study of College Housing,* Educational Facilities Laboratories, Inc., New York, 1961.

Rork, John B., and Leslie F. Robbins: *Casebook on Campus Planning and Institutional Development,* U.S. Office of Education, Washington, D.C., 1962.

Zisman, S. B., and Catherine Powell: *New Campuses for Old: A Case Study of Four Colleges That Moved,* Case Studies of Educational Facilities no. 5, Educational Facilities Laboratories, Inc., New York, 1962.

ROYCE S. PITKIN
GEORGE BEECHER

8

extending the educational environment: the community as a resource for learning

William James long ago made a distinction between knowledge about *and* knowledge of acquaintance. *The first kind of knowledge is derived from what others tell us, in speech or in writing. The other kind is knowledge derived from firsthand experience, from personal observation. This distinction between kinds of knowledge does not diminish the value of either; each has an important role to play in the education of a person. Some knowledge can be obtained only from others, simply because the experience involved cannot be duplicated; thus we read Homer and learn from him. Other knowledge can be obtained only by doing; if we would know hunger, we must not eat. But there is a vast area of knowledge that may be approached through both books and direct experience, one supplementing or complementing the other. During this century, and most particularly during the last few years, more and more American colleges and universities have come to look upon planned off-campus experience as a valid and important part of the educational process. This chapter describes some of the programs in use today and suggests their importance to American education in the future.*

BACKGROUND

Using the world for academic purposes is a time-honored practice. American college students were doing just that long before their first formal "extramural" program was born. Needy students worked their way through college; the more affluent traveled abroad during summer recess. And we may safely assume that today all colleges interact to some extent with their communities, their regions, and the world beyond. It would be difficult to create the cloistered college of academic myth.

But the lively interest shown by colleges in incorporating off-campus experiences into the curriculum is comparatively recent, and their ways of doing it are new and promising.

Perhaps the oldest program deliberately designed to make use of the world was a cooperative plan of work and study organized by the University of Cincinnati in 1906. The purpose of the plan was to give students practical experience and technical skills. Within the next several decades, a number of other institutions—most of them small independent colleges—began looking into the educational possibilities of off-campus programs. Some developed work programs, but sometimes with aims that were different from those of the original model. Others, perhaps not even thinking of any other college as a model, developed off-campus study and research programs. A listing of all the colleges and universities that today are making use of formal off-campus programs would include some of the most outstanding institutions in the country.

EXPERIENCE AND LEARNING: THE ARGUMENT

Baker Brownell has criticized American colleges for permitting themselves to be the victims of what he has called "three corrupting principles." The substance of his criticism is that higher education is ". . . still treated not as life but as a preparation for life," that the cloistered campus is unreal, and that the typical college does not relate theory to practice.[1] "If ways can be found," he writes, "whereby the student can have a significant part in events, he will respond maturely in most cases."[2]

Ways have been found, of course, and they are as varied as the colleges that have developed and adopted them. We must make a distinction between colleges that interact incidentally in many fruitful ways with their communities and colleges that consciously plan to involve their students in off-campus experience as an integral part of their education. The faculty takes a large step when it commits itself to the wider world and sends its students out to work, to study, or to observe. It must take responsibility for the quality of their performance, and even more, it must be ready to accept the students as co-workers in the educational process. This means facing many realistic questions and being willing to learn and to change with the student.

It is difficult to assess the effect of planned off-campus experience on students, but we may do so with some success by approaching the problem indirectly—by seeing what effect such programs have on the faculty.

1. The ways of evaluating the work of the student must change. The teacher will discover much about the student as a fieldworker that he might never notice or care about in class or know from reading his papers and examinations. And the teacher will see that the student is discovering much about himself that he would not find out sitting at a desk. The student in the field has more than one teacher, and he is his own teacher, too, developing many new critical standards for judging his own abilities and weaknesses. The evaluation of the student becomes much more a self-evaluation by the student. For unless the student takes an active part in the evaluation of his experience, how could the teacher know what the student has faced, has identified as valuable experience, and has gained in learning?

2. The method of planning and assigning work must change. Under the usual scheme, the teacher has been responsible for out-

---

[1] Baker Brownell, *The College and the Community,* Harper & Row, Publishers, Incorporated, New York, 1952, pp. 35–38.
[2] Baker Brownell, "The Community in College Teaching," in R. Cooper (ed.), *The Two Ends of the Log,* University of Minnesota Press, Minneapolis, Minn., 1958, p. 284.

lining the course and dividing it into a series of assignments. But when the learning is going to take place away from the campus, the teacher must consult with the student beforehand in order to accomplish academic objectives. New problems will show up, and new discoveries will bring unforeseen outcomes; the teacher must be able to assist the student to anticipate, to identify, and to make use of all kinds of learning opportunities. Good questions will be raised that will be far different from those posed in the classroom. The teacher will have to be ready to help or withhold help, gearing his response to the needs of the student. The role imposed on the faculty member is a difficult one, but it is a role that is far more challenging than the usual. The teacher must plan with the very person for whom he is planning; he must be flexible and sensitive.

Thus the off-campus programs alter the roles of teachers and, of course, of students. Students become directly involved in the planning and the evaluation integral to the teaching-learning experience. Not only does this make the entire experience more meaningful to the students, but also the direct involvement bodes well for the students' future, for they develop skills that are essential if they are to retain an interest in independent learning during the remainder of their lives—skills of self-evaluation and educational planning.

More direct support for the idea of off-campus experience may be found in the statements and writings of leading American educators. Indeed, closely related to the idea of off-campus experience are some of the ideas of John Dewey. In *Democracy and Education,* Dewey wrote: "As formal teaching and training grow in extent there is a danger of creating an undesirable split between the experience gained in more direct associations and what is acquired in school. This danger was never greater than at the present time, on account of the rapid growth in the last few centuries of knowledge and technical modes and skill."[3] As human knowledge continues to increase at a geometric rate, and as we of necessity continue to employ technical symbols to represent that knowledge, so does the danger continue to grow. The danger, the tendency to divorce out-of-school and in-school experience, affects the college student seriously and adversely. Although he is usually a young adult with a substantial amount of knowledge, a good mind, and plenty of vitality, he is usually assigned a rather

[3] John Dewey, *Democracy and Education,* The Macmillan Company, New York, 1921, p. 11.

passive and, to him, insignificant role in a world that is teeming with problems and challenges. Instead of being a contributor, the typical college student is a receiver; instead of being a participant in the world's work, he is an onlooker, a spectator.

In the classroom and on the campus, he may be presented with ideas, facts, and theories that others have developed, but he has very few opportunities to test them by his own experience. In a very real and damaging sense, the college student is too frequently forced to live without carrying serious responsibilities and to extend his childhood into his adult years. Too rarely does he find himself in situations where he is required to use his talents and his knowledge in the solution of a problem that has serious social consequences. In this setting, the development of the student as a productive personality is delayed, the rate and amount of significant learning are reduced, and many of the satisfactions of living are not realized.

But when students participate in the kinds of activities described in this chapter, they are cast in new responsible roles. They are required by the nature of their environment to do the work of adults, and what they do has significance and observable consequences; that is, what they are doing is important because it makes a difference to others. They become contributors to their society and consequently experience the rewards and satisfactions that come to those who feel they are doing something that counts and is worthwhile.

Because those with whom they work and study and live in off-campus situations accord them respect and recognition as adults, they respond accordingly and gain in self-confidence. Because they must put their theories to the test of practical conditions, and their knowledge to work on problems that have to be solved, their learning is enhanced, and their understanding increased. The more they derive satisfaction from their work, the more they are motivated to learn and to do. As a result of their off-campus experience, the students see teachers and studies in a different light and thus are able to make better use of the resources for learning on the college campus.

Surely, the consequences of such programs are difficult to assess statistically. But this much is clear: The question of what is education can no longer be answered with a pat formula. If the student learns with greater self-motivation and at the same time sees a direct connection between his campus study and his personal experience, who can regret the passing of an academic routine?

THE PROGRAMS

The many colleges that are now making deliberate use of the resources of the world have developed programs suited to their own needs and educational philosophies. Some look upon such programs as adjuncts to an existing program—a stimulus and a supplement. Others integrate off-campus programs into their curricula and make of them fundamental elements.

Despite the great diversity, it is possible to classify off-campus programs by approach: work, research and study, service, and foreign experience.

It should be noted that some colleges make use of more than one of these approaches; a few colleges make use of all four. It should also be noted that frequently the educational objectives of two institutions may be quite different even though both have programs that use similar approaches, and that the objectives of another two institutions may be the same, even though they are employing different approaches.

A new look at work programs

Off-campus work programs may represent an old concept, but not a stagnant one. The last few years have witnessed a number of significant developments in cooperative plans.

A vital distinction must be made at the outset between *campus work programs* and *cooperative programs*. A campus work program may be of great benefit to students and to the institution, but it makes only limited use of the wider community for educational purposes, and its effect on students and on the character of campus life is inevitably different from the effect of cooperative programs. (The Blackburn College plan is an example of a campus work program. Students fire furnaces, perform clerical duties, and are involved in maintenance, construction, and virtually all college operations.) Under a cooperative program, students work off campus. Some cooperative plans are limited to work experiences in the communities surrounding the college; others may extend across the nation or throughout the world.

A second distinction must be made between cooperative programs that are designed for *vocational* ends and those which are designed for purposes of *general education*. The general education type of program may also have vocational consequences, but the emphasis is on the acquisition of a mature outlook rather than skills, on emotional and intellectual development rather than career exploration. (The Drexel Institute of Technology has a vocationally oriented cooperative program, for example, whereas Goddard College's non-resident work term was designed for its general educational consequences.)

Interest in both kinds of cooperative programs—the vocational and the general—received new impetus within the last few years as a result of the Study of Cooperative Education, which was reported in *Work-Study College Programs,* by James W. Wilson and Edward H. Lyons.[4] Many of the values of these programs, as cited by the authors, are similar to those described for other programs which seek to make extended use of the community as a resource for learning. They include the tying of theory to practice, increased motivation and interest of the student in academic work, speed-up in the maturing process, greater experience with the skills of human relations, self-testing in the world of work, and closer touch of the faculty with the outside world.

As a result of the study and of the decision by the National Commission on Cooperative Education to encourage more colleges to consider the adoption of such programs, it is likely that new programs will be developed within the next few years. And the chances are that the new programs will vary as widely as those in the past.

Not only has there been a great variety among colleges using cooperative programs, but also, from a historical point of view, there has been variety within the colleges. Two examples will illustrate the evolution of such programs.

In its early years, Bennington College often made provision for nonresident study in meeting a student's special interests. When the college lacked the facilities needed by a student to pursue some individual interest, she could go elsewhere in the United States or to a foreign country and obtain credit for her study there. The program assumed a somewhat different and more formal structure with the introduction of a winter field and reading period, which in 1943 was transformed into what is now known as the "nonresident term." The term lasts nine weeks; during this time the student is supposed to make her own way in the world. Some find work in shops, factories, hospitals, museums, or schools. The college considers the

[4] James W. Wilson and Edward H. Lyons, *Work-Study College Programs,* Harper & Row, Publishers, Incorporated, New York, 1961.

entire experience—the work and the hunting for it—a valuable one that contributes to the student's self-confidence and maturity.

Antioch College has long stressed the importance of work experience as a regular part of the educational program for all its students. In a recent review of its program, the College recognized that its plan today is different in several important particulars from the program instituted by Arthur Morgan in 1921. A college official recently wrote: "The primary objective of the cooperative program at Antioch has been, since its inception, education." However, since the 1920s, ". . . there have been changes of conception and operations . . . that have far-reaching implications." Originally, the program was limited in its geographical spread and was viewed essentially in terms of alternation of work and study. "Today we think of it increasingly as the alternation of campus studies and off-campus educational experiences," which may include foreign travel, service projects, independent study, and research.[5] Work for pay is still an important element, but the emphasis today is on exposure to a wide variety of communities and experiences, both job and nonjob. Indicative of this change is the fact that the Antioch job roster now includes over 560 cooperative employers in thirty-one states and twenty-five foreign countries.

Research and study programs

Not only do colleges extend the educational environment by sending their students out to work, but they also send them out to do research, to participate in field seminars, and to do independent study in the field. Each of these programs seeks to take advantage of the special opportunities for learning which the extramural or off-campus environment may offer. Several of these programs are described below.

RESEARCH PROGRAMS. In 1959–1960, the Associated Colleges of the Midwest[6] launched its Argonne semester program. Under this program students spend from ten to sixteen weeks at the Argonne National Laboratories as part-time research assistants to Argonne

[5] Morris Keeton, *Antioch Restudied,* Antioch College, Yellow Springs, Ohio, 1960, pp. 5–6. (Booklet.)
[6] See Chap. 11 for a description of this association as well as other interinstitutional college groups.

scientists. The laboratory is operated by the University of Chicago for the United States Atomic Energy Commission. In addition to their work as research assistants, which constitutes about one-half of their daily schedule, students participate in seminars conducted by faculty members of the associated colleges and Argonne personnel.

The assumption behind the Argonne program is that able and well-trained undergraduate students can participate meaningfully in scientific research, not only to their own benefit as students, but also for the advancement of the research program itself. The validity of this assumption is borne out by the testimony of the scientists with whom these students worked.

According to their supervisors, the students learned rapidly and required little supervision. After a brief training period, they were able to serve effectively as junior colleagues on research teams. The students themselves felt that they had experienced science in action and had gained new perceptions of the interrelations of the sciences and of the nature of scientific research. These new insights, they felt, not only were valuable in themselves but also would be helpful in arriving at more informed decisions with respect to their own careers. They were unanimous in feeling that the experience had contributed in an unusual manner to their intellectual growth and emotional maturity.

The association also provides another kind of research opportunity for students. In 1962, it opened the ACM Wilderness Field Station in northern Minnesota. The station is located in the Superior National Forest, a vast woodland in wilderness condition. The area, which is inaccessible by road and where timber cutting is forbidden, is ideal for scientific study of unspoiled nature. In its first year, twenty students participated in the program, and thirty enrolled for the second year. The teaching staff has consisted of a botanist, a geologist, and a zoologist from member colleges. The project has especially benefited from the cooperation of the adjacent Quetico-Superior Wilderness Research Center, whose director and staff work with the associated colleges group in teaching and demonstrating research methods.[7]

The National Science Foundation, in addition to its assistance to programs such as the ACM-Argonne program described above, sup-

[7] For more detailed information about the ACM program, see the fourth annual report of the Associated Colleges of the Midwest. The central office of ACM is in Room 1458, 20 North Wacker Drive, Chicago.

ports a considerable amount of individual student research. Some of these projects make use of college-affiliated research laboratories; others make use of nearby privately owned scientific and research facilities.

EXTRAMURAL SEMINARS AND OFF-CAMPUS STUDY. In 1962, Antioch College experimented with a program of field seminars for students working on cooperative jobs in New York City and in Chicago. Leo Gruliow, editor of *Current Digest of the Soviet Press,* conducted the New York seminar, which was on the Soviet Union since Stalin. Ned Goldberg, associate director of Chicago Youth Centers, conducted the other, which was entitled "The City." Both seminars were optional.

The purposes of the seminars were to use the intellectual and other resources of the extramural environments more effectively than had been the case and to provide students with subjects to study that were of great interest and concern to them. The instructors were asked to prepare syllabi, which were to include bibliographies. Students were expected to devote a minimum of seventy-two hours to seminar work—nine hours a week for eight weeks.

The Chicago seminar in particular made a great deal of use of the learning opportunities afforded by the city. The seminar sought to explore patterns of residence in Chicago with particular reference to the history of selected neighborhoods, and the participation of residents in determining local affairs and their influence on city government. The seminar sought to combine field visits with regular seminar meetings. Eight meetings were held. The first hour of each session was spent touring certain selected neighborhoods. Following their tours, students met at a neighborhood center, where they were joined by some of the local residents and political leaders and members of various professional groups.

Among the neighborhoods visited were Hyde Park, where students examined the evidence of planned physical renewal and the degree to which adequate social welfare planning had taken place; Lawndale, where students examined a community going through rapid population change and the effects of the disappearance of social control where such change was taking place; Bridgeport, for evidences of the role of sectarian influence in a small community; the Chicago Commons, for evidences of planned integration; and Hull House, where students studied the resulting conflict occurring in a community being uprooted to make way for a new university.

Aside from the uses made of the physical environment itself and the many resources within it, students listed the following as key advantages of the program: It kept them in touch with academic work; it gave them a chance to study under a nonfaculty person; and it gave them a chance to concentrate on just one subject. There were some disadvantages, too, of course; some students found it hard to obtain source materials because of lack of time or the immensity of the city libraries, and some felt that the seminars were too much of a burden when added to their busy work schedules. Without any question, most of the students considered the seminars worthwhile and wanted to see them continued.[8]

Perhaps the most intensive and extensive use of the community as a resource for learning has been made by the Putney Graduate School of Teacher Education. Every year its students have made several short trips of three to ten days and longer trips that have lasted about two months. The latter have taken them through the Tennessee Valley, the Deep South, Mexico, Sweden, and Russia. Morris Mitchell, director of the school since its inception, may be considered one of the pioneers in the conscious use of off-campus experiences as a part of higher education.

Off-campus study may be used to enrich academic experience through the use of "trailer" courses. A number of departments at Antioch College have adopted plans for such courses. For example, history students may earn extra academic credits, following completion of certain courses on campus, by doing additional historical research or study off campus to enrich their previous academic experience. The off-campus work may involve visiting historical museums, reading and interviewing, or visiting scenes of historical events. Students may pursue such studies either while on cooperative jobs in the United States or while abroad. Similarly, several of the newly developing "January-term," or quarter-off, programs seek to take advantage of community and field resources for learning by encouraging students to undertake their independent study as off-campus field projects. This is true, for example, in the programs recently adopted at Colby, Florida Presbyterian, Kalamazoo, and Beloit Colleges. The Kalamazoo and Beloit programs are reviewed in a later section of this chapter. Chapter 4 describes a number of the independent study programs.

[8] Samuel Baskin and Lindsay Mattison, "Report on Student Reactions to the Use of Extramural Seminars," unpublished paper prepared by the Office of Educational Research, Antioch College, Nov. 19, 1962.

Service programs

Many colleges and universities have long made use of community service projects as a major resource for student learning. Baker Brownell, in his previously mentioned chapter in *The Two Ends of the Log,* referred to a number of early efforts by colleges to integrate educational values with community life. Besides pioneering work at Antioch, there were programs at Berea College, in Kentucky, and at Earlham College, in Indiana. William W. Biddle stated the problem for the program at Earlham: "The neglected opportunity," he writes, "lies all about the college in accumulations of humanity, nearby and far away. A vigorous acceptance of the challenge of human development will allow each college to find a unique, socially significant focus for itself to help guide an era of change while serving the growth needs of learners."[9] At Earlham an effort was made to cross departmental lines in the college to engage a wide range of the college faculty, undergraduates, and graduate students.

In Georgia, a significant program of community work was carried on at West Georgia College. This program sought to engage the people of western Georgia during the Depression of the 1930s in helping themselves by using the leadership and resources of the College. The community becomes the training ground for leaders in many forms of education. Pioneers in the West Georgia program have moved on to wider fields: Fred Wales to community education in the now famous bootstrap operation in Puerto Rico; Prof. Harry H. Giles, of New York University, to a consulting relationship with colleges and school systems across the nation; and Edward Yeomans to the Peace Corps.

The larger university, too, develops programs that extend into its wider area. One classic example was the regional study that grew up at the University of North Carolina, attracting great interest during the Depression years of the late twenties and thirties. Two great leaders in different fields activated many students in the study and use of regional resources. Frederich Koch created the Playmakers in 1918, which was responsible for new life in community drama as well as for the exploitation of regional resources by playwrights. Howard W. Odum, from 1920 until his death in 1954,

[9] William W. Biddle, *Growth toward Freedom,* Harper & Row, Publishers, Incorporated, New York, 1957, p. 23.

developed regional analysis and theory as a leader in the field of sociology from the standpoint of Southern regionalism. The effects of these programs are still being felt today.

The Educational Resources Project, which was initiated at Goddard College in 1956, serves as an example of what even a small college can do to be of service to its neighbors while serving the educational needs of its students.

The project began with a conference of seven public school superintendents and of representatives from Goddard, the Vermont Department of Education, and the Fund for the Advancement of Education of the Ford Foundation, which assisted in setting up the program. The aim of the project was to use capable college students as aides to teachers in public schools within 25 to 30 miles of the College. It was regarded as a reciprocal arrangement through which the schools would use the students as a resource for improving the opportunities for the children in the schools, and the College would regard the schools as a resource where students could use their knowledge responsibly as semiprofessional workers.

The students worked as assistants to teachers in carrying on the ordinary programs of the schools; they also assumed direct responsibility for activities in which the teachers felt less at home, such as art, music, drama, science, and play. They made curriculum studies for the schools, set up projects to demonstrate the use of audio-visual aids, led field trips, taught conversational French, and conducted science laboratory studies.

The project was not designed for students whose major interest was education, but rather for liberal arts students who felt that working in the schools would improve the quality of their own education. Eventually the project was extended to include six other colleges—Bennington, Castleton, Johnson, Lyndon, and Marlboro, all in Vermont, and Nasson, in Maine. Thus the idea was tested in several settings and with quite different types of students. The public schools, however, were all small and largely rural.

Observers in all the colleges said that the project added a valuable dimension to the education of the students. It cast them in new and responsible roles. It required them to do the work of adults in situations where what they did had serious and observable consequences. Failure to appear at a school at the appointed time meant more than being late to a college class; it upset an entire schoolroom. It forced them to put their knowledge of psychology of child development to the test; it demanded that their idealistic, philosophical principles be reduced to practical, workable terms. And, of course, it made it necessary for them to learn in a new way, as all teachers have to learn the subjects they are called upon to teach. Perhaps one of the most important outcomes was the self-confidence students derived from the recognition accorded them by schoolteachers and children as persons with knowledge and skills of worth.

The comments of students who were in the project and their performance on the college campus provided evidence for the conclusion that working as assistants in the schools contributed substantially to their maturity, stimulated them to more intensive study, and sometimes opened the way to new and better purposes. In short, it helped them become better learners.

Brooklyn College, in an environment quite different from Vermont, also has a community service program. Since 1948, the College has required that all education majors give two semesters of voluntary service in community agencies. A survey in 1957 undertook to measure the effectiveness of the program. ". . . we may conclude that the improved preparation of our student teachers, with a wider insight into community as well as school problems and their solution," seems to result from the community participation program. The program precedes work in teaching methods and practice teaching.[10]

In 1947, Earlham College inaugurated its Program of Community Dynamics, under which students help in community efforts at the request of community groups. Students may participate in community surveys, help in settlement houses, or participate in voter drives. The communities served have been those nearby and others hundreds of miles away.

In May, 1963, the Associated Colleges of the Midwest and the Chicago Board of Education announced a Program in Urban Education, to begin in September, 1963. The aim of the program was to provide advanced education students with special preparation for teaching in large urban centers. Some twenty-four seniors were selected to teach in elementary and secondary schools. Each was to have two 6-week teaching experiences in sharply contrasting environments. The program, sponsored by a three-year grant from

[10] "The Contribution That Experience in Community Agencies Makes to the Professional Training of the Students in Our Teacher Education Program," Brooklyn College Education Department, New York, November, 1959, part 2, p. 32. (Mimeographed.)

the Danforth Foundation, includes two seminars, one in urban education and the other in urban sociology.

Colleges and their students have been of service to neighboring communities through assistance in the development of planning data. And, in the process, students have benefited.

Purdue University, for example, became involved in urban redevelopment problems in the early 1950s, when civic and industrial leaders in East Chicago sought help in the elimination of blight. Purdue's Division of Educational Reference conducted a housing survey, financed by two steel companies, and made use of fifty graduate students in the canvassing of homes.[11]

In 1961, Rutgers University set up a Division of Urban Affairs after receiving a Ford Foundation grant. Among its program aims were: ". . . [to] provide assistance and stimulation to public officials and governments . . . . [to] utilize all the communities of the state as classrooms in which to learn about and help meet the problems of urbanization."[12] Probably a clearer statement of mutual benefit cannot be found.

The Ford Foundation has played an important role in encouraging students to use the resources of the world in order to learn. In 1956, the Foundation gave support to the Citizenship Clearing House, which had been founded in 1947 by Arthur T. Vanderbilt, then dean of the New York University School of Law and later chief justice of the New Jersey Supreme Court. The aim of the clearinghouse was to bring students into active contact with public officials, to encourage a better understanding of the American political process, and to stimulate greater political activity. The Foundation grant was to help the clearinghouse enlarge its programs which included seminars, workshops, and practical political activity with the major parties.[13]

Foreign experience

Within recent years, many colleges have sought to incorporate foreign experience as a regular part of the student's college program. Several of these programs give special attention to the use of field experience and attempt to integrate nonclassroom and class-

[11] Herman R. Allen, *Open Door to Learning,* University of Illinois Press, Urbana, Ill., 1963, pp. 26ff.

[12] *Ibid.,* p. 79.

[13] *The Ford Foundation Annual Report: October 1, 1955, to September 30, 1956,* The Ford Foundation, New York, 1956, p. 63.

room experiences in learning during the student's period abroad. The Princeton International Relations Program, in which students undertake field research for a two-month period; the Columbia anthropology program, in which students work in small villages or do research at field stations in Ecuador, Mexico, and Peru; and the Goddard Comparative Cultures Program are illustrative of these programs. These programs are described in Chapter 4, which deals with study abroad. The Goddard Comparative Cultures Program is described in somewhat greater detail in the material which follows.

In 1957, Goddard College, with a grant from the Fund for the Advancement of Education, developed its Comparative Cultures Program. The program was designed to help students learn how to study a subject on their own, to assist them in discovering and using learning resources outside the campus, and to make new use of a nonresident term in furthering the educational aims of the college and its students. It aimed to introduce first- and second-year college students to the values, the ways of living and working, and the language of another people and to the people themselves.

French Canada was chosen as the region for study because of its proximity to the College; the Quebec border is only 60 miles from the campus. Students enrolling in Comparative Cultures do it as two-thirds or more of their program of studies for a semester, with the understanding that they will spend the two-month non-resident winter work term in French Canada.

As soon as a student enters the program, he begins his study of French Canada: its history, geography, economy, government, culture, and language. Early in the semester, the group visits the French-speaking city of Sherbrooke, where members of the faculty and students of the University of Sherbrooke meet them and serve as their hosts. Invariably this trip and those to other communities in Quebec stimulate the students to improve their ability to speak and understand French. A very important factor in the success of the trips has been the warm and sympathetic response the groups have received from French Canadians. Such friendliness appears to help students move from a possibly complacent detachment to a sense of involvement and a more personal interest in the entire program.

As the nonresident term comes nearer, the feeling of need for learning the language is intensified. Apparently the thought of living in a French-speaking home and working in a situation where the language used is French raises doubts among the students concerning their readiness to function satisfactorily away from the college language laboratory and the supervision of the teacher. The director of the program has noticed a quickening of the pace and an increase in the effort to speak and understand French at this time.

From 1961 to 1963, the group spent January and February in the city of Quebec, where, with the aid of members of the faculty of Laval University, the students have found places to live with French families and opportunities for work in the business places of the city. They also have met with groups of Laval students and have enjoyed in many ways the hospitality of the University. For two months they are immersed in a culture with which nearly all of them have had no familiarity and concerning which many held misconceptions prior to entering the program. In 1964 the group went to the smaller city of Trois-Rivières, which had provided equally valuable opportunities for the program in 1959 and 1960.

The effects of the program on the participants and the rest of the college are quite noticeable. Awareness of Canada's importance as a nation and a neighbor has increased greatly; appreciation of French Canada as a people, a culture, and a region has been enhanced; and interest in the French language has grown steadily. Five years ago, there was not enough interest among Goddard students to sustain a class in advanced French; now, in addition to advanced courses in French language and literature, there are courses relating to the history of France, given in French.

Because of the values perceived in the program, it was expanded in 1963 to include the study of Spanish and a Spanish-speaking culture. Students in this part of the program went to Puerto Rico for the nonresident term.

Recent variations

Several colleges, recognizing the value of all the foregoing kinds of off-campus experiences, have included all of them in their programs. This may sound like a rather ambitious undertaking, but it can be done even by colleges that have followed traditional programs for years. It is important to remember that just as there is a wide variety of programs, there is also a wide variety of involvement.

Two of the most recent efforts to use the resources of the world are to be found in the programs adopted by Kalamazoo and Beloit Colleges.

In 1961, Kalamazoo College abandoned its traditional program and introduced a number of far-reaching changes. It adopted a four-quarter calendar and an extramural program. The normal course of study runs fifteen quarters, ten on campus and five off. A typical student would spend his first three quarters in study on campus, would have two quarters of work experience during his second year, and would spend two quarters abroad during his third year and one quarter in independent study during his fourth year.

The new Beloit plan, which went into effect in the fall of 1964, provides for a three-phase college calendar: (*1*) three trimesters on campus; (*2*) five trimesters—two on campus, one off campus, and two that may be used for vacation; and (*3*) a final three trimesters on campus.

The off-campus term during the second phase may be used for independent study or research, or some other "real-world" experience in the United States or abroad, and both the vacation terms also may be used for this purpose.

It needs to be emphasized that the use of the wider community as a learning resource for college students is not limited to programs which are planned by the college or which are a part of special courses developed by college teachers. The individual student may see opportunities that have not occurred to members of the faculty, and he may plan a program of studies that enables him to exploit those opportunities. Provision for genuine independent study can facilitate this process. Elimination of the grade-point, credit-hour-marking system in itself contributes to the flexibility that is so badly needed in utilizing off-campus resources for learning.

To illustrate the great potential in the wider community for learning, two fairly typical examples from the experience of Goddard College may be cited. In the first semester of his second year at the College, a young man from a section of New York City that is largely Puerto Rican proposed to a sociology teacher an independent study of drug addiction. This student—a former member of a youth gang in his home community—had taken courses in sociology and, as a part of them, had worked as an assistant on the Vermont Youth Study, a five-year research project of the College supported by grants from the Ford Foundation and the National Institute of Mental Health. This student, who had enlisted the aid of a third-year student, proposed to try to find out why approximately half of the youth gang to which he had belonged had become drug addicts and the other half had not.

The plan for the study was approved; the two young men worked diligently to acquire an understanding of human physiology and the effects of drugs as well as a mastery of the necessary research techniques. They then interrupted their regular college schedule and went to New York for several weeks to enlist the help of the first student's former gang members. The outcome of the study may be indicated by saying that the two students accepted an invitation to present their findings to the annual meeting of the Eastern Sociological Society in Philadelphia the following spring.

Another student who had become interested in propaganda happened during his sophomore year to read an article in a 1945 issue of *Life* on the Sicilian campaign of World War II. The somewhat uncritical nature of the article stimulated this young man to speculate on the extent to which its author had reported the facts or had written a propaganda piece. In the pursuit of his desire to find out what the situation had been, he not only elected courses in history and other social sciences but also actually left the College long enough to earn sufficient money to get him to Sicily to acquire a more thorough knowledge of its people and its geography. On his return to the College, he continued to gather materials related to the Sicilian campaign and to carry a normal program of studies. In his senior year, however, he proposed as the subject of his senior independent study (which usually takes from two-thirds to all of one's study time for a semester) the Sicilian campaign. Besides reading all the materials he could find that were related to the campaign, he used his two-month nonresident work term to meet with military officials at the Pentagon, to use the Library of Congress, and to interview many men who had actually participated in the campaign. The results of his wide-ranging efforts were partially revealed in a highly readable and authentic account of the campaign, which was considerably at variance with the *Life* story written during the war.

PRACTICAL PROBLEMS

This chapter has described briefly a variety of programs designed to make use of the community in the education of the college student. Consideration must now be given to some of the practical problems involved in initiating and operating such programs: problems of logistics, supervision and evaluation, integration of experiences, and proper crediting of experience.

Virtually any planned off-campus program requires the development of "contacts." Usually, some persons or some agencies off campus must agree to participate in the program before it can work. Some colleges, of course, do send their students out on their own, but most programs require that arrangements be negotiated long before the student leaves campus.

Related to this is the problem of supervision and evaluation. First, the cooperating agency, whether it be an employer or a research laboratory, must see its role as educational. Usually colleges want to receive written reports from the agencies, which assist in evaluation of the student's experience. Second, the college must be prepared to assist the students in evaluating their own experiences. Colleges may require written reports from students; many schedule informal discussion sessions with faculty members when the students return to campus.

Probably the most important, and the most difficult, of the problems confronting a college that uses off-campus programs is relating its "extramural" and "intramural" programs. The student, of course, relates much of his academic work to his off-campus experience, and vice versa, whether or not the college tries to encourage this. But clearly, a deliberate effort to accomplish this would be of benefit to both on- and off-campus programs.

How to credit off-campus experience is a problem that is likely to receive more and more attention in the future. Some colleges set up two kinds of credits, one kind for academic work and the other for off-campus experience. Others have traditional requirements for academic credits and simply require (or permit) a certain amount of off-campus experience without credit. Some integrate the classwork and fieldwork and make no problem of credit. The more "academic" of the off-campus experiences very likely will one day be honored at most colleges with academic credit; indeed, this is already being done with the previously described program at the Argonne National Laboratory. As off-campus experience wins the recognition it deserves, other kinds of experiences probably will be granted such credit too.

THE FUTURE

"Most teachers," writes Prof. Everett K. Wilson, "probably believe that they are influential in some situations, in changing certain aspects of students' behavior. . . . The truth is that we don't know what we're doing. Nor will we know until such time as we can say what changes are wrought by whom."[14]

Read in full context, it is clear that Professor Wilson does not mean that teachers are completely unaware of the consequences of the act of teaching. But rather, he is pointing out the desperate need to answer the vital question: Who teaches what?

Those institutions that have adopted an off-campus plan as an integral part of their programs are convinced that they have great educational value. "If every student has a semester away, there will be at all times a number of students who have had a variety of experiences—residence and study overseas, social work, work-study, research, etc. The interaction of these students among themselves and with the underclassmen . . . should be enormously stimulating, and should go far toward opening closed minds and shattering the multitudinous varieties of parochialism."[15]

Such institutions are not sure who teaches what. But they do find that with off-campus experience—work, research, study—students seem to mature more rapidly; to develop a seriousness of purpose; to exhibit greater self-discipline, thereby improving their academic work; and to see their campus studies in a broader context. The entire campus seems to be stimulated. Those colleges with work programs add a few more benefits; students have an opportunity to explore careers and to attain professional skills, and they also have an opportunity not to be studying—to digest what they chewed on while on campus and to see themselves more clearly under altered responsibilities.

It is likely that in the years ahead, more and more colleges and universities throughout the United States will make more complete use of the resources of the world. The trend in the small experimental colleges possibly will become more of a national trend. The consequences for higher education may be profound.

Students fresh from off-campus experience expect more of their teachers and more of their textbooks. They are readier to question and to dispute; they have experience to back them up. Classrooms, instead of lagging behind the rest of the world by a decade, move to the cutting edge of knowledge. Yesterday's discovery is dis-

[14] Everett Wilson, "Effecting Change in the College Student: Who Teaches What?" *Antioch College Reports,* no. 4, March, 1963.

[15] "Report and Proposals of the Ad Hoc Committee," unpublished mimeographed report prepared by Ad Hoc Committee at Beloit College, Beloit, Wisc., and submitted March 5, 1963, p. 6.

cussed in the classroom today, and not in a few years, after the text-book has been published. The latest laboratory technique finds its way into a college lab, brought there by a student who used it off campus weeks before.

This is a description of what has already happened on the campuses that are making use of off-campus experiences. When the use of such programs becomes more common, the effect will be obvious and pronounced. Perhaps college teachers will have to go off campus more frequently, if they would keep up with their students. Perhaps textbook publishers will have to revise production methods and schedules. Colleges will have new notions of the resources for, and the tests of, learning.

But whatever the particular manifestations and results, this much is clear: the boundaries of the campuses are vanishing.

SOURCES FOR FURTHER INFORMATION

Allen, Herman R.: *Open Door to Learning,* University of Illinois Press, Urbana, Ill., 1963.

Brownell, Baker: *The College and the Community,* Harper & Row, Publishers, Incorporated, New York, 1952.

Carr, Lowell J.: *Situational Analysis,* Harper & Row, Publishers, Incorporated, New York, 1948.

Cooper, Russell M. (ed.): *The Two Ends of the Log,* University of Minnesota Press, Minneapolis, Minn., 1958.

Hodnett, Edward: *Industry-College Relations,* The World Publishing Company, Cleveland, 1955.

Jones, Barbara: *Bennington College,* Harper & Row, Publishers, Incorporated, New York, 1946.

Lynd, Helen M.: *Field Work in College Education,* Columbia University Press, New York, 1945.

Rosecrance, Francis C.: *The American College and Its Teachers,* The Macmillan Company, New York, 1962.

Wilson, James W. and Edward H. Lyons: *Work-Study College Programs,* Harper & Row, Publishers, Incorporated, New York, 1961.

RUSSELL M. COOPER

9

improving college teaching and administration

*T*he demands upon college teaching in the 1960s are very different from those of the 1860s or even the 1920s. The college professor can no longer be simply a drillmaster, forcing reluctant students to memorize their lessons, or merely a lecturer purveying his knowledge. Rather, with the vast libraries, laboratories, teaching aids, and other resources readily at hand, the good professor today is becoming a senior partner working with the student in searching out resources for the solution of problems. In his new role, he serves not so much as a dispenser of information but rather as designer and manager of the student's learning.

Just as the posture of the professor has changed drastically in the past century, and especially since World War II, so also has the college administrator revised his role. The educational world will *no longer tolerate institutional autocrats any more than business will retain old-fashioned captains of industry. Modern Americans, and particularly college professors, will not respond to such dictatorial leadership. The effective administrator must be a man who can serve as a leader, not a taskmaster, and who can enlist the cooperation of his staff because he is cooperative with them. He must be a partner and colleague, accepting the role of leader within his sphere but also seeking to be a stimulus and a servant in helping others achieve their special goals.*

More and more the job requirements for both college teaching and administration are demanding a new kind of expertise. As these demands increase, the need for devoting special efforts to the preparation and in-service training of these groups becomes increasingly important. Such efforts are the theme of this chapter.

PROGRAMS FOR IMPROVING COLLEGE AND UNIVERSITY TEACHING

In the traditional freedom of the classroom, each professor happily assumes that his particular approach is best—at least for him—and he naturally resents any efforts at standardization or control. Nevertheless, there probably would be wide consensus on a few fundamental principles which characterize the good teacher and which should be stressed in any program for improvement.

Before looking at the several projects designed to improve college teaching on campuses across the country, let us examine these attributes of the good teacher and some implications of each.

The elements of college teaching

Reduced to its essentials, effective college teaching would seem to involve three elements: (*1*) knowledge of subject matter, (*2*) understanding of students, and (*3*) skill in bringing these two factors together. If a professor is deficient in any one of these three attributes, he may still be a great scholar or a great humanitarian but he can hardly be a great teacher.

1. The knowledge essential for a good college teacher falls into two related categories: content of the discipline for which he is professionally responsible, and comprehension of the world in general—the latter making him a rounded human being, a fitting symbol of the cultivated life he seeks to develop in students. It is obvious that if the professor fails to know his own subject, he cannot mediate it to others. But with the enormous expansion of knowledge these days, old disciplines fragmenting into dozens of new ones, and others synthesizing into larger organized systems, the college teacher faces a formidable task in keeping abreast of new knowledge while at the same time maintaining competence in the fundamentals of his own field. Not only must he understand major principles, the best sources of data, and the methodology of inquiry, but normally he also must be able to operate at several levels: as a teacher of introductory courses, as a supervisor of student projects, and as a leader of seminars. The National Science Foundation, the National Education Association,[1] and a number of old and new professional groups are giving leadership in the reorganization and interpretation of knowledge to assist the busy professor.[2] Much more activity of this kind is needed in every field. The good college teacher must also be conversant with related fields, not only if he is to teach courses in general education, but also if he is to help give students a grasp of the larger ideas, problems, and enjoyment of our culture. The Committee on General Education of the Association for Higher Education has been particularly active in promoting studies, conferences, and publications to help professors with these larger responsibilities. Several series of publications by the American Council on Education, the W. C. Brown Company, Harper & Row, and McGraw-Hill have summarized the experience derived from leading programs in the field as guides to others. And the Association for General and Liberal Studies, founded in 1961 at Michigan State University, with its sponsored publication, *The Journal of General Education,* likewise provides continuing leadership. Some of the most promising features of this movement have already been mentioned in Chapters 1 and 2.

2. A second attribute of the good teacher is his understanding of students—their abilities and motivations—and particularly the teen-

---

[1] Dorsey Baynham, *The Scholars Look at the Schools,* National Education Association, Washington, D.C., 1962.
[2] Jerome S. Bruner, *The Process of Education,* Harvard University Press, Cambridge, Mass., 1960.

age culture that tends to color their perceptions. Professor Rice calls attention to the importance of these factors in Chapter 13.

Earlier publications by Jacob,[3] Eddy,[4] Goldsen,[5] Sanford,[6] and others have highlighted the importance of the college's campus climate in molding students and determining their educational and personal development. Penetrating studies at such institutions as Vassar, Cornell, California, and Minnesota have delineated for those institutions the character and abilities of the students they serve, all of which are germane to the task of the classroom professor. Much more needs to be done on every campus, with particular reference to the utilization of such data for making teaching more realistic.

3. As professors improve in their depth of scholarship and their understanding of students, they may be expected to seek better ways of organizing the class to help students also to become masters of the subject Unfortunately there is still a shortage of good research on the psychology of learning at the college level, though this is gradually improving in both reliability and penetration. The *Handbook of Research on Teaching*[7] presents one of the more recent comprehensive reviews of research on teaching at different levels of instruction. Included in the handbook is a chapter by Dr. Wilbert J. McKeachie, of the University of Michigan, on research on teaching at the college and university level. Some of the recent studies on the use of the independent study and the new media are described in earlier chapters of this book. One should note also the periodical *Improving College and University Teaching,* published at Oregon State University, which is making significan contribution to college pedagogy.

If it can be agreed that the above attributes are essential for the

---

[3] Philip E. Jacob, *Changing Values in College: An Exploratory Study of the Impact of College Teaching,* Harper & Row, Publishers, Incorporated, New York, 1957.
[4] Edward D. Eddy, Jr., *The College Influence on Student Character,* American Council on Education, Washington, D.C., 1959.
[5] Rose K. Goldsen, and others, *What College Students Think,* D. Van Nostrand Company, Inc., Princeton, N.J., 1960.
[6] Nevitt Sanford (ed.), *The American College: A Psychological and Social Interpretation of the Higher Learning,* John Wiley & Sons, Inc., New York, 1962.
[7] N. L. Gage (ed.), *Handbook of Research on Teaching: A Project of the American Educational Research Association,* Rand McNally & Company, Chicago, 1963.

good college teacher, let us now look at the agencies designed to help develop those qualities. There are essentially three stages in the creation of the college teacher: his undergraduate education, his graduate preparation, and his growth on the job. Each has its special contribution to make and should be examined in turn.

The undergraduate education

Until recently there has been little distinction between the undergraduate preparation of a prospective college teacher and the education of his classmates. Indeed, studies by Eckert and Stecklein[8] have shown that the typical college teacher has not even chosen the profession at the time of his college graduation. Where the future college teachers were identified early, they normally were advised to perfect their reading knowledge of one or two languages and sometimes were included in a senior seminar affording experience in independent research. Even these measures, however, have been sporadic, varying greatly from campus to campus and indeed from department to department.

The major contribution of the undergraduate years has been the emphasis upon general and liberal education, though here again programs have varied widely. In the better institutions, the individual is afforded the opportunity for substantial acquaintance with the major areas of human knowledge and is given sufficient foundation in a single discipline so that he can build upon it in graduate school. Several of the preceding chapters have already described new developments in undergraduate colleges designed to strengthen the education of all students.

The most extensive effort to date to relate undergraduate education to the preparation of college teachers is a program initiated and financed by the Ford Foundation. The Foundation inaugurated the project in 1960 by distributing 4.8 million dollars to twenty-six universities interested in developing a three-year program leading to the master's degree. Since three-fourths of the college teachers in America are now entering the profession before reaching the doctorate and since a serious shortage of teachers will probably increase this proportion in the future, it was felt that some way must

[8] Ruth E. Eckert and John E. Stecklein, *Job Motivations and Satisfactions of College Teachers,* U.S. Office of Education, Washington, D.C., 1961, p. 26.

be found to strengthen the quality of the man with a master's degree. This quality is important for the first few years of teaching, even though such persons may eventually go on to complete their training.

The Ford Foundation program calls for planning the last two undergraduate years and the first year of graduate study as a three-year block to ensure that the fundamentals are covered systematically and without duplication. To quote a report from the Foundation, all the programs stress ". . . early identification and recruitment of outstanding students; a planned sequence of courses and seminars; emphasis upon independent research and writing; completion of language requirements for the Ph.D. and preparation for the Ph.D. qualifying examination; supervised teaching of undergraduate courses; and seminars dealing with college teaching."[9]

As of August, 1964, the Ford Foundation had made grants to forty institutions for the three-year M.A. programs. The largest single grant of all was a gift of $975,000 made to the University of Chicago, which in turn was to use these funds to promote a recruitment and preparation program in thirty-five Middle Western liberal arts colleges.

This cooperative feature, wherein a university works closely with a number of smaller institutions to select and prepare students in the three-year program, already had precedents in programs associated with the Universities of Michigan, Nebraska, and Washington. An important by-product of the program has been the stimulation afforded to faculty members of the participating institutions as they become sensitized to the importance of selective recruitment and work together on curricular changes to strengthen scholarly competence within the three-year span.

While the cooperating undergraduate colleges are encouraged to improve their normal programs of recruitment, liberal education, and major concentration, nearly all of them have added a kind of honors program with special seminars, independent study, and research projects under the supervision of a local faculty committee. When the student proceeds on to his first year of graduate study, he is awarded a substantial fellowship, given supervised experience in the teaching of undergraduate courses, and offered seminars for exploring the problems of higher education and college teaching.

Participating undergraduate institutions are already testifying

[9] *Ford Foundation News Release,* Apr. 10, 1962, pp. 6–7.

to the "toning-up" effect felt in their entire program when faculty members are given released time to analyze these educational problems and to experiment with new ventures. It is too early to evaluate the effectiveness of the Ford Foundation's three-year program or to determine whether its graduates who move into college teaching jobs will be more competent than those prepared under the old system, but if thought and energy can be expected to produce positive results, the prospects would appear quite promising.

Graduate preparation

The extension of the Ford Foundation program into the graduate years highlights a growing concern about the character of graduate education as it affects the preparation of college teachers. For a long time, American graduate schools have been under attack; it has been charged that they are more interested in preparing research scholars than in developing effective classroom teachers. During the past thirty years, there has been a stream of conferences, reports, and monographs dealing with the problem.

For example, in 1935 the U.S. Office of Education completed its national survey of the education of teachers and devoted seven chapters of its report to the nature of training and to responsibilities of staff personnel in higher education.[10] In the early 1940s, a cooperative study of teacher education sponsored by the American Council on Education was completed with the publication of several volumes on teacher education, including one by Hollis entitled *Toward Improving Ph.D. Programs.*[11] The Association of American Colleges and the Association of American Universities also had committees dealing with the problem, and the President's Commission on Higher Education, which published its comprehensive report in 1947, showed great concern for the proper recruitment, selection, and preparation of college teachers.[12]

[10] Edward S. Evenden, Guy C. Gamble, and Harold G. Blue, *Teacher Personnel in the United States,* bulletin 10, vol. 2, U.S. Government Printing Office, Washington, D.C., 1935.
[11] Edward V. Hollis, *Toward Improving Ph.D. Programs,* American Council on Education, 1945.
[12] President's Commission on Higher Education, *Higher Education for American Democracy,* Harper & Row, Publishers, Incorporated, New York, 1947.

CONFERENCES ON THE PROBLEM.   A series of conferences at Lake Mohonk in 1947, Poughkeepsie in 1948, and the University of Chicago in 1948 highlighted the growing concern for the problem and led directly to a national conference on the preparation of college teachers in December, 1949.

At this national conference, sponsored jointly by the American Council on Education and the U.S. Office of Education, some 160 graduate deans and professors, together with adminstrators of employing institutions and leaders of professional organizations, devised a series of recommendations for improved selection of college teachers, for broadening and making more relevant the graduate courses included in the prospective instructor's major, for more creative and useful research experience, for seminars to promote a knowledge of teaching problems and procedures, and for an apprenticeship experience to ensure some supervised teaching before the new instructor is entrusted with a full-time teaching job.[13]

Following the conference, the American Council on Education appointed a committee on college teaching, which became especially concerned with increasing the supply of college teachers in light of impending critical shortages. In addition, it sponsored a conference of selected educational leaders in Washington in 1958, which resulted in a report emphasizing again the importance of a fresh attack upon the problem.[14]

STUDIES AND PUBLICATIONS.   This growth of interest has produced more than thirty major publications in the past five years in which individuals or professional groups have offered their analyses of the problem. One of the leaders in the attack upon the graduate school has been Earl J. McGrath, executive officer of the Institute of Higher Education at Teachers College, Columbia University, who published *The Graduate School and the Decline of Liberal Education* in 1959.[15] He charged that the graduate faculties have come to dominate undergraduate liberal arts programs in the major universities, with the result that those programs have suffered from

[13] Theodore C. Blegen and Russell M. Cooper, *The Preparation of College Teachers,* American Council on Education, Washington, D.C., 1950.

[14] Joseph Axelrod, *Graduate Study for Future College Teachers,* American Council on Education, Washington, D.C., 1959.

[15] Earl J. McGrath, *The Graduate School and the Decline of Liberal Education,* Bureau of Publications, Teachers College, Columbia University, New York, 1959.

great proliferation of offerings and undue specialization, with a consequent loss to liberal education. Moreover, he declared that the graduate schools are continuing to prepare teachers for this same kind of specialized emphasis rather than for the liberal under-graduate teaching that the nation requires. He called for graduate programs especially designed for prospective college teachers that would afford greater breadth of experience, more relevant research activities, a seminar in the theory and practice of teaching, and practical apprenticeship opportunities—much the same reforms as were urged at the Washington conference in 1949. McGrath's proposal was similar also to that of Jones in his *Education and World Tragedy*.[16] But while Dr. Jones believed that an entirely new kind of graduate school would be required, Dr. McGrath hoped that reforms could be accomplished within existing graduate schools revamped for the purpose.

In reply to these critics, Bernard Berelson published a report entitled *Graduate Education in the United States*[17] in 1960, which summarized the replies to a questionnaire distributed widely to graduate deans and professors and to undergraduate administrators and professors seeking to get their impression of the effectiveness of graduate education. Dr. Berelson concluded that the shortage of college teachers would not be as serious as some predicted and that the graduate faculties are relatively satisfied with their programs for teacher education.

Continuing the debate, Dr. Oliver Carmichael presented his *Graduate Education: A Critique and a Program*[18] in 1961, sharply challenging the Berelson findings and arguing that both supply and quality of preparation are falling far short of potential demand. Dr. Carmichael's book reemphasized the same points stressed in the 1949 conference and in the McGrath study and went further by espousing the Ford Foundation's three-year master's degree program as one important step toward solving the problem.

Meanwhile, a number of professional organizations within the disciplines had been attacking the issue as it affected their own fields of study. For example, the American Association of Colleges

[16] Howard Mumford Jones, *Education and World Tragedy*, Harvard University Press, Cambridge, Mass., 1946.
[17] Bernard Berelson, *Graduate Education in the United States*, McGraw-Hill Book Company, New York, 1960.
[18] Oliver C. Carmichael, *Graduate Education: A Critique and a Program*, Harper & Row, Publishers, Incorporated, New York, 1961.

for Teacher Education published in 1960 a two-volume report entitled *The Doctorate in Education*[19] and has set up a continuing committee to study the preparation of college teachers of education. Similarly, the American Historical Association established a committee on graduate education and, under the leadership of Dexter Perkins and John L. Snell, published a book in 1962 entitled *The Education of Historians in the United States*.[20] Other studies and conferences led to informative reports prepared by Clark,[21] Strothmann,[22] Gustad,[23] and Albright.[24]

UNIVERSITY EFFORTS. Despite the many committees, conferences, reports, and research studies, there seems to have been little impact upon the graduate schools themselves. This inertia is ascribed by some to the growing pressure to produce specialists for industry by government rather than for college teaching and also to the intense departmentalization of the universities wherein the graduate faculties in the several disciplines have greater power over curriculum and staff personnel than the graduate dean does. In any case, it must be reported that only in a few institutions have the graduate programs been significantly revamped in an effort to produce college teachers for the kind of demanding responsibilities described in the earlier paragraphs of this chapter. One example has been the Doctor of Social Science Program at Syracuse University, which has emphasized breadth of preparation along with competence in a particular discipline and which has also provided opportunities for analysis of teaching problems and for gaining intern experience. Since its inauguration in 1945, more than seventy students have received D.S.S. degrees at Syracuse, and they have been in great demand from employing institutions.

[19] *The Doctorate in Education,* American Association of Colleges for Teacher Education, Washington, D.C., 1960, vols. 1 and 2.
[20] Dexter Perkins and John L. Snell, *The Education of Historians in the United States,* McGraw-Hill Book Company, New York, 1962.
[21] Kenneth E. Clark, *American Psychologists:A Survey of a Growing Profession,* American Psychological Association, New York, 1957.
[22] Friederich W. Strothmann, *The Graduate School Today and Tomorrow,* Fund for the Advancement of Education, New York, 1955.
[23] John W. Gustad (ed.), *Faculty Supply, Demand and Recruitment,* New England Board of Higher Education, Winchester, Mass., 1959; John W. Gustad (ed.), *Faculty Preparation and Orientation,* New England Board of Higher Education, Winchester, Mass., 1960.
[24] A. D. Albright, *Preparing College Teachers,* University of Kentucky, Lexington, Ky., 1959.

On several university campuses there have been established inter-disciplinary area majors, such as Far Eastern Studies or American Studies, and these have provided breadth of preparation for college teaching and for other vocations. Similarly, there has been a measure of supervision given to graduate students enlisted to teach sections of huge undergraduate courses, but such supervision has varied greatly in character and effectiveness among different institutions and different disciplines, depending upon the interest of the senior professor in charge of the course.

ASSOCIATION FOR HIGHER EDUCATION PROJECTS. It is because of these limited and very sporadic developments in graduate preparation that the Committee on Teaching in Colleges and Universities of the Association for Higher Education has focused its effort upon influencing the grass roots of the profession. Instituted in 1959, this committee has sponsored the production of Meet the Professor, a series of telecasts produced by the ABC network dramatizing the importance and excitement of good college teaching today. There is some evidence that these telecasts created a more favorable image of the college teacher in the public mind and encouraged young people to consider more seriously the opportunities afforded by college teaching as a career.

A major interest of the AHE committee has been to define more clearly the responsibility of the graduate school and the employing institution in the preparation and in-service development of teachers and to stimulate experimental projects on many campuses that may lead to improved practice. The committee is working with regional accrediting organizations and national professional societies in the development of cooperative studies for encouraging experimental ventures, both in graduate school preparation and in subsequent in-service development. While coordinating conferences are found necessary in this new program, they are incidental to the activities on campus in which many faculty members are involved in reexamination of educational practices. From such grass-roots efforts proceeding in dozens of institutions throughout the country, one may expect an increasing flow of information concerning new and tested experience, which can then be assembled and distributed by regional and national associations to everyone interested. It may be that a cooperative attack on the problem such as is now in progress will yet result in significant change.

Growth on the job

The good college teacher is neither born nor made in any final sense but rather is in a state of constant evolution. No matter how modern and effective the graduate school, no one can expect the new instructor to emerge fully competent in every facet of his teaching task. Improved graduate preparation may help greatly, but inevitably much must be learned on the job. Whether this learning will be speedy or slow, sound or sour, will depend not only upon the aptitude of the man himself but also upon opportunities and incentives for such development.

It is not possible here to describe in detail the manifold ways in which individual campuses have promoted this in-service growth. In a doctoral dissertation on the subject, William F. Kelley, of Creighton University, identified 115 different procedures for helping college teachers, which were then being applied in colleges in the Middle West. In a subsequent questionnaire study among its member institutions, the North Central Association in 1962 elicited comments from more than 100 colleges concerning in-service programs then in progress. Reports from other regions indicate similar widespread interest.

TYPES OF CAMPUS PROJECTS. Among the most popular in-service activities is an orientation of new faculty. This frequently goes beyond a mere description of college procedures and resources to include an analysis of student clientele and an examination of pedagogical problems. Often there is instituted a faculty seminar of old as well as new members to study outstanding books in higher education, review the psychology of learning at the college level, work on improvement of classroom examinations, study the use of audio-visual aids, and consider the virtues and techniques of lecture or discussion. A summary of major problems facing new instructors, together with suggestions for meeting them, was compiled from a study of North Central Association colleges by Michigan State University and, ironically, showed that practical matters such as inadequate secretarial help, office space, and teaching aids were leading causes of frustration.[25] A somewhat similar study of orien-

[25] Harlan R. McCall et al., *Problems of New Faculty Members in Colleges and Universities,* Michigan State University Center for Study of Higher Education, East Lansing, Mich., 1961.

COOPER

tation practices in the North Central area was made by Norbert Trady, and a recently published study by the Southern Regional Education Board describes and evaluates a variety of faculty development procedures being employed in Southern colleges and universities.[26]

In some institutions, such as the University of Missouri, there has been considerable visiting of classes by the faculty as they seek fresh instructional ideas for themselves and pass on suggestions to their colleagues. Such ventures can work successfully, of course, only when there is high morale among the staff, and if administrators are involved, they must command the full respect and confidence of the faculty. Where an open-door tradition has been well established, these visits appear to have been very helpful. As a further stimulus to improvement, an increasing number of faculties are using student appraisals of instruction, anonymously and confidentially prepared, in order to give the professor access to the judgment of those most intimately involved. There is now abundant evidence that these student appraisals are on the whole reliable and, when taken seriously, can help the professor considerably in identifying points of strength and weakness.[27]

Some colleges promote teacher growth by devoting faculty meetings to a discussion of educational problems; by providing money for sending people away to professional meetings; by instituting seminars, workshops, conferences, and other means for sharing experience; by providing accessible bookshelves of professional literature; by granting sabbaticals or extended leaves for further study; and by helping to provide research grants and facilities for the systematic study of teaching problems. This is in addition to extensive provision for audio-visual devices and expert consultation on such matters as course examinations, classroom dynamics, and field services. An alert and cooperative library staff also can be of immeasurable help in keeping the faculty member abreast of current material and in promoting effective use of a well-stocked library by students and staff.

It is axiomatic that these in-service programs prosper to the extent that they reflect genuine interest and not solely the imposi-

[26] W. Starr Miller and Kenneth M. Wilson, *Faculty Development Procedures in Small Colleges: A Southern Survey,* Southern Regional Education Board, Atlanta, Ga., 1963.
[27] See, for example, John W. Riley, *The Student Looks at His Teacher,* Rutgers University Press, New Brunswick, N.J., 1950.

tion of administrators. Professors are normally proud and protective of their professional prowess, determined to maintain their independence, and resentful of external pressure, no matter how benevolently intended. They have demonstrated on hundreds of campuses, however, that many are genuinely concerned about their teaching and will eagerly cooperate in programs for improvement. To encourage and facilitate this process, a number of regional and national projects have been instituted, and these deserve attention.

FOUNDATION AND FEDERAL AGENCY EFFORTS. Two or three foundations and some governmental agencies have been particularly interested in fostering intern experiences for young instructors. For example, between 1953 and 1958 the Fund for the Advancement of Education made grants to eighteen universities to help them develop programs for inducting young scholars into the teaching profession. Typically, each young instructor (with less than two years' experience) was attached to an older staff member of his department, who served as his mentor, aiding and supervising him in the section or two he was teaching. In addition, there were extended seminar sessions, where the interns could bring their teaching problems and could collectively look at the major principles and trends in higher education. Frequently the several mentors also attended the seminars, affording opportunity for analytical discussion by both new and experienced teachers. The strengths and weaknesses of the program were summarized in a publication written by John S. Diekhoff for the fund, entitled *Tomorrow's Professors*.[28] With the termination of subsidies, these intern programs largely have been abandoned, although some institutions have continued their interest in seminars and in supervising the teaching of beginners.

A somewhat different program of faculty development has been promoted by the Danforth Foundation. In addition to approximately one hundred fellowships given each year to college graduates to encourage them to go into graduate study and become college teachers, and another fifty Teacher Grants given to college teachers in service to help them round out their graduate study, over twenty-five hundred faculty members on more than six hundred campuses have received Danforth Associate Grants. These

[28] John S. Diekhoff, *Tomorrow's Professors,* Fund for the Advancement of Education, New York, 1960.

grants are designed to foster closer social and spiritual relations between students and faculty and include provision for a one-week summer conference devoted to aspects of creative teaching.

During the past eight summers, the Danforth Foundation has sponsored three-week workshops on liberal arts education, usually on the campus of Colorado College, to which some twenty-five or thirty selected colleges have been invited to send teams of four faculty members (including a dean), with expenses partly paid by the foundation. At these workshops, participants have studied the latest developments in curriculum building, classroom teaching procedures, and personnel services, and they have developed projects of educational advance to be undertaken when they return home.

Within the several disciplines, there have also been efforts to strengthen the quality of teaching, particularly in mathematics, the natural sciences, and foreign languages. While these programs have been designed primarily for high school teachers, they have attracted an increasing number of college faculty members. In the summer of 1964, for example, the National Science Foundation sponsored about seventy-five institutes attracting approximately twenty-five hundred college teachers of mathematics, science, and engineering. With grants from the NSF, the host institutions conducted programs of from four to twelve weeks' duration, defraying the travel and living costs of participants. In addition, the NSF similarly subsidized during 1964 some thirty-five conferences of one to four weeks' duration, attracting about eleven hundred participants to work in a particular subject field.

Since its passage in 1958, the National Defense Education Act has fostered many projects to strengthen teaching in science, mathematics, and foreign languages. A total of fifty-five language and area centers have been established to offer instruction in some seventy unusual tongues. As of June, 1964, about fourteen thousand elementary and secondary school teachers, nearly one-fourth of the nation's total, had attended 301 modern-language institutes for the purpose of upgrading their instruction. These institutes have had an effect upon college teaching as well. In discussing this feature, James M. Spillane, chief of the Language Institute Section in the U.S. Office of Education, reported:

A survey conducted by the Modern Language Association among college presidents whose institutions had conducted language institutes indicated that new materials are being adopted; more stress is being put on the understanding, speaking, reading, and writing sequence; increased and more intelligent use is being made of language laboratories. There is, in short, very good evidence that college faculties are becoming more and more interested in shifting their teaching emphasis to an audio-lingual approach and in revising radically their teaching methods.[29]

Illustrative of the stimulus possible in such a program is the Cooperative College Teacher Development Program in the state of Nebraska. Under the direction of Dr. Norman Cromwell, a professor of chemistry at the University of Nebraska, and with financial support from the National Science Foundation, the program provides opportunity for science teachers in colleges in this state to continue their graduate study and research. The project seeks to strengthen the teaching capabilities of professors, interest promising graduate students in science teaching as a career, and knit together the scientific profession of the state in an exchange of ideas and services. More specifically, the program includes special seminars and courses, a statewide faculty development council, opportunity for college faculty members to continue their study at the University of Nebraska, and provision for extended visits of outstanding scholars and scientists to various college campuses.

PROGRAMS OF PROFESSIONAL ORGANIZATIONS. The most extensive and persistent project for faculty improvement is that sponsored by the North Central Association of Colleges and Secondary Schools. Inaugurated in 1941 for twenty-eight selected liberal arts colleges, it has gradually expanded, until today it embraces approximately one hundred liberal arts and teachers colleges of the Middle West. Originally financed by the Carnegie Corporation, it is now carried entirely by contributions from the participating colleges, who agree to conduct a project of self-study and to share their findings with the other participants. Three workshops, each of four weeks' duration, are conducted each summer at the Universities of Minnesota and Michigan, where representatives from the colleges may study current developments in higher education and prepare for stronger leadership in projects back home. The program is carried forward through the leadership of a part-time director; ten coordinators, who were chosen from the participating colleges to visit the cam-

[29] James M. Spillane, "The Turn of the Tide in Modern Language Teaching," *Higher Education*, vol. 18, no. 8, p. 12, June, 1962.

puses once a year; a monthly news bulletin with a packet of ex-change materials emerging from the campus studies; a loan service of books and filed resource materials relating to higher education; and occasional intercollegiate conferences and research projects. During its twenty-three years of operation, this program has done much to strengthen intercollegiate cooperation in the Middle West and to help faculty members become more effective professional leaders.[30]

Similarly, the efforts of the Association for Higher Education's Committee on Teaching, mentioned previously, are concerned as much with the in-service development of college teachers as with their recruitment and professional preparation. One of the concerns of this committee is to determine if possible the locus of responsi-bility for the main aspects of teacher improvement. For example, should the graduate school or the employing institution be held re-sponsible for familiarizing the young teacher with teaching re-sources in his field, the use of audio-visual aids, and the prepara-tion of valid examinations? Which should provide supervised ex-perience in classroom discussion leadership? If the teacher is to participate in integrated general education courses, is it the respon-sibility of the graduate school or of the employing institution to help him become acquainted with those related disciplines necessary for competent instruction? Who should familiarize the young teacher with the current issues and trends of higher education so that he may participate constructively on college committees? And who will teach him the rudiments of counseling so that he may work effectively with individual students?

At the present time, most of the responsibilities just mentioned are assumed by neither the graduate school nor the employing in-stitution—at least to any substantial degree—which accounts for the floundering of many instructors during their first years of teach-ing. If some division of responsibility can be accepted all around, both graduate school and employing institutions might be expected to take such clearly identified obligations more seriously, and teach-ing in the colleges could then be expected to rise toward the level demanded today.

[30] For a discussion of recent developments in the North Central As-sociation's program, see Richard H. Davis, "College Teacher Project: A Summary Report," *North Central Association Quarterly,* vol. 27, pp. 251–258, Winter, 1963.

IMPROVING COLLEGE AND UNIVERSITY ADMINISTRATION

As noted in the early paragraphs of this chapter, most college administrators come from the teaching ranks, and many of their leadership functions continue to be "teaching" in the best sense of the term. Since individuals tapped for the purpose could be expected to have superior ability and extended campus acquaintance, it has seemed to some a bit presumptuous to worry about their qualifications and training. Perhaps this explains why there have been so few programs and so little research devoted to the improvement of college administration.

During the past five years, more than twenty volumes have appeared describing various aspects of college administration, written from a historical, theoretical, or pragmatic point of view. These are filled largely with accounts of prevailing practice, which presumably would be suggestive for college administrators who cared to read and profit from such summaries, but almost none of the publications have dealt with matters of preparation and in-service improvement. Some work of note has been done concerning public school administration, but little concerning administration at the college level.

Unfortunately, the kind of amateurish leadership that sufficed reasonably well fifty years ago is not adequate for modern institutions, with their multimillion-dollar budgets, their hundreds of fiercely independent faculty members, and their critical place in American society. Academic leaders today (we are not here concerned with nonacademic personnel) would include primarily the presidents, deans, and department chairmen. While the roles of these individuals vary somewhat according to level and circumstance, all must possess a peculiar and almost paradoxical comination of virtues. They must be wise and judicious in their handling of personnel whether in the selection of faculty members, the maintenance of staff morale, or the determination of promotions and tenure. At the same time, they must be widely acquainted with the educational issues involved in curriculum reform, improvement of instruction, and utilization of counseling services. They must be efficient in the handling of multitudinous daily details, understand the elements of finance and accounting, and contemplate the mysteries of an IBM machine. On top of all this, the president in particular must be adept at public relations, friendly to the alumni, and persuasive with men of wealth.

Considering the heavy load of responsibility carried by top administrators, it is small wonder that President Dodds, of Princeton, stated in his book *The Academic President: Educator or Caretaker*,[31] that many chief executives become so enmeshed in a network of supporting activities (such as business management and public relations) that they cease to be educational leaders. And in the absence of creative leadership, all the paraphernalia of efficient institutional management may be of little avail; it may result only in the systematic entrenchment of mediocrity.

University contributions

Because of the new and exacting demands now placed upon college administrators, universities in recent years have been developing programs of professional training for the task. Though imaginative in character, these programs are still very limited in scope. However, they are growing in quality and enrollment and may mark an important trend for the future.

The most extensive of these university programs is conducted by the Center for the Study of Higher Education at the University of Michigan. Under the direction of Algo Henderson, and with substantial grants from the Carnegie Corporation and the Kellogg Foundation, the center fosters programs for the preparation of both college teachers and college administrators. There are a few Michigan Fellowships in College Administration for persons with the doctorate or the equivalent to spend a year of intensive study on administrative problems. There are also graduate fellowships in higher education for persons with one year of graduate training or the equivalent to help them lay a foundation for future administrative activity; and there are fellowships in community college administration to assist persons looking forward to junior college leadership.

In addition, the center has sponsored nine annual Institutes on College and University Administration; approximately sixty presi-

[31] Harold W. Dodds, *The Academic President: Educator or Caretaker?* McGraw-Hill Book Company, New York, 1962.

and Harvard have already been mentioned, and occasional conferences have also been held at Chicago, Pennsylvania State, and a few other places.

Still more has been done by the administrators themselves through their professional organizations. For example, the American Association of Colleges for Teacher Education sponsors each summer a School for Executives, where presidents and their wives spend a week discussing educational and administrative problems. The Association of American Colleges, in cooperation with Cyrus Eaton, has developed a series of annual seminars at which liberal arts college presidents discuss great books that probe deeply into philosophical and educational issues. The Liberal Arts Study of the North Central Association conducts each spring, just prior to the association's annual meeting, a two-day workshop for college presidents at which some educational issue or innovation is reviewed.

Annual conventions of associations representing institutions, such as the American Council on Education, the regional accrediting associations, and those related to particular types of institutions, devote many of their sessions to topics designed to help presidents formulate and implement educational policy. At some of these, such as those of the North Central Association and the Southern Association of Colleges and Schools, special sessions are conducted by deans and are concerned even more explicitly with problems of educational leadership.

At the annual meeting of the Association for Higher Education, several discussion groups are devoted to administrative problems. An analyst highlights central factors of an issue, and the administrative officers then pool their thoughts and experience. The AHE also has sponsored a series of summer Washington Seminars for College and University Presidents to help new administrators become acquainted with activities and personalities of the Federal government as they relate to higher education. With the increasing meshing of governmental and educational activities, this program helps administrators to make use of available Federal assistance and discriminatingly to select projects in line with their own institutional purposes.

Since 1948, Oklahoma State University has sponsored an annual Summer Conference of Academic Deans. Sixty or seventy deans and their wives, from a dozen or more states, spend three days in lecture and discussion on a theme of current educational im-

dents, deans, and other administrative officers spend a week durin June analyzing problems of higher education under the stimulu of national leaders in the field. Similarly, there have been insti tutes and seminars for groups such as the Michigan Association of Church Related Colleges, the Michigan Junior College Adminis-trators, and others. The Michigan center has also fostered a number of research activities whereby the six staff members and their graduate students have published a series of monographs and journal articles relating to problems of college administration.

At Teachers College of Columbia University, there has long been a heavy emphasis upon educational administration, and under the leadership of Karl W. Bigelow, this has been extended to the col-lege field. Dr. Bigelow has prepared an annotated bibliography, *Selected Books for the College and University Administrator,*[32] and has directed a doctoral program for persons preparing for adminis-trative positions in higher education.

Harvard University has for several years conducted an Institute for College and University Administrators; presidents and other top officials have been invited for a week of discussion built around concrete cases arising in the field. Other major universities such as Minnesota, Chicago, California, UCLA, Stanford, Ohio State, Florida State, and the Catholic University of America have developed within their Colleges of Education a special concern for administrative problems in higher education and have provided opportunities for graduate students to achieve their master's and even a doctor's degree in that field. While in all these cases the number of degrees granted has been modest, there is here a solid foundation of interest and experience that, with adequate financing, could be an important factor in preparing administrative officers of the future.

In-service projects

The need of the profession, however, cannot wait for the maturing of graduate programs. Hence, as is the case with college teachers, there have developed in recent years a number of institutes and seminars to aid men already in service. The institutes at Michigan

[32] Karl W. Bigelow, *Selected Books for the College and University Administrator,* Bureau of Publications, Teachers College, Columbia University, New York, 1958.

portance. While initiated and hosted by Oklahoma State, the summer conference now has its own organization, and a committee of participants aids in its planning. Through the years, the mimeographed volumes of proceedings resulting from these conferences have made a significant contribution to the literature on college administration.

While this discussion is concerned primarily with *academic* administration, it is important to recognize the important contribution of the University of Omaha, which for over ten years has sponsored an annual one-week institute for persons involved in college business management, attracting nearly 200 people each year. The institute deals intensively with such problems as purchasing, accounting, auxiliary enterprises, personnel, and the like. One of the purposes is to emphasize ways in which competent business managers can reinforce and promote the educational enterprise.

Internships

In addition to conferences and seminars to improve administrative officers, there has been a growing interest recently in the use of internships for training young and promising administrators. The largest of these programs is that recently undertaken by the American Council of Education, under a $4,750,000 grant made to the council in October, 1964, by the Ford Foundation. This program provides for a total of 300 internships to be awarded over a five-year period to outstanding young men and women in their late twenties or early thirties. Interns participating in the plan spend a full year as assistants to college presidents, provosts, deans, or other administrative officers on some campus, preferably other than their own. During the internship period, they are paid their full salaries plus travel and moving allowances for themselves and their families. The internship program also provides for a series of seminars to be held at the beginning and end of the internship year.

On a smaller scale, the Ellis L. Phillips Foundation provides for a similar program of internships. This program makes available six internships a year to young men and women who wish to enter academic administration. As in the ACE program, the interns are paid their full salary and expenses to spend up to a full year as associates attached to some administrative officer in a university of their choice. A sponsoring committee, with Ellis L. Phillips, Jr. as executive director and Esther Raushenbush as program chairman, selects and works with the interns to assure optimum experience. Another type program is the Leadership Training Project sponsored by the North Central Association and directed by Dr. Norman Burns. Under this program, fifteen young men in teams of three are chosen to visit five institutions for one week. These visits, plus the associated seminars, are designed primarily to train competent examiners for North Central evaluation committees, but in addition the men gain invaluable experience for possible administrative responsibilities later on.

Research required

The field of college administration, like that of college teaching, needs much greater research than has so far been produced. Most books and conferences on the subject describe existing practice, but few can present well-validated evidence of what constitutes *superior* practice.

For example, the methods of dealing with faculty personnel are critically important in building a strong institution, and yet they are only moderately understood. What are the best means of faculty procurement? What criteria should govern promotion in rank, and what evidence should be sought to demonstrate whether a man has fulfilled them? Why are some faculty members so much more productive than others, and how can true scholarship and teaching skill be nourished in all?

Or consider the problems of university organization. How can power and responsibility be delegated without creating divisive little empires? Are departments too autonomous, too fragmented? What effect does the present system of faculty rank have on morale and productivity?

How should broad university policy be formulated? Should it come from the top or the grass roots or from some combination? How can faculty be utilized in making important but complex decisions without interfering unduly with their primary scholarly commitments? How can such decisions derive from careful consideration of all factors, properly assembled, rather than from political pressures of campus power centers?

And through it all, how can better communication and understanding between administration and faculty and between the several units be achieved? Why do some institutions exhibit friendly cooperation and trust among these groups, while others reflect a virtual cold war?

In tackling such questions as these, educational administrators might consult more closely with those in business and public affairs. It is ironic that on the same campus there may be departments of public administration, business administration, and education administration, with almost no interchange between them. Actually, many of their problems are similar, and each could learn much from the others.

A LOOK AHEAD

From the activities described in this chapter, it is evident that some programs for improving college teachers and administrators are beginning to take shape. There is still great need for research to identify and refine the more effective teaching and administrative procedures, but systematic inquiry into these matters is now going forward in scattered sections of the country.

Moreover, significant efforts are now under way to recruit more college teachers into the field and to strengthen their preparation. The Ford program is helping to select promising young men and women and prepare them through the master's degree, while a few graduate schools are beginning to explore ways of improving the teaching component of their doctorate. And instructors out on the job are getting some reinforcement through campus orientation activities, special institutes and conferences, and their professional organizations.

With faculty members, as with their administrators, all these efforts are still very feeble, considering the gigantic character of the educational task. Several concrete steps are now indicated if the profession of higher education is to gird itself to face the onslaught of huge student enrollment while at the same time meeting new demands for increased competence:

1. All segments of higher education—graduate schools as well as employing institutions—must rouse themselves to the impending faculty crisis and develop imaginative programs to meet it before it is too late.

2. The problem must be attacked at the grass-roots level, through the specific offerings and requirements of graduate schools and through aid to instructors in enriching their actual classroom performance. Conferences and workshops, researches and reports, and exhortations of lay and professional leaders—all these factors can help, but they clearly are not enough. Improvement can come only as those persons immediately responsible for college teaching are moved to reassess and reorganize the quality of their effort.

3. While any solution must rest ultimately in the hands of the thousands of people who are involved in recruitment, graduate preparation, and in-service performance of college teaching, there must obviously be some stimulus and coordination for such effort if it is to proceed smoothly and promptly. The recent development of a National Council on College Teaching, composed of representatives from many disciplines and professional organizations concerned with higher education, may prove to be an effective coordinator for this purpose. Ultimately progress will require leadership and cooperation at the local, state, regional, and national levels, and such collaboration is now beginning to take place.

4. A comprehensive national program of these dimensions will cost money. Substantial sums may be forthcoming from private and governmental foundations, but institutions likewise must reexamine their operations to make sure that adequate college teacher preparation and dynamic classroom performance become a charge of major importance. Funds can provide time, and time can bring thought and experimentation. And, as these activities among faculty members on campuses throughout the country move forward toward ever more competent instruction, with a sharing of experience to give mutual stimulation and support, the quality of learning in college will surely improve. Similar efforts among administrators will undoubtedly redound to the improvement of total institutional practice and be a further reinforcement for the teaching enterprise.

In summary, higher education has become critically important to society in this modern age, as a fountain of trained talent and a generator of fresh knowledge. New demands are pressing upon the teacher as well as upon the administrator, who must so operate the institution that the teacher can work at his best. The improvement of both functions will be a growing concern of the decade ahead.

SOURCES FOR FURTHER INFORMATION

Axelrod, Joseph: *Graduate Study for Future College Teachers,* American Council on Education, Washington, D.C., 1959.

Berelson, Bernard: *Graduate Education in the United States,* McGraw-Hill Book Company, New York, 1960.

Blegen, Theodore, C., and Russell M. Cooper: *The Preparation of College Teachers,* American Council on Education, Washington, D.C., 1950.

Bolman, Frederick deW.: "Administrative Structures," paper presented at Seminar in Higher Education, Rutgers University, New Brunswick, New Jersey, July 21, 1964.

————: "They Had Stars in Their Eyes," paper presented at Institute for College and University Administration, Harvard University, Cambridge, Mass., June 26, 1963.

————: *Toward Better Preparation of College and University Administrators,* National Education Association, Washington, D.C., 1964.

Carmichael, Oliver C.: *Graduate Education: A Critique and a Program,* Harper & Row, Publishers, Incorporated, New York, 1961.

Gage, N. L. (ed.): *Handbook of Research on Teaching: A Project of The American Educational Research Association,* Rand McNally & Company, Chicago, 1963.

House, Raymond (ed.): "Toward Better Preparation of College and University Administrators," Proceedings of Sectional Meetings, National Conference on Higher Education, Association for Higher Education, Washington, D.C., 1964.

Kelley, Fred (ed.): *Improving College Instruction,* American Council on Education, Washington, D.C., 1950.

Lunsford, Terry F. (ed.): "The Study of Academic Administration," papers presented at the fifth annual Institute on College Self Study, University of California, Berkeley, Calif., July 22–

26, 1963, and Western Interstate Commission for Higher Education, Boulder, Colo., 1963.

McGrath, Earl J.: *The Graduate School and the Decline of Liberal Education,* Bureau of Publications, Teachers College, Columbia University, New York, 1959.

W. HUGH STICKLER

10

the college calendar: what kind of a school year?

For many years the standard academic calendars have been
of two kinds: semester and quarter. Of these plans, the semester
plan has been far the more popular; some 85 per cent of American
colleges and universities operate under this system. Under both
semester and quarter plans, the academic year is organized so that
students are expected to attend college for a period which may
vary in length from thirty-two to thirty-six weeks.

The big debate in college and university circles today centers
around the year-round academic calendar, a calendar which provides a minimum of forty and often as many as forty-eight weeks
of classes per year and which permits the student who desires
to do so to earn the baccalaureate degree in three rather than the
usual four calendar years without requiring him to carry
more than a "normal" full-time course load.

The present concern for finding ways of providing more
"stretch" to the academic year grows out of a variety of considera-
tions. Chief among these are the desire to provide high-quality
education for an increased number of students seeking entrance
to our colleges and universities, the problem of costs, and the press
our colleges and universities have been feeling to put their
plants, staffs, and financial resources to maximum use.

This chapter reviews the evolution of year-round-calendar plans.
It discusses educational and administrative considerations in
the adoption of year-round calendars, types and basic charac-
teristics of these year-round plans, some of the problems associated
with year-round operation, financial implications, and possibilities
these plans may hold for the future.

WHY THE YEAR–ROUND CALENDAR?

The idea of the year-round calendar is not entirely new. During both world wars, a number of colleges adopted year-round academic calendars as emergency measures and then dropped them as soon as possible. One college on the West Coast has operated on the trimester calendar since 1946, and another in the Middle West since 1949. For years, dozens of institutions have offered four full quarters of academic work, and many institutions operating on semester calendars have long offered summer-session programs enabling the student to earn the baccalaureate degree in three years.

Why, then, all the recent and current concern about the year-round academic calendar? It has to do with the seriousness of purpose, the nature of the educational emergency, and the magnitude of the educational problems that confront us; it also has to do with the emerging character of the year-round program.

Heretofore, summer sessions have been academic appendages. Characteristically, they have not been an integral part of the school-year calendar. Usually they have been of less than full regular term duration. Curricular offerings in summer sessions have been sharply limited, sometimes even to the point of being fragmentary. Enrollments have been limited—frequently numbering not more than 20 or 30 per cent of normal full enrollments—and a "different type" of student has typically gone to summer school. Summer-school students in general have been older than students attending college during the regular academic year. Public school teachers and graduate students have been conspicuous by their presence, and undergraduate students by their absence. In the year-round academic calendars now being widely considered, summer terms would cater to all students, would provide extensive and balanced curricular offerings, and would become an integral and regular part of the total school-year program.

The student: some educational considerations

Frequently cited as educational reasons for the change to a year-round calendar are the following:

1. Knowledge is expanding at an enormously rapid rate; more time is needed to deal with it. The year-round calendar meets this need by putting more weeks of the calendar year to use.
2. Curricula—especially graduate curricula and curricula in the professions—are getting longer and longer; any calendar scheme that will shorten the overall educational process and get the graduate into his lifework while still young and vigorous is all to the good.
3. A liberal education or a professional education alone is no longer adequate; in order to follow a productive career in today's world, the graduate must have both. Under a year-round academic calendar, "both a liberal and a professional education often can be acquired within the time span formerly devoted to one or the other."[1]
4. Year-round campus operation generates greater seriousness of purpose on the part of the student. It advances the view that time is a precious human resource. It affords better opportunity for the student to move through his educational program at an accelerated speed if he cares to do so.

Summarizing the academic reasons for introducing a year-round

[1] Edward Harold Litchfield, "Trimester: Education of Superior Quality in a Shorter Length of Time," *College and University Business,* vol. 31, p. 25, July, 1961.

226   STICKLER

calendar at the University of Pittsburgh, Chancellor Litchfield, of
that institution, said: "We believe that such a calendar makes
possible a more complete education, provides a more flexible
means of coping with the expansion of knowledge, and encourages
the entry of people into professional life at an earlier and more
productive age."[2]

The college: some administrative, financial, and other considerations

Reasonable and logical though the academic reasons are, it is not
likely that we would be hearing much about the year-round academic calendar were it not for the compelling administrative advantages it offers. During the next decade all colleges and universities will be faced with the problem of unprecedented numbers
of students knocking on their doors and demanding educational
services. The essential consideration here is to find and use wisely
the resources that will be required to deal with these enormous
numbers of students. Principally these resources are three in
number: physical facilities, faculty and staff, and money. The year-
round calendar provides assistance with regard to better use of
all three.

EXTENDING THE COLLEGE'S PHYSICAL FACILITIES.   College enrollments will double within the next ten years, but in that period of
time institutions of higher education cannot double their physical
facilities. We simply must use our college and university plants
more efficiently than we do at present. No longer can we afford
the luxury (the academic waste!) of using our facilities only a few
hours a day or of letting our campuses lie idle one-fourth of every
academic year. Rather, we must insist on better utilization of academic space; we must increase instructional time by changing
the 8 A.M. to 5 P.M., five-day-a-week schedule (Monday through
Friday) to 7 A.M. to 10 P.M. (or later), 5½- or six-day-a-week
schedule (Monday through Saturday). Finally—and of major concern here—we must extend our calendar year from thirty-two to
thirty-six weeks to forty to forty-eight weeks. By one or more of
these procedures, or by some combination, our capacity to serve
additional numbers of students—insofar as physical facilities are

[2] *Ibid.,* p. 25.

concerned—can be enormously expanded. John Dale Russell has stated: ". . . if classrooms were used to the greatest extent possible during the day and evening and all through the year, present classrooms could handle four times the present number of students."[3] To be sure, there are numerous and formidable obstacles to theoretically perfect utilization of academic space, but the opportunity for improvement in utilization of facilities is immediately obvious.

MAKING FACULTY AND STAFF RESOURCES GO FURTHER. Turning to the problem of providing faculty and staff to serve our vastly expanded student enrollments, we find a similar situation; demand far exceeds supply. Nobody claims that college faculty members can teach around the calendar year after year. Although the report of Nelson Associates[4] to the State University of New York recommends no addition to the annual faculty work load, there is a growing feeling that faculty members in general can and are willing to work longer per year provided, of course, that equitable salary adjustments and suitable leave periods are made. The year-round academic calendar is one way of making faculty and staff resources go further. More will be said on this point later.

DISTRIBUTING THE COSTS. Consider money resources, particularly money not used for faculty salaries. Dormitories must be paid for, whether or not they are occupied. Library resources are there whether or not students use them. Buildings and grounds must be maintained whether school keeps or not. Some 35 per cent of the average college or university budget in this country goes to overhead, and it remains constant whether the academic calendar operates nine, ten, eleven, or twelve months a year. Year-round operation distributes overhead costs over a larger volume of educational accomplishments, and the relative cost for overhead per unit goes down.

[3] Quoted in Sidney G. Tickton, *The Year-round Campus Catches On,* Fund for the Advancement of Education, New York, 1963, p. 6. For a fuller discussion of this problem of better utilization of plant and teaching resources, see Professor Russell's chapter in this book, Dollars and Cents: Some Hard Facts.
[4] Nelson Associates, *Increasing College Capacity by Calendar Revision: A Report to the State University of New York,* privately printed, 1961.

228   STICKLER

Chancellor Litchfield, in summarizing the administrative reasons for going to a longer academic year, says:

In general we can say that if we are to meet the needs of the coming generation of students, we must make our resources go further by more intensive use. Failure to do so means either a poorer quality of education for a large number of students or a refusal on our part to educate many young people who are qualified for an education. In our view neither alternative is likely to help our nation in the competition for survival.[5]

OTHER CONSIDERATIONS. Our nation today confronts worldwide responsibilities greater than it has ever faced before. Busy minds, greater respect for time, and deep concern for the full use of human abilities and resources—all concomitants of year-round campus operations—will put America in a better position successfully to discharge those responsibilities.

Finally, year-round operation brings educational institutions into line with the pace of the times. The unhurried academic life of yesteryear grew out of an agrarian society. This leisurely pace interspersed with long vacations can no longer be justified. The times demand a quickening of pace in our colleges and universities to bring them into step with the pace of our national life. Year-round campus operation is one way of meeting this demand.

TYPES OF YEAR–ROUND CALENDARS

Several types of calendars have been devised to achieve year-round operation. In a paper read at the tenth annual meeting of the Southern Association of Land-Grant Colleges and State Universities, Newman[6] listed seven such calendars; a thorough search of the literature and review of practices would undoubtedly reveal at least that many more.[7] Yet in the main, year-round academic calendars

[5] Litchfield, *op. cit.*, p. 26.
[6] James H. Newman, "Year-round Operation of Universities," paper read at tenth annual meeting of the Southern Association of Land-Grant Colleges and State Universities, New Orleans, La., October 8–9, 1962. (Mimeographed.)
[7] Robert L. Lathrop, of the University of Minnesota, in a mimeo-

fall into some variation of one of three basic categories: quarter, semester, and trimester.

Variations of the quarter system

The quarter system has typically operated in three regular terms per year, each of ten, eleven, or twelve weeks' duration. The fourth quarter, if operated at all, has generally been a summer session outside the regular program. Typically it has had a different emphasis and has served a different clientele. If the fourth quarter were reconstituted, however; if it were made an integral part of the regular academic program; and if it catered to the regular student clientele, it might very well serve the purpose of a year-round academic calendar of the sort here being considered. Few, if any, institutions have yet met these criteria in full. Some, however, are on their way to achieving this goal.

Three variations of quarter systems merit consideration. Pennsylvania State University in June, 1961, shifted from a semester to a "term" calendar. (Penn State prefers not to use the word "quarter," although the calendar in general seems to be a modification of the quarter system.) Important is the fact that the summer term is an integral part of the total school year. Each term is ten weeks long, instead of fifteen, as under the semester system. Class periods, however, have been increased from fifty to seventy-five minutes in length; hence in a given course a student receives as many minutes of instruction under the term system as he did formerly under the semester system. Credit is awarded in semester hours, not quarter hours. A student typically graduates in twelve terms. If he goes straight through college, he can complete work for the baccalaureate degree in three calendar years.

Kalamazoo College divides its academic year into four 11-week

graphed memorandum to the Senate Committee on Institutional Research, dated May 1, 1962, says: "With very little searching it was possible to identify almost a dozen distinct proposals for calendar revision. It seems reasonable to presume that a more extended search would uncover several more. As some of the more thoughtful authors suggest, the particular division of the calendar is less important than the educational thinking which precedes and follows it, and many of the desired outcomes are possible under a variety of calendar arrangements. The unique advantages of one calendar division over another are often untested or only submitted to subjective evaluation."

quarters. The student typically takes three subjects rather than the usual five or six. Most courses require more than the usual amount of independent study and less than the usual amount of dependence on classroom activities. "The plan differs from other quarter plans in that not all quarters are spent on campus. Credit is given for time spent in study abroad and for career and service activities off-campus."[8] The student may complete the baccalaureate degree in either a three-year or a four-year pattern, but in every instance he spends two or more quarters away from the college.

Dartmouth, Carleton, Coe, Lawrence, Monmouth, and a number of other colleges now operate on the so-called three-three system— only three courses per quarter for three quarters or terms a year. Although not a year-round calendar per se, the ". . . three-three 'plan' . . . is admirably suited for . . . transition to a year-round operation, for the summer term can be exactly the same in length as the other three terms. . . ."[9] Some of the colleges presently operating on the three-three calendar have already made plans to launch the fourth, or summer, quarter. This extension of the current calendar should put each of these colleges on a year-round basis and enable the student, if he wishes, to earn the baccalaureate degree in three years.

Variations of the semester system

The semester calendar is the most widely used academic calendar in the nation today. Many institutions on the semester plan offer summer sessions of six, eight, nine, ten, eleven, or twelve weeks' duration. Within a calendar year they may be in session from forty to as many as forty-eight weeks. Inherently, however, the two-semester-plus-summer-session plan is not a full-blown year-round calendar. Summer sessions in institutions operating under this plan are generally "different." The summer term is shorter than the other terms of the academic year; thus the academic cadence is irregular. The emphasis is different, the curriculum is curtailed, many of the regular faculty members are not in residence, enrollment is sharply reduced, and the programs cater largely to older

[8] Weimer Hicks, "The Kalamazoo Plan," *Saturday Review,* vol. 45, p. 52, Dec. 15, 1962.
[9] Joseph E. McCabe, "The 3–3 Plan," *Saturday Review,* vol. 45, p. 55, Dec. 15, 1962.

students, public school teachers, and graduate students. The summer session does not articulate fully with the regular program. Although the campus is busy many weeks per year and although it is entirely possible within this arrangement to earn the baccalaureate degree in three calendar years, the overall program lacks cohesiveness and integration; it does not meet or even approach the optimum conditions for operating a year-round academic calendar that will be mentioned later in this chapter. So while the two-semester-plus-summer-session calendar meets the letter of year-round operation (i.e., forty or more weeks of classes per year and provision for the student to complete the baccalaureate degree in three years), it scarcely has the new character of the year-round academic calendar to be noted later.

Trimester systems

In recent years the trimester calendar has emerged as a plan of year-round operation. Although a misnomer, the word "trimester" seems to convey the intended meaning; apparently it is firmly established in our educational lexicon. Under the trimester plan, the year-round academic calendar is composed of three 15- to 16-week terms, all of equal or nearly equal length. The third, or summer, trimester may or may not be divided into equal terms. At present some thirty-five institutions either operate on the trimester calendar or have made the basic decision to shift to this type of year-round operation in the foreseeable future.[10] Among the major institutions now using this calendar are the University of Pittsburgh and the state universities of Florida. As more and more colleges and universities consider the possibility of year-round operation, the trimester calendar will undoubtedly receive increasing attention.

Actually, the trimester plan is an extension of the regular semester calendar, the third, or summer, trimester being an integral part of the total academic calendar. In the Florida institutions—and possibly in others—it should be noted that although the number of weeks of instruction per term has been reduced in the trimester calendar, the length of class periods has been extended, so that in a given course the student now receives as many minutes of

[10] This is the approximate number of institutions operating on, or committed to, the trimester calendar at the time of this writing. However, the picture with regard to trimester operation is changing rapidly.

classroom or laboratory instruction under the trimester system as he formerly received under the semester system.

Anyone who has been in a college or university when it shifted from a semester to a quarter calendar, or vice versa, knows that such a shift is a major undertaking. It should be immediately obvious, however, that shifting from semester to trimester operation is a relatively simple matter. The expression "relatively simple" is used because there is still much to do in curriculum consideration, course sequence determination, faculty rotation, and the like. But individual courses usually do not require major surgery; thus shifting from a semester to a trimester system is simple indeed when compared with shifting from a semester to a quarter calendar or from a quarter to a semester calendar. It will be remembered that about 85 per cent of American colleges and universities currently operate on the semester calendar. The relatively simple transition from a semester pattern to a trimester pattern constitutes reason to believe that, given time, the trimester plan may emerge as the commonly accepted type of year-round academic calendar. This line of reasoning is supported by the findings of Easton.[11] After analyzing ideal mathematical models for year-round operation, he concluded: ". . . the greatest increase in student capacity, the highest efficiency of operation, and the lowest cost resulted from a trimester operation with three entering classes per year, each of the same size."[12]

It may be noted in passing that Grayson Kirk, the president of Columbia University, also favors the trimester pattern of calendar organization.[13]

THE YEAR–ROUND CALENDAR: SOME BASIC CHARACTERISTICS

The year-round academic calendar has been defined as one which provides for forty or more (usually more) weeks of classes per year and which permits the student who desires to do so to earn the baccalaureate degree in three rather than the usual four calendar

[11] Elmer C. Easton, *Year-around Operation of Colleges,* Engineering Research Bulletin 41, Rutgers University, New Brunswick, N.J., 1958.
[12] *The University Calendar,* American Association of Collegiate Registrars and Admissions Officers (Committee on the University Calendar), American Council on Education, Washington, D.C., 1961, p. 15.
[13] Grayson Kirk (as told to Stanley Frank), "College Shouldn't Take Four Years," *Saturday Evening Post,* vol. 232, pp. 11ff., Mar. 26, 1960.

years without requiring him to carry more than a normal full-time course load. There is more to year-round operation, however, than the number of weeks utilized by a college or university within a given calendar year. If the summer term is unequal in length to the other terms, if it offers only a limited curriculum, or if it caters to a particular clientele (for example, public school teachers) rather than to all students, it may meet the letter of the definition, but it does not meet the spirit of the new character of year-round operation.

Optimum conditions for operating a year-round academic calendar include the following:

1. The terms should be of equal length, character and status. "Terms equal in length provide the most workable conditions for achieving equality in character and status. Terms equal in character (i.e., in such factors especially as breadth of course offerings, student activities, etc.) make them, in effect, interchangeable with one another. This eliminates the problems created by a term which meets the needs of only a portion of the student body, and which therefore has limited enrollment potential. Terms equal in status (i.e., in such factors especially as rate of pay for instruction, tuition fees, room charges, etc.) are seen as such by faculty and students and the effect is to make the terms equally desirable, removing obstacles to equalized term enrollments."[14]

2. There should be equal numbers of admissions every term and equal numbers of enrollments every term. Equal numbers of admissions every term are needed to assure equal numbers of enrollments every term; and equal numbers of enrollments every term are essential for the year-round calendar to operate at full potential.

3. Course and curricular offerings should be equalized. A full complement of courses and curricula should be offered every term in order that all levels of students may be adequately served and in order that the terms may be interchangeable.

4. The faculty should be equitably paid and equitably utilized. The principle of equal pay for equal periods of work is important to the long-term success of year-round campus operation. Equitable use of faculty time—including teaching, research, service, and regular leave—will have to be achieved.

5. Physical-plant utilization should be equalized throughout the year. Additional faculty members (to provide for regular leaves and faculty rotation while the program continues in full force) will re-

[14] Nelson Associates, *op. cit.*, pp. 18–19.

quire additional offices; air conditioning will frequently become a necessity; and additional housing may need to be provided for continuing education activities. But since the physical plant is an impersonal aspect of the program, it generally will provide no real obstacle to year-round operation.

6. *The year-round program of the college or university should be integrated and unified.* A single integrated, unified year-round overall program should chracterize the institution operating on a year-round academic calendar. The terms—be they quarters, semesters, or trimesters—should be interchangeable. They should be looked upon as incidental divisions for convenience of a program that essentially is of one piece, a sort of seamless garment.

The factors just noted are conditions for *optimum* operation. This does not mean that all these requirements must be met in full in order to make the year-round academic calendar feasible. It does mean that the operation of the calendar becomes increasingly successful and efficient to the degree that these conditions are met.

SOME PROBLEMS ASSOCIATED WITH YEAR–ROUND OPERATION [15]

There is no reason to believe that full-scale year-round-calendar operation will come into the American system of higher education as a matter of course or without pain. Year-round operation solves some problems; it creates others.

Educational problems

Some of these problems are educational in character. For example, as yet the educational effects of longer-period–shorter-term operations of extended duration have not been adequately appraised, nor has the effect of intensive and continuous year-round operation on

[15] Reference is made to W. Hugh Stickler and Milton W. Carothers, *The Year-round Calendar in Operation: Status, Trends, Problems,* SREB Research Monograph no. 7, Southern Regional Education Board, Atlanta, Ga., 1963. The portion of this chapter which considers some of the problems associated with year-round operation draws substantially from that publication.

the long-range quality of higher education been adequately determined. What about the total research effort of the college or university? Whether it is enhanced, unaffected, or diminished by year-round operation is not yet fully known. These problems do not seem to indicate inherent characteristics of year-round operation which would reduce educational quality; in fact, preliminary and incomplete evidence seems to show no deleterious effects upon the total educational effort of an institution. But more—much more—evidence is needed; these problems should be studied intensively and head on.

Administrative problems

Also, there are administrative problems. Undoubtedly the most difficult of these administrative problems is that of getting faculty members to teach and of getting students, especially undergraduate students, to go to school in the summertime. Traditional patterns of college attendance are deeply ingrained in faculty, students, parents, and the various academic publics; all resist change. Eric Walker, the president of Pennsylvania State University, refers to this custom of going to school during the winter months but not during the summer months as an "American folkway." Yet, unless the summer term is attended in stride by quantities of regular students, there is no real year-round operation, regardless of the name given to the calendar. Relief for this problem may be in sight. Pressures for admission within the next few years will undoubtedly force many students to go to college whenever they can, including during the summer session. But for the next few years—until the flood tide of students engulfs our campuses and makes summer attendance virtually obligatory—the problem of recruitment for the summer session will continue to be real and difficult.

Under a year-round calendar, there is a general speedup of institutional operations. Things move at a faster pace. The admissions office works longer and harder; another registration period is necessary; more grades must be distributed; and possibly another commencement exercise will be arranged. Business operations are intensified and are more extensive; student personnel workers have more to do; and housing and feeding services have more customers and a longer work year. The problem of maintaining the physical plant is made more difficult when there is less time with students off campus. Classroom and dormitory painting, building renovation, street alterations, and the like are not as easy to schedule and carry out. These problems attendant to the general speedup of year-round operation are by no means insurmountable, but they must be taken into account.

Then, too, there are financial problems with which the administration must necessarily be concerned. Sufficient funds must be obtained for equitable term-to-term, year-round operation. Money may come from more students paying more tuition and fees, from additional legislative appropriations in the case of public institutions, from other sources, or from various combinations of these sources, but it must be forthcoming. The financial implications of year-round operation will be discussed further later in the chapter.

Problems associated with the faculty

Special problems may be encountered with regard to the faculty. In some cases there will be recruitment problems. Some potential faculty members simply will not like the year-round calendar and will not be attracted to it—at least until it becomes far more common than it is at present. Others will not like the salary provisions of the full-schedule plan, especially if it involves a system of pay other than that of equal pay for equal work.

Under the traditional academic calendars, different faculty members have used the summer months in different ways. Some have taught in summer sessions in other institutions; year-round operation may preclude this practice or at least make it more difficult in the future. Young faculty members not yet holding the doctorate frequently continue graduate study during the summer months; this may not be so easy to plan under the year-round calendar. Many professors use the summer for intensive and sustained research; year-round operation may in some cases necessitate teaching instead. For college teachers, summertime has traditionally been travel and vacation time; in some cases this may have to be changed. And in the long haul, year-round operation may produce very real problems with regard to family vacations, especially in families having school-age children.

Educators, even under the familiar calendars, have never been able to agree as to what constitutes an adequate and appropriate work load for a faculty member. Under year-round operation, the problem of faculty work load is intensified. How much should a typical faculty member teach per term? How much faculty research should be expected? What about other faculty responsibilities—committee work, service activities, consulting, and the like? What should be the length of the work year for the faculty —three quarters out of four, two trimesters out of three, individually negotiated leave, or no limitations at all on employment and work load per calendar? And is sabbatical or other regular leave even more important under year-round operation than it is under the traditional calendars? It is entirely possible—and highly desirable—for a year-round operation to be successfully installed without requiring year-round teaching on the part of individual faculty members. The institution, not the individual college teacher, operates on a year-round basis, year after year.

Adequate and equitable pay for faculty members may constitute a problem. In this connection current practices vary widely. Some institutions have established the principle of equal pay for equal periods of service, but most institutions pay less for the summer session than for the other terms, even though all terms are of the same length. Faculty members have difficulty in reconciling such discrepancies. Problems such as these ought to be resolved on a fair and equitable basis; the writer believes that the solution lies in acceptance of the principle of equal pay for equal work.

Problems associated with students

Students also have problems with regard to year-round operation. First, there is the problem of articulating transfers between high school and college, between junior college and senior institution, and between one senior institution and another. When different institutions have different calendars, the starting dates may not articulate, and time lapses may ensue. This becomes a particularly important problem when an institution is trying to equalize admissions and enrollments from term to term. A partial solution may be found in provisions for "trailer" groups. At least two institutions operating on the trimester calendar employ the trailer principle. The winter trimester begins in early January, but in order to pick up midyear high school graduates, these colleges start trailer sections in February (carrying an accelerated and reduced load for a shorter period of time). In like fashion, the spring or summer trimester begins in late April, but in order to pick up the May-June crop of high school graduates, additional trailer sections are started in June. By the next trimester in each case, the trailer student is placed in a regular schedule.

There is also the problem of length of school year for individual students. Should college attendance be continuous or intermittent? Surely, acceleration by the student is not a necessity, not a *sine qua non*, for successful year-round operation; the central feature is balance by means of equal term enrollments, whether the student is accelerating or is attending on a normal but staggered schedule. A year-round calendar should permit a student to accelerate, but he should not be required to do so.

There may be a problem in some cases regarding student course load. The academic pace in year-round operation is fast. Perhaps most students will be able to handle a normal course load and make normal progress with it. Some, however, may wish to reduce their course loads—at least until they get their "academic legs" and feel confident that they can proceed satisfactorily with the usual course load.

What about the student's extracurricular activities? Under the year-round calendar, will it be "business as usual"? Can a student expect to move at the faster academic pace demanded by the full-schedule calendar and yet participate in extracurricular activities on the scale to which he has been accustomed? Answers, of course, will differ with individual students. Some will be able to take both the year-round curriculum and extracurricular activities in stride. Probably most students, however, will find it necessary to cut back somewhat on participation in the extracurricular program.

Financial problems for students may attend year-round campus operation. Full-schedule operation in itself will not increase the overall cost of a college education; in fact, it may reduce the total cost somewhat. But if the student wishes to accelerate, the year-round calendar will necessitate more concentrated spending over a shorter time span. In this case, however, the student will complete his college education sooner than is usual and will enter into his lifework at regular earning capacity at an earlier age. Some students will elect to borrow money and stay in college for longer stretches of time. Most institutions which have gone to year-round operation in recent years have found it advantageous to increase rather sharply their student loan funds. On the other hand, however, the student who must interrupt his college work to earn money for college expenses may find that the year-round calendar is an asset. Instead of competing with large numbers of other college students for summer employment, he may find it to his advantage to attend the summer term and to work during some other term when temporary jobs are more readily available and when pay is possibly better. In any event, the student's ability to pay for his total college education is not adversely affected under the year-round plan.

MAINTAINING A YEAR–ROUND BALANCE: DEALING WITH THE PROBLEMS OF THE SUMMER TERM

As has been indicated, one of the major problems the year-round colleges face is that of getting students to go to school in the summertime. This picture may change in the next few years in that pressures for admissions may force students to go to college whenever they can, including during the summer term. In the meantime, institutions will have to resort to inducements to get regular students to attend the summer sessions; many inducements are being systematically offered at present.

A common inducement, of course, is to accelerate the academic program. Under this plan an undergraduate student can complete the baccalaureate degree in three years or less, and a professional or graduate student can complete his advanced program in significantly less time than it would otherwise take.

Some institutions indicate that students may enter only at certain times; some require students to preregister and to pay fees in advance for a whole year; some offer remedial work in the summer only; some insist that students on probation attend the summer session; one requires marginal students whose cumulative grade-point averages are under C to attend the summer trimester; and still others offer their most attractive courses and programs (for example, a fine-arts program with Broadway stars, symphony orchestra, and well-known guest artists) during the summer session.

One institution features a summer program in "rapid reading." A number of colleges and universities offer full- term or even full-year courses in seven to eight weeks, but only in the summer.

At least two colleges reduce student expenses for the summer term. One institution, for example, reduces tuition for the third trimester from $375 to $250, and dormitory rental for the third trimester from $80 to $60, a net saving to the student of $145 during the third, or summer, trimester. Some colleges are giving dormitory priorities to year-round students.

At low personal cost to the students, two or more institutions encourage their students to study in foreign countries (Europe and elsewhere), provided they attend a summer term to balance the time element.

A number of colleges help students secure jobs for the fall or winter terms with the understanding that the students will make up the time by attending an equal number of summer terms. A common physical inducement to summer attendance is complete air conditioning of libraries, classrooms, food services, and even dormitories.

All these devices—and still others yet to be invented—are being or will be used to lure quantities of regular students into attending the summer sessions. Whether the measures here listed will accomplish their goal remains to be seen. There is reason to hope, however, that with the buildup of pressures for college admission and following a period of transition in college-going habits, the goal of substantially increased summer attendance may be increasingly achieved.

FINANCES AND THE YEAR–ROUND CALENDAR

Decisions regarding an institution's academic calendar should not be made primarily on the basis of financial considerations. However, the cost of higher education to the individual student, to the sponsoring agency or tax unit, and to the nation as a whole will be so great in the years immediately ahead that any financial advantages merit serious attention. In institutions operating on year-round schedules, these financial advantages may not be inconsequential.

The use of coordinated full-year calendars on a substantial scale is a relatively new phenomenon in American colleges and universities. As yet it is too early to make precise financial analyses of these new operations. However, some insights into the financial consequences of using full-schedule calendars are possible.

In a survey of year-round programs completed in 1963, the writer (*1*) made extensive and careful study of the literature pertaining to year-round operations, (*2*) received written replies to questions asked of some forty–fifty institutions now operating on, or committed to, full-schedule calendars, and (*3*) visited a dozen or so year-round institutions and conversed widely with persons involved in year-round operations. On the basis of these experiences, he makes the following judgments regarding the financial implications of year-round campus operation:[16]

1. To the student, the cost of a college education in a year-round institution will be no greater than it would be under a traditional calendar; it will probably be less.

2. Year-round operation characteristically results in material increases in the salaries of college teachers.

3. Preliminary evidence indicates that in a well-run year-round operation, increased productivity more than compensates for the increased cost of current expenses. There is good reason to believe that the average cost per quarter hour, per semester hour, or per trimester hour will be reduced.

4. Auxiliary activities such as dormitories, dining halls, and bookstores are almost certain to show net economic advantages.

5. Probably the most important economies can be made as a result of savings in capital outlay for additional buildings and equipment. An institution operating on a year-round calendar can accommodate more full-time-equivalent students with the same physical plant. Over a period of years, lower capital costs per student station are almost sure to result.

While no financial gain can inevitably be implied, the potential economies in using the year-round calendar are manifestly there. But a word of caution is in order. Year-round operation with a summer program comparable to that of other terms, with reduced per-credit-hour operating costs and with savings in capital outlay for buildings, will not prove feasible for any institution until it has reached the point where it cannot accept all qualified applicants for the fall period or until that point is expected in the near

[16] The writer shared these experiences with his colleague, Milton W. Carothers. An outcome of their study was Stickler and Carothers, *op. cit.* Dr. Carothers concurs in the author's judgments here expressed regarding the financial implications of year-round operation.

future. As a general rule, successful year-round operation will be dependent on an oversupply of qualified applicants for the peak period.

SUMMARY, CONCLUSIONS, AND IMPLICATIONS FOR THE FUTURE[17]

McKenna is undoubtedly right in contending that ". . . the academic calendar may be described as being in a state of transition between the traditional pattern of the nine-month academic year and the proposed full utilization of the calendar year."[18] It is possible, nevertheless, to draw some conclusions about the year-round movement to date and to make, with some measure of confidence, projections concerning its future.

The movement toward year-round campus operation, which has shown substantial growth during the past five years, will continue to grow. As college enrollments mount during the next five to ten years, interest in the full-schedule plan will be intensified, and many additional institutions will adopt year-round calendars.

Various patterns of year-round calendars will emerge, but the strong tendency in the long view will be toward the new goals of (1) terms of equal length, equal character, and equal status; (2) terms having approximately equal admissions and approximately equal enrollments and (3) equal pay terms for members of the faculty and staff. Interchangeability of terms is highly desirable for a successful year-round campus operation.

Although no one system of year-round operation is likely to be established, the trimester calendar seems likely to emerge as the model plan. In theory, it has been shown to be the most efficient plan, and it provides the easiest transition from semester operation to full-schedule operation.

In institutions on the year-round calendar, intensified efforts have been and are being made to integrate and unify the academic year and to establish better balance among the terms. Particular attention is being given to the summer session in order to increase

[17] This portion of this chapter draws substantially from Stickler and Carothers, *op. cit.* See footnotes 15 and 16.
[18] David L. McKenna, "The Academic Calendar in Transition," *The Educational Record,* vol. 43, p. 68, January, 1962.

enrollments, to upgrade its character and status, and to bring it into line with the other academic terms.

The most important single obstacle currently militating against successful year-round operation is student and faculty apathy, if not outright resistance to attending college during the summer session. Until this "American folkway" of attending college in the winter but not in the summer is changed, year-round campus operation will be a struggle. But mounting enrollments and pressure for admission may change this "habit" sooner than most people think.

Intensive and extensive studies need to be made of the effects of year-round operation on the quality of the institution's total educational program. There would seem to be nothing inherent in the year-round calendar which would militate against academic excellence—in fact, year-round operation may well enhance the academic program—but much more evidence is needed before firm conclusions can be drawn.

There is considerable preliminary evidence indicating that successful long-term year-round operation will result in substantial economies to the institution. It can be said with reasonable assurance that the unit cost per full-time-equivalent student will not be increased as a result of year-round operation and that it probably will be decreased.

The major institutional economies will result from (*1*) more efficient utilization of the physical plant and facilities and (*2*) long-term savings in capital outlay for buildings and equipment. There will probably be savings in operations once the program gets fully under way.

Preliminary evidence also indicates that long-range financial advantages will probably accrue to students who attend colleges and universities employing year-round calendars. At least the potential benefits are there.

Before an institution moves into full-scale year-round operation, there should be enrollment pressure and pressure for admission adequate or more than adequate to fill the institution to capacity during the period of maximum enrollment. For some time to come —at least for the next few years—successful year-round operation will be dependent in considerable measure upon an oversupply of applicants for the peak (usually fall) term.

Finally, it should be noted that further experimentation with year-round calendars is both inevitable and desirable. All the answers are not yet in. Continuing evaluation of all aspects of year-round operation—academic aspects, financial aspects, aspects of faculty and student acceptance, and others—is essential.

To summarize, the question that can be asked about the future of year-round academic calendars is: Will they work? The answer must be an unequivocal "yes." Although planned under a variety of patterns (e.g., quarter, semester plus summer session, trimester) and although attended by many problems—but what college or university is without problems?—they have been tried in institutions of all sizes and have proved to be successful in operation. As has been indicated, the biggest problem is—and for some time will continue to be—the changing of people's attitudes toward year-round college attendance. Nevertheless, "Year-round operation seems to be accepted as an inevitable part of the future for most colleges and universities in American higher education."[19] And the reason for this inevitability is very simple: there is no alternative.

SOURCES FOR FURTHER INFORMATION

"Colleges Can Operate All Year," *Saturday Review,* reprint from the Dec. 15, 1962, issue.

Easton, Elmer C.: *Year-around Operation of Colleges,* Engineering Research Bulletin 41, Rutgers University, New Brunswick, N.J., 1958.

Henderson, Algo D.: "A Critical Look at Year-round Operations of Institutions," *Current Issues in Higher Education, 1962,* pp. 161–164, Association for Higher Education (NEA), Washington, D.C., 1962.

Hungate, Thad L., and Earl J. McGrath: *A New Trimester Three-year Degree Program,* published for the Institute of Higher Education by the Bureau of Publications, Teachers College, Columbia University, New York, 1963.

Kirk, Grayson (as told to Stanley Frank): "College Shouldn't Take Four Years," *Saturday Evening Post,* vol. 232, pp. 11ff., Mar. 26, 1960.

Litchfield, Edward H.: "The Trimester System," *Saturday Review,* vol. 45, pp. 50–52, Dec. 15, 1962.

[19] *Ibid.,* p. 68.

McEntire, Davis: "The Academic Year: Nine Months or Twelve?" *AAUP Bulletin,* vol. 49, no. 4, pp. 360–364, December, 1963.

McKenna, David L.: "The Academic Calendar in Transition," *The Educational Record,* vol. 43, pp. 68–75, January, 1962.

Nelson Associates: *Increasing College Capacity by Calendar Revision: A Report to the State University of New York,* privately printed, 1961.

Rauh, Morton A.: "College the Year Round," *Antioch Notes,* vol. 38, April, 1961.

Schoenfeld, Clarence A., and Neil Schmitz: *Year-round Education: Its Problems and Prospects from Kindergarten to College,* Dembar Education Research Services, Madison, Wis., 1963.

Stickler, W. Hugh, and Milton W. Carothers: *The Year-round Calendar in Operation: Status, Trends, Problems,* SREB Research Monograph no. 7, Southern Regional Education Board, Atlanta, Ga., 1963.

Tickton, Sidney G.: *The Year-round Campus Catches On,* Fund for the Advancement of Education, New York, 1963.

The University Calendar, American Association of Collegiate Registrars and Admissions Officers (Committee on the University Calendar), American Council on Education, Washington, D.C., 1961.

Webb, David C.: *Year-round Operation of Universities and Colleges,* Canadian Foundation for Educational Development, Montreal, 1963.

"The Year-round School," *Theory into Practice,* vol. 1, no. 3, College of Education, Ohio State University, Columbus, Ohio, June, 1962.

KEVIN P. BUNNELL
ELDON L. JOHNSON

11

interinstitutional cooperation

C*ooperation among groups of colleges or universities can hardly be said to be new. Some ancient universities were, and still are, the aggregate of cooperating collegiate parts. However, recent rapid growth has raised interinstitutional cooperation for the first time to the level of a new educational dimension.*

Two or more institutions join together to share staff, students, and services. Several colleges in close proximity learn to substitute cooperation for long-standing competition. Institutions hundreds of miles apart in distance but close together in objectives cooperate to do something better together than they could do separately. All the institutions in the same state or region band together for common good, as commonness can be agreed upon. Public institutions in a single state find cooperation a more

*harmonious and economical means of living together in the shared
service of the state; others are bound together by law and
consolidated governing boards to put an end to unwholesome
competition. Like-minded institutions join together to form a new
companion institution. Smaller colleges cooperate to gain the advantages of largeness. Large universities cooperate to avoid small
programs everywhere. Joint experimentation has appeal in terms
of bolstering confidence, sharing risks, and broadening the base of
comparison, and pieces of incompleteness are fitted together to
make whole programs.*

 *This chapter reviews developments in interinstitutional coopera-
tion. Attention is directed to the forces that have given impetus
to the development of interinstitutional groups, the advantages and
the limitations of these groups, the kinds of interinstitutional groups
that have been developed, and the possible uses these groups
hold for cooperative planning in the future.*

INTERINSTITUTIONAL COOPERATION: SOME MOTIVATING FORCES

Educational groupings of all kinds have emerged from the American penchant for organization, but the favorites of the past were
function-centered rather than institution-centered. They came into
being for professional purposes, shoptalk, annual meetings, public
relations, and influence of public policy. Now a new type of organization is rapidly multiplying—a partnership or consortium of
institutions for the advancement of institutional goals through cooperative educational programs. These combinations seek not to
project themselves more favorably but to change themselves in
complementary concert with others. They are operational and
program-oriented. They exist solely for educational improvement,
both directly and through increased managerial effectiveness.

 Cooperative combinations of institutions of higher learnings are
entered into for a host of reasons and because of the advantages
they offer. Some want a common voice and a common front in
behalf of some goal or in response to some fear. All presumably
want a new dimension, with somebody and some machinery at the
center concerned with the new overall perspective—at least an
organizational means of discovering commonness and going for-

ward together. In educational combinations, there are economies of scale, in money, in efficiency, and in capacity to negotiate with outside parties. There are gains in complementary specialization. There are, in short, obvious advantages in shared burdens, shared techniques, shared specializations, and shared experiences. The advantages of the common market and mutual aid have caught on in education as well as in diplomacy. Theodore S. Distler, executive director of the Association of American Colleges, recently said to his large and influential constituency: "For most colleges the only solution that I can see is for them either to enter into some kind of alliance with a university—where one is within reach—or to join a group of like-minded colleges in providing facilities that no one of them could provide for itself."[1]

Interinstitutional cooperation can be put to almost any use, but its great growth in recent years suggests the emergence of new factors on the educational scene. Among them is the rapid expansion of knowledge, tending to make every institution short-handed, incomplete, and malformed somehow. Cooperation is a means toward completeness. Other factors are the widening gap between needs and resources, the pressures of student enrollment, the appeal of quality as a competitive weapon, the deafening demands of society for specialized competencies, the "collusion" and administered arrangements in what used to be the "free market" of students and faculty, and the growing flexibility of academic life, calling for year-round operation, off-campus residence, part-year enrollment at another college, and overseas study centers. To many of these new problems, joint institutional effort seems to be the logical answer, or at least an intermediate answer, until every cooperator is ready or willing to "go it alone." This groping for completeness, not in meeting the old demands but in dealing with the new challenges, is the main spur to interinstitutional cooperation. Indeed, colleges may soon experience pressures so great that, as one perceptive and experienced observer has said: "They will need every help they can be given, including the frequently neglected help they can give each other."[2]

[1] "Report of Executive Director," *Liberal Education*, vol. 49, no. 1, p. 128, Association of American Colleges, Washington, D. C., Mar., 1963.
[2] H. W. K. Fitzroy, "Interinstitutional Cooperation: Hope and Reality," in John J. Wittich (ed.), *Proceedings of the Conference on College and University Interinstitutional Cooperation, Princeton, New Jersey, April 1962*, College Center of the Finger Lakes, Corning, N.Y., 1962, p. 17.

The new organizations for cooperation rest on what the co-operators have in common. The most potent bonds are common geography, common new funds, common danger, and common new purposes. Common background exerts much less influence than might be supposed, as testified to by the fact that tight federations have not arisen even among colleges closely tied to the same church. Indeed, cooperation of the earliest kind arose in many cases from such competitive interests as athletic relations and fund raising.

As a result of these developments, many cooperative centers and associations now exist. Typical examples will be given later. More than twenty, excluding fund-raising and athletically oriented groups, were represented at the first national conference on inter-institutional cooperation, held at Princeton, New Jersey in April, 1962. They reflect the emergence of "centers" closely related geographically and "associations" more related in purpose and prospect than in geography. They also reflect cooperation ranging from the informal and natural to sophisticated planning and joint new program operation, including even new institutions.

ADVANTAGES

Most of the cooperative schemes emphasize excellence and effi-ciency. They seek to coordinate, but they also attempt to innovate, to conserve, and to expand. Four common objectives and advantages will illustrate this.

To present a united front. The augmentation of strength by joint action is nowhere more apparent than in negotiations with outside parties—government, foundations, universities, and other associa-tions. This is one of the economies of scale. A group of federated colleges can better deal with, and gain concessions from, a large university. Large universities acting together can better deal with, and gain concessions from, the Federal government. The con-sortium idea has appeal as a means of amplifying independent voices and commanding increased attention. It is also, at its mini-mum, a mode of self-help and mutual aid, whatever the external relationships are.

To provide new opportunities. With the limitations of all institutions and with the growing specializations and new emphases (e.g., on non-Western studies), all kinds of cooperative possibilities emerge to give students better choices than they would otherwise enjoy and faculty members better opportunities for research or other creative work. Specialization can be dovetailed and made complementary rather than duplicative. For students, this may mean a wider choice of courses or even of a career, an opportunity for study abroad, access to new visiting professors, preferential admission to a professional school, or a kind of specially arranged advanced standing for graduate school. For the faculty, it may mean refresher seminars, planned apprenticeships for beginners, new research possibilities, leaves tied to reserved places abroad or in larger institutions, teaching exchanges, and summer activity relevant to professional advancement. These advantages emerge from the pooling of resources and from agreements conferring benefits on both the "have" and the "have-not" institutions joined in common purpose. Cooperation can thus mean significant enrichment for both students and faculty.

To save. While economies can be made through combined services and improved efficiency, the mere spending of less money is not the chief advantage. In fact, interinstitutional cooperation of much imagination is likely to lead to new financial commitments in behalf of better educational results. But whatever is to be spent can be more effectively and efficiently spent by sharing, by division of labor, and by avoiding duplication or wasteful competition. Direct economies range from reduced insurance rates and chartered-plane savings to the advantages of group purchase of elaborate equipment. What may be more important in terms of both dollars and education is the economy resulting from the division of areas of specialization for graduate or professional study, rotation of summer-school obligations, pooling of needs for space and staff overseas, and sharing of other new-program costs. In any case, cooperative educational enrichment without the costs of competition is the kind of savings sought. It is also a fact that cooperative savings on the managerial level soon reach a point of diminishing returns.

To experiment and innovate. Many tantalizing educational experiments call for institutional comparisons, enlarged staff or other resources, and a daring that welcomes and needs strong company. With the demands of society and hence career opportunities for students changing rapidly, many institutions are tempted to make innovations that may change their traditional character and call for staff and overhead disproportionate to student demand. Meeting such temptations through the associated endeavor of several colleges permits each to gain something from the strength of all or from some who act on behalf of all. This may be done by embarking on an entirely new overall venture divorced from, but supported by, each cooperator (e.g., a professional school, a graduate school, a summer field camp). It may be done through an agreed-upon development at one college in behalf of all (e.g., a teacher preparation program, a nursing program, or special language programs). Much innovation in education, as in other economic sectors, tends to make exacting demands in terms of men, money, and materials. Other innovations with appeal limited to a particular campus, and perhaps more demanding of imagination than finance, may still benefit from company and collective aid in experimentation and evaluation. In either the major or the minor cases, therefore, cooperation among institutions has its strong appeal. Improvement can be sought by example and experiment, each institution serving as a potential stimulus to every other member. The standard of the best tends to become the ambition of all. Whether the confrontation of cooperating institutions, officers, and faculties can be given credit for emerging new ideas, the cooperative device is often an improved means of carrying them out.

LIMITATIONS

All the cooperative associations of colleges and universities have built-in limitations, necessarily and understandably. Rarely, if ever, can they submerge or override the autonomy of the member institutions or put a member under any obligation contrary to its will. Their powers are derived, not original. They have no constituency of their own and no basis for separate loyalty. They may be fortunate in having no alumni, but that fact points also to their limitations. The loosest association has limitations in purpose; the tightest federation has limitations in method. It is in the nature of a federation, as someone has said, to be designed to keep too much from happening.

Communication is probably the greatest problem and limitation. Everything depends on awareness of common purposes and of advantageous differences. Yet how is this to be brought about? The obvious and significant can be agreed upon at once; the really significant takes painful effort. Vaguely common sentiments give rise to the organization, but clear identification of, and dedication to, common goals must precede effective action. This is difficult enough within a college. The difficulty is compounded in a collection of colleges or universities. Systematic machinery for deliberation is ordinarily limited—there is no senate, no body of delegates except a small governing board, and little means of feedback to the campus. Reliance must be placed heavily on *ad hoc* conferences, special committees, and rare meetings of the governing board. In an organization sensitive to the independence of its members, unusual care must be taken to keep everybody in agreement and to keep everybody "in the know." Arriving at a consensus is sometimes delicate and often cumbersome. In case agreement is not apparent, or if disagreement is clear, there is no alternative to careful and time-consuming polling, conferring, weighing of suggestions, repolling on revisions, and finally explaining the composite of all to the satisfaction of each. Organization, geography, motivation, outstanding commitments, and tradition all make communication in cooperative association inherently difficult. When machinery comes into being, it functions much more like the United Nations than a congress or a parliament; discussion is the chief lubricant.

Self-interest of member institutions is natural and unavoidable, but candor requires that it be recognized as an ever-present limitation in cooperative effort. This explains the ease with which new projects can be undertaken, as contrasted with the difficulty of obtaining cooperation on the old. Vested interests, loyalties, commitments, and prestige become involved whenever familiar problems have already been solved on the several campuses. When the amalgam of loyalties and tensions—affecting faculty, administration, students, alumni, trustees, and donors—which produced the X College way of doing this or that is multiplied by the number of colleges in the association, not many new and acceptable ways of "improvement" are possible. Colleges, like individuals, have trouble with "mine" and "ours." Cooperative projects are fortunate if they get warmly enthusiastic, rather than coldly intellectual, endorsement as "ours." Some officers experienced in cooperative ways of education would incline to the conviction that the weakest colleges are the most cooperative and that the strongest are the least cooperative—that cooperation is in direct proportion to weakness. So far as this is true, it is a reflection of an understandable desire to place energies where gains can be made. The college that can do everything for itself has less reason to rely on others. On the other hand, it can and has been argued that strong institutions are in the most advantageous position to cooperate, as they often demonstrate. Cooperative associations encounter self-interest and limitation in another way; if a common problem is discussed and thought urgently ripe for action, the action may be taken by the separate colleges rather than through the common organization.

The danger of uniformity also presents a limitation which is more feared than real but which is real because it is feared. Few centers or associations for cooperation have any of the hallmarks of the tyranny or of the persuasiveness required to produce much uniformity among their members. Nevertheless, every such organization at some time must face the challenge: What are you doing to recognize that we are unique rather than to make us all alike? While this recognizes a limitation, it overlooks the fact that cooperation can accentuate differences by giving them a secure place in a new totality.

Money is not the measure of all things, but it is sometimes a useful measure of priorities. Limited funds result in limitations in cooperative associations for higher education. The college that will not enter a cooperative venture unless some outside source pays the bills does not have much confidence in what it is undertaking. By no means do association efforts all call for money, but where efforts do require money, its absence cannot be compensated for by cooperation. Almost all the criteria one could apply to the financing of interinstitutional organizations—the amount spent, the way it is raised, the haphazard and unconventional support, the divorce from both gains and ability to pay—indicate that the importance of these cooperative groups can easily be overestimated in the total scheme of things educational. Whether these associations could wisely use more resources at present may be open to argument, but that doubt eloquently testifies to the limitations on what they are presently able to do. Mere coordination is not expensive; program operation is. Representing old constituencies is not expensive; managing a new one is. Few associations operate really major programs on their own (measured by the members' own major programs), and even fewer have any new overall organizational program to manage. This is not to say that they should but merely to recognize them for what they are—inherently limited but as useful as the members wish them to be.

Another limitation is that of fitting organizational and representational machinery to the tasks to be done. A dilemma exists. Most cooperative arrangements are predicated on extreme simplicity of organization and effectuation of purposes through the members. This means that there may be alarm when the central secretariat expands and, paradoxically, dissatisfaction if more tasks are foisted upon the members. One cannot get organized to do what the other does not want to do within an organization committed to doing it somehow. Central secretariats normally tend to expand and take on more and more functions. That is one danger. New cooperative commitments are normally assigned to collegiate machinery already overoccupied with existing independent commitments. That is another danger. Steering between dangers is the real problem and the real art.

Whatever the solution, if it is addressed to a task of significance it calls somewhere for officers and representation of the interests involved. Officers, powers of office, interests to be represented, and means and organs of representation are some of the issues. It matters greatly whether or not there is a central headquarters with officers; whether the representatives are president- or faculty-elected or are spokesmen for each college or for each curricular area; whether the expectation is coordination of what is found or innovation of what is needed; whether decision-making power resides at one place or another; and whether the consent of persons who must be relied on can be obtained and used.

The limitations here are universal: choosing and fitting the organizational form to the task and, to complicate matters in cooperative endeavors, harmonizing a new governmental form with the existing ones out of which it grows.

Three other limitations are also worthy of mention. New and experimental organizations without campuses, students, faculty, or big budgets sometimes have problems of attracting and retaining topflight leadership. They are likely to succeed in proportion to the educational significance of the tasks they are willing to undertake.

Another limitation exists in the general reluctance of all academic personnel to tamper with the "free market" of students. Yet if students in an association of colleges are to have guaranteed or reserved opportunities at special places (e.g., a university abroad) or places of specialization (e.g., professional or graduate schools) or are otherwise to be favored by mutual agreement, the free market has to surrender to some control.

Finally, for collegiate cooperation, the residue of general common interest is limited by all the specialized interests served through other organizations in the field of higher education. The new interinstitutional centers and associations have to do what a plethora of educational organizations do not already do, and they must represent what these organizations do not already represent. They have to put broad, institutional interests together in a world overflowing with fragmented, subinstitutional representation.

All these limitations, however real, should be kept in perspective. Like many organizational limitations, they may restrict at one point but liberate at another. They set free new powers. They open up opportunities heretofore closed. They certainly do not make agreement easy, but agreement is given a new dimension and a higher ceiling of possible success.

The preceding generalizations about interinstitutional cooperation can be given further point and relevance by describing and commenting on several programs that illustrate some of the major forms of organization for interinstitutional cooperation: (*1*) interstate compact agencies, (*2*) the larger corporate groups for cooperation, (*3*) smaller multilateral arrangements with a minimum of organizational structure, and (*4*) bilateral programs.

PROGRAMS
Interstate compact agencies

In the years immediately following World War II, educators and government officials in all the states became aware of the shortage of educational facilities, particularly at the advanced levels. They began to consider seriously how they could cope with the vastly increased numbers of students who would be seeking higher education. In the late 1940s, in the South and in the West there were tentative probings into the possibility of interstate cooperation. Could the states share scarce graduate and professional facilities? Could they use their higher educational resources cooperatively, not only to meet the demands of students, but also ultimately to improve economic and social conditions within their borders? The answers to these questions were sought not only by educators but also by state legislators and governors. They decided they could cooperate and that the best device for doing so was a treaty or compact among the states. By 1955, the three existing interstate compact agencies had been established. They were eventually to unite thirty-five states in the search for excellence in higher education. The New England Board of Higher Education (NEBHE) serves the six New England states; the Southern Regional Education Board (SREB) joins sixteen Southern states; and the Western Interstate Commission for Higher Education (WICHE) serves thirteen Western states, including Alaska and Hawaii. Each of these organizations has a governing board or commission made up of persons appointed by the governors of the member states. Their basic operating funds come from state appropriations. All three of them supplement these funds with moneys from public and private granting agencies. In the case of the Western Interstate Commission for Higher Education, every dollar of state funds is currently matched by about $4 from outside the states.

It is important to keep in mind that the regional compact agencies are organizations of *states,* not of *institutions.* In this sense they are different from all the other cooperative bodies and arrangements described in this chapter.

Although the regional compact agencies were founded primarily to promote interstate rather than interinstitutional cooperation, they have been responsible over the past ten or twelve years for developing many cooperative interinstitutional arrangements. Some of these arrangements are described below.

NEW ENGLAND BOARD OF HIGHER EDUCATION.   Under a plan sponsored by the NEBHE, the six New England state universities have agreed to open certain of their more specialized curricula on a regional basis. Out-of-state students admitted to regional programs are charged in-state tuition. Thus a student from Rhode Island may study forestry at the University of Maine, and a Maine student may take dairy management at the University of Vermont. Students benefit from the program by enjoying a much wider selection of courses than is available within their own states, and the universities benefit by having a larger universe of students to draw upon in filling their less common programs. In the past year, nearly fifty courses of study were available under the New England regional program, and about 350 students were enrolled in regional curricula.

SOUTHERN REGIONAL EDUCATION BOARD. The SREB has encouraged a wide variety of cooperation among the universities in its region. Southern institutions have cooperated in planning and conducting specialized graduate summer sessions in the agriculture sciences, statistical methods in biology, business, and the health sciences. They have encouraged cooperation in producing definitive textbooks in certain uncommon fields. With SREB encouragement, some Southern institutions have cooperated in recruitment by jointly preparing brochures designed to counsel prospective teachers and students in such areas as the master of arts in teaching, forestry, and agricultural science.

Almost since its beginning, the SREB has worked actively to encourage cooperation among states and among institutions in the uses of educational television. It has sponsored numerous meetings and has provided professional consultants to assist colleges and universities in planning, developing, financing, and using systems of educational television stations and campus facilities.

In the South, over sixty schools of nursing are now working together and with the SREB to improve graduate education for nurses, research, continuing education, and the use of instructional media.

In the field of mental health, the SREB has encouraged major Southern universities to cooperate in planning to meet the educational needs of persons working in the mental health field.

WESTERN INTERSTATE COMMISSION FOR HIGHER EDUCATION. The WICHE has recently followed New England's lead in establishing an exchange program for students, called the Western Regional Student Program. The program will operate much the same as that in New England, the main difference being that there is a potential participation of 146 public institutions throughout the West instead of six, as in New England. The program will attempt to move students across state lines into uncommon curricula that can benefit from increased enrollments and a larger pool of students from which to choose. As is true in New England, the WICHE's role is organizational and administrative. Participation in the Western Regional Student Program is voluntary on the part of both the institutions and the students. The WICHE will publicize the new program, keep the necessary records, and encourage institutions to join in the new cooperative venture. This program is so new that there has been no opportunity to evaluate its effectiveness.

In its early days, the WICHE was instrumental in the establishment of the Western Association of Graduate Schools. This is essentially an organization to establish communication between the graduate schools in the West, particularly between the graduate deans. Until 1964, the WICHE served as secretariat for the WAGS; the organization has now become completely independent. The WAGS deans meet periodically to discuss problems of graduate education in the West, to recommend research on graduate education, and to discuss new curricula or the revision of existing programs.

Like the SREB, the WICHE has stimulated cooperation among Western schools of nursing. Using the device of an advisory council of nursing specialists, known as the Western Council on Higher Education for Nursing, the WICHE has helped Western nursing schools to find the way to cooperation for the improvement of nursing education at all collegiate levels, including graduate programs for the preparation of nurse-teachers and nurse-researchers. The basic source of the nursing council's energy and its success is the enthusiasm of the deans and faculties of Western schools of nursing. With foundation assistance, the WICHE maintains a nurse-consultant who works closely with the council to stimulate cooperative action.

The WICHE has also sought to promote interinstitutional cooperation in solving the educational problems which cluster around the mental health field. The need for interinstitutional cooperation arises from the fact that there are few curricula specifically designed to train persons to work with the mentally retarded, juvenile delinquents, or the mentally disturbed. New curricula to train people for research and work in these fields are needed; they are not needed in every Western university or, indeed, in every Western state. The WICHE has encouraged key university persons, first to become aware of the need for specialized programs for research and training in mental health, and second to agree among themselves where centers of excellence in certain fields shall be established, thus avoiding needless duplication of programs.

Not all interinstitutional cooperation is voluntary. Many states have established statewide coordinating agencies that enforce intrastate cooperation. Cooperation stimulated by the interstate compact agencies is voluntary. If this is so, by what means have they been able to foster interinstitutional cooperation? The two forces that work most strongly in their favor are their ability to marshal *facts* and their capacity for region-wide *organization*. The facts are that certain specialized programs are extremely expensive to organize and operate; that many kinds of teaching, research, and service can be done more effectively by universities working together than by one institution working alone; and that the range and quality of opportunities required by college and university students in the 1960s will tend to outstrip the capacity of any one institution. The staffs of the regional compact agencies have been the means for organizing the processes of cooperation; the substance of cooperation and the success of it are in the hands of the institutions.

The larger corporate groups for cooperation

The years since World War II have seen the growth of another form of educational cooperation—corporate cooperative groups of *institutions*. Urged on by visions of collective strength, groups of colleges and universities in all parts of the land have formed corporations or have entered into other kinds of voluntary formal agreements to secure for themselves the economies of large scale and the efficiency of specialization.

Like the interstate agencies, these institutional groups are governed by boards of directors and are administered by full-time professional staffs. In most cases the presidents of the participating colleges constitute the governing boards; they determine the kinds of cooperation to be attempted, and they determine how deeply their joint efforts shall penetrate the structures of their institutions.

One of the first groups to be established after the war was the Richmond Area University Center. Started in 1946 by eleven

Virginia institutions with widely varying purposes, the center today has twenty-four members, who cooperate in numerous ways,
including operating an FM radio station, maintaining a central
film library, and sponsoring visiting scholars as well as musical and
dramatic events.

Another corporate group is the College Center of the Finger
Lakes, an aggregation of seven small colleges in south and central
New York State. Founded in 1961, the center maintains an office
in Corning, New York. Among its efforts have been block bookings
of performing artists, workshops on problems of college teaching
and administration, a cooperative visiting scholar program, and
joint publication of a scholarly journal.

An even newer corporate cooperative venture is a consortium
of five major universities in the District of Columbia area, which
began to function in early 1964. This group of universities—
American, Catholic, Georgetown, George Washington, and Howard—will cooperate at the graduate level to provide a wider
variety of student opportunity and to improve the overall quality
of graduate teaching and research.

More detailed descriptions of three other corporate groups will
suggest the realities and the potential of this means of cooperation
among institutions of higher learning. Two of these, the Associated
Colleges of the Midwest and the Great Lakes Colleges Association,
are groupings of small colleges. The other, the Committee on
Institutional Cooperation, is an association of complex universities.

COMMITTEE ON INSTITUTIONAL COOPERATION. The Committee on
Institutional Cooperation is an association of eleven large Middle
Western universities that have established a central office to
facilitate voluntary cooperation. Members of the group are the
"Big Ten": Illinois, Indiana, Iowa, Michigan, Michigan State,
Minnesota, Northwestern, Ohio State, Purdue, and Wisconsin, plus
the University of Chicago.

The CIC might be described as a startling educational achievement. Each of the participating institutions is really a "multi-
versity," offering an almost endless variety of programs. Why
should anyone look to another to supplement its offerings? Why
should there be an abatement of the traditional competitiveness
long stimulated by athletic rivalry? Should not state lines and
great distances continue to keep these institutions apart? Part of
the answer to these questions lies in the fact that the demand for

learning and the quantity of knowledge have grown so rapidly in the past decade that no one institution can possibly offer all the courses, all the research opportunities, and all the contacts with distinguished teachers that its students need.

In 1958 the Committee on Institutional Cooperation, made up largely of top-level deans and vice-presidents representing the eleven institutions, began to explore ways to work together. They began by identifying areas of teaching and research that were too costly or too specialized for one university to undertake. An ultimate objective was to improve educational and public services at minimum cost.

During the six years of its history, the committee, its administrative staff, and the faculties of the universities have developed a wide variety of cooperative programs in their attempt to move "from hope toward harmony."

Perhaps the most widely publicized effort is the CIC traveling-scholar program. Beginning in the fall of 1963, graduate students have been able to cross institutional lines to study at other CIC universities. The students benefit by gaining access to library collections, research facilities, and specialized courses. The participating universities are able to devote more of their resources to building existing strengths. Traveling scholars are registered at their home universities and pay fees there, but they have access to the resources of eleven universities.

The CIC has sought to develop cooperation in several foreign-language areas. A series of summer institutes in Far Eastern languages provides a variety and depth of study opportunities far beyond what any one university could offer. A committee of CIC liberal arts deans is working on a master language plan for the eleven universities. While continuing to offer the traditional Western languages, the universities would cooperate in developing programs for the teaching of twenty-six less common languages and dialects, with each institution developing its strength noncompetitively in a particular language area. Presumably when the plan is implemented, the traveling-scholar idea will give students easy access to the languages offered by any of the eleven universities.

The CIC is now either practicing or planning for other forms of interinstitutional cooperation. These include coordination of study-abroad programs, a joint study of ways to stimulate economic growth in the Middle West, joint preparation of alumni publications, and cooperative production of television courses.

In all its efforts, the CIC strongly emphasizes faculty participation in planning. To encourage faculty participation, the CIC has obtained foundation funds for "seed grants." These grants pay the cost of meetings by faculty groups to work out ideas for cooperation. Many of the CIC's programs have developed out of these faculty deliberations.

The literature of the CIC emphasizes repeatedly that the committee and its staff are determined to avoid the trappings of bureaucracy and that they do not possess authority over any member institution. The staff prefers not to originate ideas for cooperation, hoping rather that they will come from the faculties and staffs of the universities. Once established, cooperative programs are administered cooperatively; there is no tyranny of the majority, and the central staff seeks to disengage itself from projects when they become operative.

A statement in the 1962–1963 CIC annual report sums this up very well: "The success of the CIC idea depends upon those to whom a sharing of resources would be most meaningful. The CIC provides an organizational framework for cooperation and strives to encourage promising ventures within this framework; its future remains in the hands of the faculties and administrators it was formed to serve."

This paragraph hints at some of the similarities and dissimilarities between an association of cooperating universities such as the CIC and regional compact agencies. The one is a voluntary organization of universities; the other is a grouping of states voluntarily committed to cooperation by their participation in an interstate compact. The constituency of the compact agencies is extremely broad. They answer ultimately to all the people of the compacting states. The constituency of the CIC and similar associations is the faculty, the staffs, and the students of the cooperating universities. Like the CIC, the compact agencies have no formal authority over any part of their constituencies. They cannot dictate policy to the states or to any institution in the states. They prefer that expressions of need for their assistance come from the universities, the legislatures, or the general public. Both organizations are committed to providing a framework for cooperation which will strengthen higher education. Their ultimate purposes are similar; their organization to achieve these ends is different.

THE ASSOCIATED COLLEGES OF THE MIDWEST.   In 1958, ten Middle Western liberal arts colleges (Beloit, Carleton, Coe, Cornell of

Iowa, Grinnell, Knox, Lawrence, Monmouth, Ripon, and St. Olaf) joined in forming a corporation that would enable them, while maintaining their full independence, to strengthen their educational programs by accomplishing collectively what they could not accomplish individually. The central office, in Chicago, operates under the president of the association, Dr. Blair Stewart, former dean of Oberlin College.

At the outset, the colleges hoped that their joint efforts would carry them into such areas as standardization of admission procedures and scholarship qualifications, pooling of library resources, establishment of a joint office for student recruitment, sharing of faculty, expansion of cooperative arrangements for faculty recruitment, and promotion of joint purchasing, research, and fund raising.

One of the first achievements of the new association was a program in cooperation with the Argonne National Laboratory, a center for research into the peaceful uses of atomic energy. The program makes it possible for faculty members in such disciplines as physics, biology, chemistry, and mathematics to gain extended access to rare, highly expensive equipment at the laboratory. Thus qualified teachers in liberal arts colleges have research possibilities and personal associations with other researchers comparable with opportunities available only in large institutions. Opportunities are also available at the laboratory for advanced students from the ten colleges, who may spend a semester in research and study under the guidance of highly qualified specialists on the laboratory staff and the visiting ACM faculty then in residence.

Because of their willingness to join in the quest for research funds, the ten colleges have achieved a place of leadership in the field of language teaching. Using funds from the U.S. Office of Education, they are undertaking experiments in language teaching designed ultimately to improve the quality of language instruction in American secondary schools. The project places special emphasis on experimentation with methods of teaching, including the use of language laboratories.

A desire to secure the advantages of large scale has led to the associated colleges' cooperative purchase of insurance and a resultant sharp downward revision in their rates, as well as the rates to a number of other institutions in the Middle Western region. Other cooperative enterprises include the joint collection of NDEA loans, the operation of a wilderness-area field station, self-studies of institutional characteristics, and student and faculty conferences and seminars on current issues. Overseas opportunities for both staff and students have been organized in locations representative of the world's major cultures. ACM-sponsored student groups have participated in an experimental work-study program in India. The colleges have also developed a program for cooperation with Cuttington College, in Liberia. This effort will help Cuttington to meet urgent staff needs and to develop its library, while enabling the ACM colleges to strengthen their African studies programs.

THE GREAT LAKES COLLEGES ASSOCIATION. One of the newer corporate groups, the Great Lakes Colleges Association, was organized in 1961, with twelve participants: Albion, Antioch, Denison, DePauw, Earlham, Hope, Kalamazoo, Kenyon, Oberlin, Ohio Wesleyan, Wabash, and Wooster.

Through cooperative research, experimentation, and action the group hopes to strengthen academic programs and improve managerial effectiveness. According to its descriptive leaflet: "It aspires to be in some respects a university made up of colleges geographically separated. It is interested in promising educational innovations and particularly in those activities which one college is not likely to undertake or could not so well carry on alone."

Though still in its infancy, the association has drawn a design for its future which outlines five broad program areas encompassing everything the group is doing or planning. These are international education, graduate education, faculty development, educational research, and a visiting-scholar program.

A comprehensive program of non-Western or intercultural studies has been launched with both campus and overseas dimensions. With foundation support, funds for retraining and research are available to involve the faculties as deeply as possible. Overseas centers for student instruction and faculty research are being set up in locations representative of several major cultures. A Near Eastern operation is already launched in cooperation with the American University in Beirut. A pilot group is paving the way for a continuous relationship with Waseda University, in Tokyo. The most ambitious overseas program is the Latin-American Center in Bogotá, opened in 1964. The center combines special facilities and programs supplied by the association with complementary facilities and programs in three Colombian universities. A preparatory stage for certain students will also be offered during the summer in cooperation with the University of Guanajuato, Mexico.

Two other major programs provide marine biology opportunities for students and staff through a formal agreement with Florida State University and its laboratories at Alligator Harbor and also for research on the improvement of teaching under a U.S. Office of Education grant. The latter is concerned with self-instruction techniques and will test programed materials, produce new ones, and appraise useful applications in liberal arts colleges. It is organized under a separate full-time director located at Hope College and seeks to achieve its ends by wide faculty participation and released time for specific assignments.

Multilateral arrangements with a minimum of organizational structure

Throughout the country there are many enclaves of cooperation, some recently developed, which engage several institutions in informal cooperative arrangements. Three such groups, each composed largely but not exclusively of liberal arts colleges, are located in Massachusetts (Amherst, Mount Holyoke, Smith, and the University of Massachusetts); Pennsylvania (Bryn Mawr, Haverford, Swarthmore, and the University of Pennsylvania); and California (the Claremont Colleges, Occidental, the University of Redlands, and Whittier).

These three groups have a number of characteristics in common. Each is made up largely of liberal arts colleges, with the Massachusetts group involving a state university. The cooperating institutions are located close enough to one another so that transportation of students or teachers among colleges is feasible, if not always easy. The disciplines and services touched by these cooperative efforts are many rather than few, and the areas of cooperation tend to change over time in response to changing faculty strengths and student needs. The administration of the arrangements among the participating colleges tends to be informal and adjustable to evolving realities rather than highly structured.

AMHERST, MOUNT HOLYOKE, SMITH, AND THE UNIVERSITY OF MASSACHUSETTS. A brief description of cooperation among the four Massachusetts institutions will serve as a model of the possible rather than as a definition of all that can be achieved under such an arrangement.

The original objective of the program, now substantially achieved, was to make it ". . . easily possible for any student in any one of the four institutions to take for credit any course in any of the other institutions, provided he has the approval of his dean for so doing."[3] Thus, in the recent past, a University of Massachusetts student was able to major in Russian by taking courses at Smith, and a Smith student was able to take a course in biology at the University of Massachusetts that was essential to her major but not available at Smith that semester. Students at the four colleges have enriched their studies in such disciplines as music, political science, cryptography, mathematics, economics, and art. The four colleges awarded their first corporate doctor's degree in 1961.

Together these four institutions are able to recruit and hold highly competent specialists by offering advantages usually found only in the largest universities. Cooperation enables them to attract enough students for certain advanced specialized courses to make them economically feasible. Furthermore, the exchange of students and faculty seems to put both on their mettle and evoke a quality of performance by both above that normally expected.

Professor Sidney R. Packard, of Smith College, who coordinates the program, described its effects as follows:

This interchange of students and instructors, deliberately planned, has made the educational potential in this valley progressively available to all students in our four institutions, under reasonable controls. The sending institutions . . . can be depended upon to see to it that the migrating student is of adequate calibre scholastically and of high motivation. An important secondary result of these interchanges has been inevitably a closer relationship among the four departments in a single subject and a growing tendency of these departments to think cooperatively in their planning for the future, both in course offerings and appointments.[4]

One of the most obvious forces which has brought the Massachusetts group together has been the desire to take advantage of geographical proximity and the potential for complementary specialization. The four colleges have lived together for a long time, but apparently only in recent years has the rationale of

[3] Sidney R. Packard, "Academic Cooperation," *The Educational Record*, vol. 40, p. 360, October, 1959.
[4] *Ibid.*, pp. 360–361.

cooperation overcome the tradition of isolation and perhaps some sense of competition.

An interesting characteristic of this union of institutions is that it operates with a minimum of administrative machinery. The group has the services of a coordinator, whose responsibility is not to command but to unify the collective wills and minds of the cooperating colleges. Occasionally the presidents meet to review the status of the cooperative relationships.

Apparently the real strength of this cooperative enterprise lies not in complex structure but in the collective vision of potential advantages held by those who must make the cooperation work. Without this kind of vision—this will to work together rather than to duplicate and compete—even the best-organized venture in academic cooperation will not long endure.

An implied objective of cooperation among these four institutions is to gain the completeness of the largest universities without paying the price in dollars and size. Student access to a shared and compounded variety of specialized course offerings and other educational opportunities is an example. These colleges have purchased such advantages at low cost indeed. No teacher was asked to stop teaching a treasured course. No basic internal administrative changes were required; there was not even an effort to standardize the academic calendars of the four colleges. They have, in a sense, had their cake and eaten it too.

This is the kind of cooperation that can most easily succeed. Difficulties are more likely to arise when interinstitutional cooperation demands basic internal changes that are essentially subtractive rather than additive—when a department must stop giving a major because it is being offered by a stronger department at a nearby cooperating institution or when a researcher must refrain from seeking a grant on his own because a group of researchers from several cooperating universities or colleges can command more money to do a similar piece of work on a larger scale.

Bilateral programs

ALFRED–SYRACUSE. Alfred University, located in southwestern New York State, provides study through the master's degree for schoolteachers and school administrators living within a 40- or 50-mile radius. More than 100 miles separates Alfred from Syracuse University, which offers the doctorate in education. These two institutions have joined in a transfer-of-credit agreement, which provides that Syracuse doctoral candidates from the Alfred area may take a substantial portion of their course work at Alfred. Candidates' programs are planned jointly by Alfred and Syracuse faculty members. Because Alfred area educators may take half, and occasionally more than half, of their doctoral work within commuting distance of their homes, the required time away from home and job and thus the expense of obtaining a degree are substantially reduced.

The continuance of the program has hinged on its popularity with doctoral candidates and on its acceptance by the faculties of the two institutions. Faculty acceptance may be attributed, in part at least, to the fact that the program requires no fundamental curricular changes at either institution. Thus it poses little or no threat to those who must make it work.

The primary source of any potential difficulty would seem to be the attitude of the Syracuse faculty toward accepting Alfred courses in lieu of those offered at Syracuse. The history of relationships between Alfred and Syracuse may explain why this has not been a major barrier. Because they are located some distance from each other and because they are different in size and purpose, relations between Alfred and Syracuse have tended to be of a cooperative rather than a competitive nature. The Syracuse graduate school has supplied a number of Alfred's faculty members, and at the time this particular program was launched, one of the chief administrators of Syracuse was an alumnus and member of the board of trustees of Alfred University. These factors have contributed to the successful joining of the two in a cooperative enterprise which capitalizes on the special capabilities of each and which at the same time makes doctoral study in education more readily available to the teachers and administrators of the Alfred community.

FLINT JUNIOR COLLEGE—THE FLINT COLLEGE OF THE UNIVERSITY OF MICHIGAN. The bilateral relationship between Flint Junior College and the Flint College of the University of Michigan is far more complex than the Alfred-Syracuse arrangement. The Flint College of the University of Michigan offers only junior- and senior-level courses. Flint Junior College is a two-year community college under the city Board of Education. The two colleges have joined in an effort that makes optimum use of funds from municipal and state sources to provide, in one community, educational opportunities encompassing all four years of college. There is an arrangement whereby students enrolled in one college may be permitted to take courses in the other. At the end of each semester, the educational-services ledger is balanced, and the creditor institution is reimbursed.[5]

The two colleges share certain physical facilities, including a library. The operating expenses of the new Mott Library are shared on a pro rata basis, and acquisitions by either college are catalogued and shelved together.

These arrangements are formalized by a written agreement between the Flint Board of Education and the Regents of the University of Michigan.

Because of their closeness, the physical problem of moving students from one college to the other is minimal. Furthermore, communication among faculty members and administrators is easy enough to permit each institution to become familiar with those characteristics of the other that bear on successful cooperation.

Like Syracuse and Alfred, the Flint colleges have purposes that tend to be complementary rather than competitive. Consequently, cooperation is likely to suffer little from the rivalry that may exist between two neighboring institutions with overlapping objectives.

This type of cooperative enterprise confers many of the economies of larger size. Thus library and audio-visual services and some teaching can be provided at a considerably lower cost than if each institution supplied its own.

In contrast to the Alfred-Syracuse arrangement, the Flint program is complex, reaching into many departments and service units of both institutions. Greater complexity means greater exposure to logistical as well as human relations problems. While the Alfred-Syracuse program can and does function with little administrative participation, the Flint program requires the attention of a broad array of personnel, including academic administrators, department heads, and fiscal officers. Clearly, interinstitutional cooperation of this order requires strong staff support. Beyond this, geographical proximity is helpful, a conjunction of institutional interests and objectives is essential, and the determination of people of good faith to make it work is mandatory.

[5] Clyde E. Blocker, "A Cooperative Experiment in Higher Education," *Higher Education,* vol. 14, p. 13, September, 1957.

All these partnerships in behalf of excellence in higher education suggest that voluntary cooperation can be extremely effective;
that the spirit of cooperation is more important than structure; that
economy in dollar terms alone is rarely a sufficient reason for
cooperation; that it is desirable to avoid, especially at the outset of
a cooperative enterprise, arrangements that threaten those who
must make the idea work; and that communication is essential to
interinstitutional cooperation, which is the essential mission of all
these groups.

FUTURE USES

A combination of academic pressures, experimentalism, and curiosity brings many inquiries to persons connected with cooperative
ventures. Is this something our group of colleges or universities
can do, too, with great advantage? There is no easy or certain
answer. It depends on objectives, history, personalities, geography,
willingness to sacrifice, and perhaps a host of other factors or combinations. The history of what is being done in interinstitutional
cooperation is so diverse that it seems to hold something for everyone and every purpose, from one end of the spectrum to the other.
At the easy and obvious end, the question is: Do the gains justify
all the effort and machinery? At the difficult and more obscure end,
the question is: Can enough effort and machinery be brought together to produce the desired gains?

In other words, cooperation obviously can give strength on certain common matters, some so minute as to raise questions about
the justification of the joint attention given or the joint effort
exerted. Joint purchases of antifreeze or joint arrangement of a
round robin for lectures hardly calls for incorporation, a board of
directors, councils, and a central secretariat. The machinery should
be commensurate with the objectives, not disproportionate to the
projects undertaken. At the other extreme, however, some objectives are so grandiose or exacting that they can hardly be matched
by implementing machinery or the common surrender to a common task. This is likely to be the case if the establishment of a
brand-new overarching institution is contemplated.

Interinstitutional cooperation has its inherent limitations. It is
and can be made useful if not too much is expected of it. Its cur-

rent popularity probably outruns its merits in the majority of situations. In some respects, it is a hard device. It calls for unusual motivation and behavior, no less human because it is related to colleges and universities. When really important matters are at stake, will the college act with others or for itself? Will "our own" be more attractive even than something that promises to exceed the sum of the parts?

The appropriate question for institutions contemplating possible cooperation is not: What do we have in common? Rather, it is: what can we do better in common, and what *will* we do? The answers are very different. The active doing together, in contrast to the passive "having" together, calls for purpose, organization, means, and will; and in proportion as these are understood and supplied, cooperation offers a valuable new dimension.

SOURCES FOR FURTHER INFORMATION

Chambers, M. M.: *Voluntary Statewide Coordination in Public Higher Education,* University of Michigan, Ann Arbor, Mich., 1961.

Ertell, Merton W.: *Interinstitutional Cooperation in Higher Education,* University of the State of New York, Albany, N.Y., 1957.

Fields, Ralph R.: *Interinstitutional Cooperation among the Associated Colleges of the Mid-Hudson Area: A Report to the Council of Presidents,* Associated Colleges of the Mid-Hudson Area, Poughkeepsie, N.Y., June, 1964. (mimeographed.)

First Annual Report, Associated Rocky Mountain Universities, Boulder, Colo., 1960.

"Interinstitutional Cooperation in Graduate Education," *School and Society,* vol. 91, April, 1963.

Johnson, E. L.: "Cooperation in Higher Education," *Liberal Education,* vol. 48, December, 1962.

Martorana, S. V., James C. Messersmith, and Lawrence O. Nelson: *Cooperative Projects among Colleges and Universities,* U.S. Office of Education, Washington, D.C., 1961.

Oliver, Kenneth: "The Small College and the Big Crisis," *College and University,* vol. 36, pp. 7–13, Fall, 1960.

272   BUNNELL AND JOHNSON

Packard, Sidney R.: "Academic Cooperation," *The Educational Record,* vol. 40, pp. 358–363, October, 1959.

Stewart, Blair: "Cooperation by Independent Colleges: The Associated Colleges of the Midwest," *Liberal Education,* vol. 47, pp. 360–366, October, 1961.

Wittich, John J. (ed.): *Proceedings of the Conference on College and University Interinstitutional Cooperation, Princeton, New Jersey, April, 1962,* College Center of the Finger Lakes, Corning, N.Y., 1962.

JOHN DALE RUSSELL

12

dollars and cents:
some hard facts

*I*n 1957–1958, *educational and general expenditures for the*
nation's institutions of higher education were put at 3.6 billion
dollars. One recent estimate indicates that these expenditures will
rise 170 per cent, to 9.8 billion dollars by 1969–1970.[1]

The tremendous amounts of funds now being required in higher
education and the prospects of even greater expenditures in the
decades ahead have been the cause of great concern to those
responsible for college and university management. It seems clear
that all the present sources from which financial support is drawn
will need to be tapped to the utmost to meet the increasing

[1] Mel Elfin, Bernard Asbell, Alvin Toffler, Margaret Farmer, and James
J. Morisseau, *Bricks and Mortarboards: A Report on College Planning
and Building,* Educational Facilities Laboratories, Inc., New York, 1964,
p. 12.

demands. It is equally clear that new sources will have to be
discovered and new methods of obtaining supporting income
developed.

This chapter is concerned with the problem of financing higher
education. Attention is given to some factors affecting current
needs for funds, economies that might be achieved in the present
operation of colleges and universities, and prospects for future
support as they relate to endowment earnings, philanthropic gifts,
and tuition and to local, state, and Federal governments.

SOME FACTORS IN THE CURRENT SITUATION

The poverty of colleges and universities is notorious and perennial. While various phases of the financial problem affect different kinds of institutions in different ways, there is sufficient commonality of situations within the colleges and universities of the country to warrant a general discussion of the problems. The current situation can best be considered in relation to two basic categories commonly used in financial accounting and reporting: (1) current funds and (2) capital funds.

Factors affecting the need for current funds

Current funds are those which may be used up in a relatively short period of time, such as a year, for the ordinary operating expenses of the institution. They include funds for salaries and wages, supplies, utilities, and maintenance.

Most colleges and universities have always faced a struggle to get enough current-fund income to maintain their customary levels and volume of service. Although this situation has existed ever since there were colleges, several aspects are relatively new and can be expected in the future to become more and more serious.

INCREASING ENROLLMENTS.   The number of students who want higher education and for whom it must be provided is rapidly increasing. The current high levels of college enrollment in the

United States seem certain to double within the next ten or fifteen years, barring unforeseen contingencies.

Some colleges probably will choose not to accept an increased number of students; they will become more selective in their admissions policies. Such colleges and universities will avoid the need for additional current-fund support that arises from the pressures of expanding enrollments. The number of institutions, however, that will choose this course probably will be small.

A substantial part of the increased enrollment will be served by newly established institutions, particularly the new public junior colleges. Chapter 1 indicates that 146 institutions of higher learning were established between 1961 and 1964. These newly established institutions, however, may tend also to contribute to the trend toward increasing enrollments, especially those which are located in communities where the residents previously had little or no opportunity to attend college while living at home. The location of an institution in such a community tends to increase the percentage of high school graduates going on to college from that community. Thus the establishment of new institutions will bring only small relief of pressures for increasing enrollments at existing institutions.

Most colleges and universities now existing will therefore find their enrollments continuing to increase rapidly for the next two decades. These institutions must find new current support, at least in proportion to the increases in enrollment, if the quality of their services is to be maintained. There are some institutions whose present volume of service is below the level for efficient operation; these can expand enrollments with a rate of increase in expenditures somewhat less than the rate of increase in number of students. Some of the additional students, for example, will only fill up classes that are presently smaller than they need to be and will not require additional faculty members for the instructional program. But most colleges of 1,000 students or more that are at present operating economically will be forced to add current-fund income as rapidly as enrollments increase if they are to maintain the present quality of their services.

RESEARCH. Long recognized as a function of higher education, research today is making extraordinary demands for increased support. Most junior colleges and many liberal arts colleges do not consider research an important function in their programs; such institutions may escape severe pressure to obtain additional funds for the support of research. Even such institutions, however, experience some pressure for research support because of the tremendous prestige of this activity in the academic world. Capable young scholars, invited to join the teaching staff of such a college, sometimes are reluctant to accept appointment unless assured of funds for research and some release from a full teaching load to give them time for research and writing.

At the opposite extreme are a few universities and institutes of technology so noted for their interest and success in research that they are almost overwhelmed with requests to undertake specific research projects, usually accompanied by ample funds. Agencies such as the Federal government and industrial organizations are eager to purchase the services of institutions where there are faculty members considered especially competent to carry on the needed research. In some of these institutions, the dollar volume of so-called contract research is greater than that of the total instructional program for students. In one respect a financial problem does not arise in the institutions carrying a big program of contract research. Some projects, particularly those from certain agencies of the Federal government, do not provide sufficient support to cover the additional overhead costs that research imposes on the university. Thus the institution may have to curtail some other activities in order to carry the temptingly large research projects it undertakes.

In between the two extremes—the colleges in which little or no research is supported and the universities enjoying bountiful support from outside agencies for limited kinds of research—are large numbers of universities and some colleges which feel great pressure to increase their research activity and which must seek funds for its support. Institutions ambitious to move up on the scale of academic recognition generally try to follow the route of increasing the volume and quality of research by faculty members. This route to enhanced status in the academic "pecking order" is usually much speedier than any corresponding effort in improving the quality of instruction. The policy of increasing research activity usually involves the bringing in of some new (and hitherto unneeded) faculty members, usually in the highest salary brackets. In exceedingly fortunate circumstances, a university may even be able to snare a Nobel Prize winner at a salary totally incongruent with the salaries of the most capable members of the present faculty, who have long rendered faithful and effective service. If the university is fortunate enough to have a faculty member who is becoming noted for his research (or his ability to wangle research contracts from the Federal government), his salary must be advanced rapidly if he is to be retained in the face of competitive bids from other universities. All this is expensive and creates a demand for sharp increases in the level of financial support for current operations.

Funds for the support of research in certain aspects of science and technology are at present rather abundantly supplied by the Federal government and by industry. Correspondingly generous funds to support research in the humanities and the social sciences are not available from these sources. Universities that have some conscience about a research program that is appropriately balanced among the various fields of knowledge face a difficult problem in finding the necessary supporting funds.

IMPROVEMENT IN QUALITY. It is not sufficient merely to get the additional current funds that are necessary to provide instructional services to rapidly increasing numbers of students or to extend the research services of a college or university. Most institutions feel an urgent need for funds to improve the quality of their services, particularly in the instructional area. In fact, the better the college now is, the more urgent is the feeling of need for improvement. Most such improvement comes quickly to be translated into a necessity for additional supporting funds.

Realization of the need for improvement in faculty salaries is today widespread among college and university authorities. The annual studies of salary scales by the American Association of University Professors and the accompanying rating of institutions have provided stimulation for, and a sense of urgency concerning, the provision of better faculty salaries. Enough institutions are now seriously attempting to upgrade salaries so that the competitive market is deeply affected. Well-qualified scholars for faculty positions are, furthermore, in short supply, and this at a time when increasing enrollments require the employment of additional instructors. Thus the demand for faculty members of superior qualifications, urgently needed for the improvement of the institution's services, will most certainly force a continued rise in salary rates. The result is a heavy additional burden on the current-fund budget, which must be met by an increase in supporting income.

Costs of higher education, other than faculty salaries, are also rising. A competent professor should be provided with adequate clerical and other assistants. Unionization of the plant staff and other nonacademic employees, coming increasingly to be the pattern in institutions located in cities, generally forces the adoption of higher wage scales and costly fringe benefits. There is scarcely an item used in higher education that has not had its unit cost increased markedly in recent years. Institutions are constantly adding new equipment or processes; these are not mere "gadgets" to satisfy the manipulative instincts of staff members but in most cases are introduced as a means of directly improving the institution's services. A good example is the language laboratories recently installed in many colleges and universities over the country. The effectiveness of such an installation in the improvement of language instruction is amply demonstrated, but the whole setup requires new money from somewhere, and it usually must be staffed and operated by additional personnel. The net effect is indeed an improvement in services but also an increase in the needs for current-fund support.

GRADUATE AND ADVANCED PROFESSIONAL STUDIES. A substantial part of the increased demand for higher education in these times is occurring at the graduate level and in advanced professional studies. Costs per student tend to run much higher in curricula for students who already hold the bachelor's degree than in courses for undergraduates. Programs at the Ph.D. level are particularly expensive to maintain when competent staff members and adequate facilities are provided. The graduate-level courses tend to be highly specialized, and classes are usually much smaller than at the undergraduate level. The net result of increases in enrollment of advanced students is thus a requirement for larger amounts of supporting income per student than would be needed for corresponding increases of undergraduates.

The problem of increased enrollments in graduate and advanced professional studies is at present a concern chiefly at the universities. The Federal government now offers some assistance, through funds provided by the National Defense Education Act, to institutions introducing new programs for the Ph.D. degree or expanding present programs at that level. There is no corresponding aid for new or expanded programs at the master's degree level. Current conditions force every institution engaged in teacher preparation to consider seriously the advisability of offering graduate studies at least to the master's degree level. Only with this fifth year of studies can the program for teacher preparation be considered reasonably complete.

Too often, institutional authorities are induced to set up a new program of graduate study on the promise that "it won't cost anything." Some superficial reasoning or hastily accumulated data may indicate such a probability, but this is rarely found to be the case in actual practice. If the new program is truly offered at the graduate level and does not consist solely of some renumbering of present undergraduate courses without changing their content, it will inevitably entail additional cost. The emergent program of graduate studies is in many institutions an important new burden on the current operating budget.

Factors affecting the need for capital funds

The second major category in financial classification is known as "capital funds." Outlays are included in this category when they provide things that are relatively permanent, such as land, buildings, and major improvements. It is characteristic of most capital outlays that they are nonrecurring; that is, the same sort of expenditure is not repeated year after year. Thus the building of a new library is not an anuual occurrence but is an extraordinary event and usually takes some kind of extraordinary financing.

PHYSICAL-PLANT FACILITIES.   Today colleges and universities need new capital funds mostly for the expansion of physical-plant facilities. Mention was made earlier of the extraordinarily large increases that are occurring in enrollments, which may be expected to continue at least for the next twenty years. The additional students will need additional classrooms, laboratories, libraries, and dormitories and more of the other kinds of buildings usually required on a college campus.[2] Building costs tend to be high. It is almost frightening to realize that in the next ten or fifteen years, colleges and universities in the United States will have need for twice the plant facilities now in use.

ENDOWMENT.   Another kind of capital fund is endowment, defined as assets held by the institution in perpetuity, to be used for no purpose other than the production of income. The capital of the

[2] For a fuller discussion of developments in this area, see Chap. 7, Facilities and Learning: An Overview of Developments.

endowment fund is kept invested, and the income received from it is used to support the operation of the institution.

Traditionally, heavy emphasis has been laid on the accumulation of endowment by colleges and universities. For many years the accrediting agencies set rigid standards of endowment holdings as a major requirement for membership and recognition of privately controlled institutions of higher education. This emphasis has changed somewhat in the United States during the past two or three decades.

Every institution naturally welcomes gifts to its endowment fund, and many are actively seeking to increase the amount of their endowment. The "new" factor in the situation, however, is that institutions are not under the extreme pressure they formerly felt for increases in endowment funds. Perhaps this is only because the other needs seem so overwhelmingly great.

SOME POSSIBLE ECONOMIES IN INSTITUTIONAL OPERATIONS

One way of meeting the problem of increasing costs in higher education is to improve the efficiency and economy of institutional on-going operations, so that present resources can be used with maximum effectiveness and so that facilities can be utilized as fully as is consistent with a good quality of service. This is by no means a new idea in higher education. Economies in operation were introduced by most colleges and universities during the Depression of the 1930s. But when times are relatively prosperous and only normal growth is being experienced, most institutions, facing new developments they wish to undertake, find it easier to go out and get new money. Currently, however, when additional expenditures seem imperative and when corresponding increases in supporting income do not seem immediately possible, many institutions look for economies in their operations and exploit this method of balancing the budget. A few examples might be mentioned of areas in institutional operations that are likely to yield "pay dirt" when examined for possible economies. The mention of these examples is possibly hazardous, for it must not be assumed that each possibility applies equally to all institutions. Yet there is a strong probability that most institutions would find opportunity for economy in operations in one or more of the areas cited below.

Plant-space utilization

Could more students be accommodated in the present classrooms and laboratories without impairing the quality of the instructional program? If so, the needs for additional capital outlay funds might be scaled down a bit. Around 15 or 20 per cent of the current operating expeditures of colleges and universities is devoted to plant operation and maintenance, and an overextended plant throws an unnecessary burden on the annual current operating budget. To assist in making analyses of plant use, the American Association of Collegiate Registrars and Admissions Officers has prepared a manual[3] giving directions for collecting and organizing the data on use of classrooms. The resulting analysis permits direct comparison with the results of similar studies in other institutions.

In half the institutions in the country, the average general classroom is occupied by a class less than twenty-one class periods per week, an average of a little more than four hours a day on the basis of a five-day week. For teaching laboratories, the corresponding figure is seventeen class periods per week, or a little more than three hours a day on the basis of a five-day week. The range in utilization is wide, both for institutional averages and for individual rooms or different buildings in a given institution. Even in a college where the overall utilization is low, it is common to find some one or more buildings in which the classrooms are used thirty-five or more periods per week on the average. The question immediately arises as to why the utilization in all buildings, and hopefully in all institutions, cannot be pushed up to this figure. Indeed, some few institutions do report an average use of classrooms for thirty-five periods or more per week, but almost without exception these are located in the larger cities and have a heavy program of evening and night classes; use of rooms for evening programs for part-time students may push up the average utilization by ten or fifteen periods per week.

Another view of the utilization of instructional space may be obtained by looking at the number of periods per week that the average classroom seat or laboratory desk is occupied. In the typical situation, when classrooms are in use only about half the

[3] John Dale Russell and James I. Doi, *Manual for Studies of Space Utilization in Colleges and Universities,* American Association of Collegiate Registrars and Admissions Officers, Ohio University, Athens, Ohio, 1957.

seats in the rooms are occupied by students. In half the colleges and universities in the nation, each classroom seat or laboratory desk is occupied only eleven periods per week or less (a little more than two hours a day on the basis of a five-day week). Thus it would be theoretically possible to accommodate almost twice the number of students presently enrolled, without organizing any more classes or building any more classrooms, just by filling the seats that are now vacant in the rooms when classes are meeting. One must hasten to point out that this theoretical improvement in utilization is scarcely worthy of consideration as a practical matter, for it would force students to attend institutions where space is available and to take courses they do not want or need, merely because seats in the class were available.

Improvement in the number of periods per week classrooms are occupied by classes usually means the scheduling of classes at hours that are presently unpopular, such as those in the late afternoon. This is likely to meet with resistance, and usually the courses at those hours will be avoided by students if at all possible. Changes in the habits of students (and professors) seem difficult to effect by administrative means. Any institution, on the basis of a survey of its instructional-space utilization, can readily calculate how many additional students it could accommodate under given conditions of class scheduling and other factors. With few exceptions, institutions generally would find room for considerable expansions in enrollment in the present instructional space without too drastic an alteration in the work habits and mores of faculty members and students.

It should be noted that instructional space is only a fraction of the total physical-plant space in the typical college or university. Requirements for other kinds of facilities, such as residence halls, dining rooms, libraries, administrative offices, faculty offices, conference rooms, auditoriums, gymnasiums, etc., must be considered when estimating the maximum number of students that can be accommodated in the present plant. Quite commonly one of these kinds of facilities proves to be the bottleneck that limits the acceptance of additional students. Often a relatively small capital outlay to relieve such a bottleneck may open up possibilities for accommodating substantially larger enrollments in the institution.

The traditional academic year of nine months has often been mentioned as a cause of low utilization of physical plants in educational institutions. Chapter 10 presents a discussion of the advantages and disadvantages of year-round-calendar plans and of the possibilities these plans hold for increasing the carrying capacities of colleges and universities.

Instructional programs

In the typical college or university, more than half the budget for all current educational and general purposes is expended for the function of instruction, with faculty salaries as the principal item under this function. The sheer size of the expenditure for this function suggests the possibility of a search for economies in its operation. Analyses of the instructional programs in many colleges and universities have found large opportunities for savings, which might be used to improve the salaries of the competent members of the faculty or for other urgent purposes. The analyses deal with such factors as the average size of classes in the various subjects and at different academic levels, the percentage of classes that are smaller than necessary, the teaching loads of faculty members, and the ratio of student credit hour to full-time-equivalent member of the instructional staff.

The greatest opportunity for improving efficiency in the instructional program lies in a conservative attitude toward adding new staff members. The plea of a department for an additional instructor should be justified, not on the grounds of the natural inclination to gain prestige by expanding the staff, but on the coldly appraised needs of the program of instruction that must be maintained. The proliferation of course, mostly with enrollments of fewer than ten students, is one of the surest ways of dissipating not only financial resources but, even worse, also the time and energy of scholars at a time when competent faculty members are in extremely short supply.

Mechanization of processes

Many universities and some colleges have introduced new electronic computing and recording mechanisms, which enable certain operations to be performed with far less manpower and in a much shorter time than by older, manual processes. Among the functions for which electronic tabulation is especially useful are financial accounting, payrolls, student registration in classes, recording of students' grades, computation of students' grade-point averages, and reporting of enrollments. New developments and particularly the availability of service centers where the data on punched cards can be processed, without the institution actually having to install the very expensive machines on its premises, have made the process valuable for one or more functions in almost any college.

Offices of institutional research

There is a distinct trend among well-administered universities (and some colleges as well) toward the setting up of an office or bureau of institutional research to facilitate studies of operational problems. Such an agency is usually attached directly to the highest administrative level in the institution, preferably the office of the president or of the executive vice-president. The office of institutional research is assigned specific responsibility for carrying on studies needed for the making of important decisions regarding policy or procedure.

Improvement in the efficiency of institutional operations has a double effect on finances. The primary goal is to save money that may be used to better advantage. Such a saving, if there is no adverse effect on the quality of justifiable scope of the program, is the equivalent of a gift of the same amount.

Even with the maximum attention to internal economies, colleges and universities in the United States are going to continue to need rapidly increasing amounts of financial support during at least the next two decades. Belt tightening is usually a "one-shot" procedure; once it has been accomplished, it cannot be repeated to show still further economies in the same procedure. Where are the funds to come from that will be so vitally needed for the support of higher education in the years immediately ahead? What new sources are being developed, and what trends are evident in present sources? In the remainder of this chapter, each of the major possible sources of increased income for higher education will be examined.

SOME SOURCES OF SUPPORT: PROSPECTS FOR THE FUTURE

Earnings of endowment and other invested funds have long been a mainstay in the financial support of colleges and universities. Back in the 1880s, when reliable reports about income and expenditure for higher education first became available on a nationwide basis in the United States, endowment earnings were supplying more than half the income used for current educational and general purposes. At present in the United States, endowment earnings supply less than 5 per cent of the total income of higher education used for educational and general purposes, and this percentage shows no signs of increasing. It is true that some favored institutions hold large endowments and receive a very substantial share of their income from that source, but there are also large numbers of colleges and universities with no endowment at all or with only limited amounts of productive funds.

The decrease in the percentage of current support from endowment income does not mean that the totals of endowment investments or the amounts of income therefrom are diminishing; indeed, they increase regularly. But the increase in endowment capital and investment earnings is not as rapid as the increase in total expenditure.

The reduction in the share of support provided by endowment earnings is not due solely to the failure to increase the capital of endowment as rapidly as current educational and general expenditures have increased. Interest rates are substantially lower than they were in the earlier decades of this century. With ordinary "safe" investments yielding only about 4 per cent, it takes 1.5 million dollars of endowment investment to yield the same dollar income that 1 million dollars yielded when it could be invested at 6 per cent.

Another factor in the situation is the tendency, during the past quarter century, for college and university boards of trustees to invest substantial portions of their endowment funds in common stocks. This was originally viewed as a hedge against inflation and as a means of stabilizing the purchasing power of the income from investments. Both these objectives are highly commendable. In many institutions, however, the investment program began to be motivated by the idea of increasing the capital of the invested funds through the rise in value of the securities held. In such circumstances, the principal objective of the investment program was diverted from its true purpose—earning income for the support of the institution's current operations—to an ulterior purpose of capital gains for the increase of the endowment holdings. Almost inevitably, under such a plan a large part of the securities purchased and held were "growth" stocks and had low price-earnings ratios. In other words, current income for the support of the institution's operations was sacrificed in order to take on a speculative risk of increasing the endowment capital.

Professors' salaries, as everyone knows, are paid out of income, not out of the "book value" or the "market value" of the securities in the endowment portfolio. Thus the investment manager may make a highly gratifying report to the trustees that the common stocks in the endowment portfolio now have a current market value of double the book value, or the amount of endowment funds invested in them. But if these securities are paying dividends amounting to only 1½ to 2 per cent of their market value, the support of the institution's current operating program is in no way advantaged and may actually suffer. This shift in emphasis in the investment program was occurring at the very time when faculty salaries, relative to purchasing power and relative to salaries in other callings, were falling far behind.

The future prospects for increased support from endowment earnings are not bright. There is no hope that gifts to endowment can possibly come in as fast as the new demands for support arise in the next ten to twenty years. A gift of 1 million dollars to the endowment fund will provide in perpetuity about $40,000 annually in additional support to the current operating budget of a college. The same gift, if made not as an endowment but as a fund expendable over a ten-year period, will provide about $120,000 a year for the ensuing ten years. In the present situation, a college is better off to have assurance of $120,000 additional income each year for the next ten years than to have assurance of $40,000 a year in perpetuity. The improvement in an institution's program that is made possible by a substantial increase in current-fund income over a period of ten years is perhaps the best guarantee that by the end of the period, the college will be in a most favorable position to continue to attract even larger gifts for its support.

Philanthropic gifts

Philanthropic gifts from nongovernmental sources also provide financial support for higher education. In the past, the great bulk of the philanthropic gifts to colleges and universities has been designated for capital purposes, particularly for additions to endowment funds and for physical-plant facilities.

Ever since about 1930, a number of crystal gazers have been forecasting a drying up of the stream of philanthropic gifts. These observers have believed that the accumulation of large personal fortunes, such as supplied many notable gifts to higher education in earlier decades, was no longer possible under the modern system of taxation and economic organization. The forecasts have proved to be wide of the mark, at least in the conclusion about the trend in total gifts and grants from private sources to higher education. Colleges and universities have continued to receive philanthropic gifts, as they did in the past, in large as well as small amounts for all purposes.

What is new in the field of philanthropic giving to higher education is the relatively large increases in the amounts for *current,* as well as for capital, purposes. In the cases of the gifts for current purposes, the entire amount can be used for such objects of annual expenditure as faculty salaries, scholarships, library books, and other operating expenses of the institution. Gifts of this sort only two or three decades ago provided less than 5 per cent of the support for the total current educational and general expenditures in American higher education. Today almost one-tenth of the total support is derived from such gifts. The increase has been principally due to new trends of giving from three important sources.

Corporations. It had long been held that corporations were forbidden by law to make charitable donations. The decision of the court in the Standard Oil case completely reversed this line of legal reasoning, and corporations may now legally make contributions to charitable organizations. Large numbers of corporations now annually make gifts to institutions of higher education, and the amounts of income from this source are often substantial.

Alumni. Sporadic drives among alumni for contributions have long been characteristic episodes in the financial history of a great many colleges and universities. During the past two or three decades, the program of alumni contributions has been systematized into annual giving campaigns. These are usually well organized and have proved increasingly productive in most institutions. In each of a number of colleges and universities, the annual "gift" from alumni for current purposes totals 1 million dollars or more.

Church groups. A great many of the so-called "church-related" colleges and universities have long had some support from their constituent churches for current operating purposes. Many of the church groups in recent years have taken renewed interest in providing more substantial support than formerly for their institutions of higher education and have stepped up markedly the level of their contributions.

Typical of this trend are the end-of-year figures from the *Higher Education Report* of the Methodist Church, which show an increase in giving to higher education of more than $4,540,000 between 1960–1961 and 1962–1963. During 1962–1963, over $17,223,000 was contributed to higher education through Methodist annual conferences. The figure for the year 1960–1961 was $12,681,715.[4]

Foundations. It has been chiefly during the twentieth century that the endowed foundation has emerged as a source of substantial support for higher education. The number and strength of the foundations having an interest in higher education have grown rapidly during the past two decades. A few of them have truly tremendous sums to distribute. The foundations have provided funds for endowment, for plant facilities, and for current operating purposes. Institutions under public control, as well as those which are privately controlled, have been beneficiaries of foundation grants. Foundation support of higher education is quite commonly characterized by two sorts of restrictions. Under the first type, the grants are frequently on a matching basis, the institution being obligated to raise an amount proportionate to the foundation's gift. Formerly the matching was on a one-to-one basis, but it has been pushed up, until now one of the largest of the foundations typically requires an institution to provide $5 from other sources for every $2 given as a grant, and sometimes the matching is on a one-dollar-for-three basis. Under the second type of restriction, the grants are nearly always limited to some specific purpose or project, usually relatively narrow in scope, something that the institution is not now doing and would not do without the added funds provided by the philanthropy. Thus a college is likely to feel pressure to come up with some novel proj-

[4] Dr. Woodrow A. Geier, director, Department of Information and Publications, Board of Education, the Methodist Church, Division of Higher Education, Nashville, Tenn., letter of Sept. 9, 1964.

ect or new program, known to be within the interest of the foundation, in the hope of attracting favorable attention to its appeal for a supporting grant.

On the whole, support from endowed foundations has been both welcome and beneficial to the colleges and universities of the country. Occasionally fears have been expressed that with so much money at their disposal, the authorities in charge of the foundations may be able subtly to control the direction of American higher education or to exert an exterior form of control over the supposedly independent colleges and universities.

The increases in philanthropic giving to higher education have been definitely stimulated by a number of factors:

1. A fairly generous deduction is allowed for charitable contributions in computing Federal (and most state) income taxes. A taxpayer in the higher brackets can make a very substantial contribution without affecting his own net income.
2. The establishment of the Council for Financial Aid to Higher Education has done much to stimulate philanthropic giving to colleges and universities, especially by corporations. The council, with headquarters in New York City, has maintained an effective staff for publicizing the needs of higher education and for the encouraging annual gifts to colleges and universities.
3. The Advertising Council of America in recent years has made higher education one of its special annual projects. Advertising space in all sorts of media—newspapers, magazines, billboards, car and bus cards, etc.—has been donated by large advertisers and used effectively to call public attention to the needs of colleges and universities for financial support. Because of this publicity, there can scarcely be a citizen anywhere in the country who has not been informed of the fact that higher education urgently needs increased financial support.
4. The Alumni Council, a federation of the alumni organizations of a large number of colleges and universities, has been effective in working out plans and disseminating information about programs of alumni giving.
5. In a majority of the states, the stronger privately controlled colleges and universities have formed associations or "foundations" for fund-raising purposes. They pool their efforts at soliciting funds from corporations, and each member institution shares in the total gifts on a formula basis. In the usual

procedure, the presidents of two institutions go together for a visit to a top executive of a corporation to solicit a gift, not to their individual institutions, but to the foundation. This procedure has been effective in developing mutually beneficial contacts between the institutional presidents and the corporation executives, with each gaining a new respect for the other. These state foundations are federated in a national organization, effectively staffed for assisting the local efforts, with headquarters in New York City.

6. The job of fund raising for higher education is rapidly becoming a profession. Men are becoming available who have been specifically trained for this kind of work and who have been successful at it. Increasingly, colleges are placing such officials on their administrative staffs.

The forecast for continued support of higher education by philanthropic gifts is entirely optimistic. The dollar volume of such support is still relatively small, in comparison with the total needs of higher education, but the significant fact is that the total current income from this source has been increasing faster than the total expenditures for educational and general purposes.

Student fees

Institutions of higher education have for centuries depended on student fees as a major source of financial support. The chief new development to be reported concerns the rapidly increasing fee. The charging of fees is not universal among institutions in the United States, however, and the degree of dependence on student fees varies greatly among institutions. Privately controlled colleges and universities in general depend heavily on student-fee income for their support. Some privately controlled colleges and universities have almost no other source of financial support, and the income from student fees supplies 95 per cent or more of the current operating budget. At the other extreme are a few privately controlled institutions that charge no fees whatever to students. These institutions limit their enrollments and their programs of instruction to what can be supported by their income from endowment and from philanthropic gifts. For the entire country, student fees annually provide about 60 per cent of current costs in institutions under private control.

Publicly controlled institutions generally charge fees that are much lower than those charged by privately controlled colleges and universities. The state institutions generally have two different rates of fees, one for residents of the state and the other, typically much higher, for nonresidents. In the typical state university or college, student-fee income provides about 20 per cent of the support needed for the current educational and general program. Many junior colleges charge no tuition fees; this is the practice throughout California, the state having the largest number of junior colleges, and also in a number of individual junior colleges in other states.

Traditionally in the United States, student fees have been a source of support for only the current operating budget of the college or university. A new development that has made considerable headway during the past two or three decades is the levying of charges on students to support capital outlay programs, particularly for additions to physical plants. In most colleges and universities of the country, the permanent dormitories constructed since the end of World War II have been financed in large part by borrowings from the Federal government, under special provisions enacted by Congress. The loans are expected to be repaid from the earnings of the facilities. The institution, in borrowing the funds, agrees to set the charges to those occupying the facilities at a rate that will provide an annual surplus over operating costs sufficient to meet the charges for interest on the loan (at a relatively low rate) and the amortization of the principal. Thus at the end of the mortgage period, some thirty, forty, or fifty years after construction, the institution will own a debt-free building that will have been paid for, in large part at least, by charges levied as fees against students.

In many institutions, all students are assessed a special "building fee," the proceeds of which are used to finance the construction of general-purpose buildings, such as a library or classroom building. In a number of states, the publicly controlled institutions of higher education are authorized to borrow funds for constructing buildings, the security for the loan being the pledge to charge students a special fee large enough to meet annual charges for interest on, and repayment of, the loan.

The general trend in the amount of fees charged the individual student has been steadily upward for at least the past one hundred years. When the dollar amounts of the average fee charged per student are plotted year by year over the period since 1860, the resulting curve is exponential and is positively accelerated. The rate of increase has been spectacular since the end of World War II, and apparently no slackening of the trend is in sight.

Careful studies have repeatedly shown that the cost of college attendance is a serious barrier to the continued education of many highly capable high school graduates. Consequently, almost all colleges and universities have some provisions for financial assistance to students in the form of scholarship grants, loan funds, and part-time employment.

However, recognition of the inadequacy of institutional funds for financial assistance has led the Federal government, under the National Defense Education Act, to provide funds for long-term loans to students. The new Federal funds have made it possible for a student to begin a program of borrowing in his or her freshman year and to continue the borrowing through five years of college attendance, with five years after graduation in which to repay the loan.

The policy of supporting higher education in part by money borrowed by students, which they must repay shortly after graduation, is a curious modern-day reversal of the traditional practice of one generation providing the support for the education of the next generation. Normally it is expected that the student's fee for attending college will be paid by his parents—indeed the term might better be "parent fee" instead of "student fee." But when students borrow the money to pay their fees, expecting to repay the loan after graduation, *their* generation is supporting its own education. The preceding generation—after getting *its* education at the expense of the generation that preceded it—has failed to provide for the education of the following generation. The national student loan program apparently has been adopted without adequate consideration of the significance of abandoning a centuries-old tradition.

The charging of fees to students in publicly controlled colleges and universities is something of an anomaly, for public education at other levels, elementary and secondary, has long been free to the pupil in every state in the country. In a day when higher education is recognized as vital to the public welfare, just as elementary and secondary education have long been recognized, it would be logical for colleges and universities under public control to be tuition-free. Historically, the student-fee system in public higher education is a carryover from the days when all higher education was privately controlled. The early constitutions of several Middle Western states promised a tuition-free system of education extending through the state university, but this promise has never been realized in practice. In some states even today, the charges to students cannot be labeled a "tuition" fee but must be given some other designation, such as "maintenance" fee, because of constitutional restrictions. Even if the authorities that determine state policies in higher education were disposed to reduce student fees or to abandon them altogether as a source of support, they would doubtless find great pressure to continue the fee system. The privately controlled institutions often feel at a competitive disadvantage with respect to their ability to attract students because of the relatively low fees charged in the state colleges and universities.

Trends in support from student fees are somewhat difficult to forecast. It seems probable that privately controlled colleges and universities will generally continue to obtain at least the present percentage of their total support from student fees. To do this, while the cost per student continues to rise, will mean that most privately controlled colleges and universities will increase their charges to students. As in the past, increases in the rate of fees charged will to some extent be offset by expansions in the program of financial assistance to students in the privately controlled institutions.

There is a possibility that locally controlled junior colleges or community colleges, maintained as a part of local public school systems, will increasingly adopt the policy of keeping tuition charges at a minimum or of charging no fees at all. Among some leaders in state universities and colleges, there is a tendency to try to hold the line against further increases in fees for residents of the state or even to advocate reductions in fee charges. The fees charged in publicly controlled institutions for nonresidents of the state, however, may be expected to increase very substantially. If past trends continue, members of the state legislatures can be expected to continue to bring pressures on the publicly controlled colleges and universities to obtain maximum support from sources other than appropriated tax funds and to suggest increases in student fees rather than increases in appropriations.

Government appropriations

Appropriations of funds from governmental sources have long been the major support of publicly controlled higher education in the United States. Three levels of government—local, state, and Federal—contribute funds for the support of higher education.

LOCAL GOVERNMENTS. More than three hundred units of local government—cities, counties, or school districts—maintain junior colleges or community colleges in the United States. These institutions in almost all cases receive a substantial part of their support from the tax moneys of the local governmental unit that maintains them. The number of these locally controlled community colleges is steadily increasing. A few of the larger cities also maintain a municipal university and support it from tax-derived funds. In general, the support of an institution of university proportions proves to be a heavy burden on the taxpayers of a municipality, and the number of such universities is decreasing. A recent study reports that only a dozen remain in the United States.

STATE GOVERNMENTS. The bulk of the funds used for the support of publicly controlled higher education in the United States comes from funds appropriated by state governments. Every state has at least one state university, which receives appropriated funds for its support, and all the states except those with the smallest populations maintain several colleges or universities. There are almost four hundred state-controlled institutions of higher education in the United States.

In addition to the support from state-appropriated funds to the state-controlled institutions of higher education, there is a general tendency for the state to appropriate funds for distribution to its local junior colleges or community colleges. This financial assistance is usually distributed on a formula basis, somewhat like the provision of state funds for the maintenance of locally controlled elementary and secondary schools.

Some states in which there are municipal universities give some support from state-appropriated funds to these institutions.

Sometimes this support is limited to a particular phase of the program of the municipal university, such as a medical school, teacher preparation, or the junior college function of the first two college years. Most municipal universities that do not now receive financial assistance from their states are trying to get it. Some have in the past found that the step from state financial assistance to direct state control is an easy one and have changed their status from that of a municipal university to that of a state-controlled university.

A few states make grants of appropriated funds to privately controlled colleges and universities, although in most states this is considered unconstitutional. Pennsylvania leads all other states in the amounts given to privately controlled universities. Maryland gives annual grants to the Johns Hopkins University for the maintenance of its School of Engineering and smaller amounts to a number of other privately controlled colleges for teacher education. Florida appropriates state funds to support a medical school at a privately controlled university.

A number of states appropriate funds to maintain a system of scholarship assistance for residents of the state. Perhaps the best known of these state scholarship systems is that in New York, where the so-called Regents Scholarships have a long history of providing financial assistance to high-ranking graduates of the state's high schools. A number of states in the South have provided scholarship plans, supported by state-appropriated funds, to enable Negro students to attend institutions in other states for programs not offered in any public institutions open to Negro students in their home state. Scholarship funds, it should be noted, are *not*, technically speaking, a financial support for higher education. They are rather a form of public welfare grant, merely enabling some students to attend college who would probably otherwise not find attendance possible.

FEDERAL GOVERNMENT. The government of the United States has long provided support for higher education, and the grants through congressional appropriations in recent years have increased rapidly in amount and also in the variety of programs supported. Every state upon its admission to the Union, since the admission of Ohio, in 1803, has received grants of Federal lands for the support of higher education. The Morrill Act of 1862 made further land grants to each state as an endowment for a new kind of college, which today is known as the "land-grant college." Subsequent extensions of the Morrill Act have provided Federal funds to these institutions for agricultural experiment stations, for the support of their general instructional programs, and for agricultural extension services. Federal funds for the college-level preparation of high school teachers of vocational subjects were provided in the Smith-Hughes Act of 1917; in subsequent acts the amounts of the funds were increased, and the scope of the programs aided was expanded. The preparation of reserve officers for the armed forces has been carried on at Federal expense in selected colleges and universities since 1920. Grants and loans for new construction were made to publicly controlled colleges and universities by the Federal government during the Depression of the 1930s under the Public Works Administration and the Works Progress Administration.

During World War II, the Federal government made heavy use of colleges and universities for providing specialized training of men and women in the armed forces, with full payment for the staff and facilities used. The GI Bill of Rights, although not designed as an aid to higher education, had a distinctly stimulating effect on colleges and universities. The program of the disposal of surplus government property, in effect since the close of the war, has been of inestimable benefit to hundreds of institutions, providing them with land, temporary buildings, and usable equipment of great variety.

Since 1940, the Federal government has given rapidly increasing support to research in institutions of higher education. Whether this can be classified as "support" of higher education is debatable. It is much more like the purchase of services, for the grants are almost invariably for specific projects, the results of which are expected to be valuable to some Federal agency, such as the Department of Defense.

Several Federal agencies, notably the National Science Foundation, are authorized to provide fellowships from Federal funds for advanced students in subjects thought to be currently vital to the national welfare, particularly the sciences. The National Defense Education Act of 1958 broke new ground in that it provided fellowship grants to students and funds to institutions for the extension of programs at the doctor's level into new fields or for the expansion of existing programs at that level. As previously noted, the act also provided loan funds for students, but these are properly construed as funds for aiding students and not as a direct aid to the operation of institutions of higher education.

Prospects for additional government support

The prospects for the needed additional support for higher education may be examined for each of the three levels of government—local, state, and Federal.

LOCAL GOVERNMENTS.   Increased support from tax sources in local governments (city, county, or school district) may be expected, but support from this source probably cannot expand as rapidly as enrollments increase in the next decade or two. Enrollments in locally controlled institutions of higher education, principally junior colleges or community colleges, will tend to increase much faster than the tax base of the units supporting these institutions. The rate of increase in total support from local governments will be controlled much more by the increases in the local tax base than by increases in enrollments.

Two factors will work toward an expansion of the total volume of support from local governments. The first is the creation of new community colleges or junior colleges in new locations, thus bringing in the resources of a new taxing unit for the support of higher education. The second is the probability of a new policy in the states where community colleges are becoming well established. By this policy, every local school unit not maintaining its own community college will be required to pay the transfer tuition charges of its residents who attend any community college in the state. This step is important, for it marks acceptance of the principle that every qualified citizen has the right to expect his own local community to provide fourteen years or grades of schooling, just as at present the right of every qualified citizen to twelve years of public school education is recognized in every state. When this step is taken, practically every local school unit, not just those that maintain junior colleges, will be providing basic support for higher education.

The other form of support of higher education from local governmental units, the maintenance of municipal universities, seems not to offer much prospect of increase. In general, the municipal universities get their local public support from a tax base that is restricted to the corporate limits of the city. The wealth that now tends to be heavily concentrated in suburban areas cannot be taxed for the support of the university as long as it remains a "city" institution. Efforts to widen the local tax base to include suburban territory are usually not looked upon favorably by the citizens. The readiest solution is to widen the base of support by seeking state grants, and from this it is but a step to the change of name and control from "municipal" to "state" university.

STATE GOVERNMENTS. If past trends continue, support from state governments can be expected to increase, but under the present revenue systems of most states, the limits of expansion are being reached. It seems clear that the greatest share of the burden of caring for the rapidly expanding enrollments will fall on the state-controlled colleges and universities. Most observers believe that the states will do well to maintain their appropriations for current operating expenses at the present amounts per student enrolled. Even this, in the period of most rapidly expanding enrollments, will put a severe strain on the tax resources of most states. In addition to the requirements for current operating expenses, a staggering sum will be needed for capital outlay purposes. It is difficult indeed to see how the states can meet the projected capital outlay needs under the present methods of financing new-plant construction.

Certainly the heavy investments in higher education that most states have been making in recent years will eventually begin to affect the economy and should produce a favorable change in the tax base that will later make the burden of support for higher education easier to bear. Probably these economic benefits of the expanding program of higher education cannot make themselves felt in time to meet the demands for tax support that will mount rapidly in almost every state during the next ten to twenty years.

What is needed is some kind of a breakthrough in the system of taxation at the state level to permit the raising of adequate revenues to finance the program of higher education. This would require invention of a new tax, comparable to the invention of the gasoline tax for financing highways. The prospects of such an invention for the benefit of higher education do not at present seem bright.

FEDERAL GOVERNMENT. As has been noted earlier in this chapter, the Federal government is already heavily involved in the support of higher education. The trends would indicate a continued rapid increase in the amount of support from Federal sources. Most Federal grants in the past have been limited to narrowly defined purposes, such as the land-grant colleges, vocational education, or research in certain highly specialized fields. The amount of Federal funds received in the past that has been available for the unrestricted use of the institution in support of its general operating budget is very small indeed. Yet this is the sort of support that is most useful and most needed in the current situation.

It should again be emphasized that Federal loans to colleges for dormitories, grants for fellowships for graduate students, loan funds for college students, and the purchase of institutional services are not "support" for higher education. Most certainly the institutions of higher education welcome these manifestations of Federal interest and concern about their activities, but none of these programs contributes a dime toward meeting the expenses a college or university must bear in providing instruction for its students. (An exception is the limited number of fellowship grants that carry, in addition to the stipend to the student, a grant to the university toward the support of the program the student is carrying.) In fact, some of these Federal programs actually subtract from the institutional funds available for providing education to students. An example of such a program is one involving research grants that have limits on administrative overhead below the actual costs to the university. Another example is the student loan fund, which places the burden of collecting loans (which are 90 per cent Federal money) on the institution, with no reimbursement for the expenses of collection.

The Federal government is undoubtedly able to bear the burden of increased support of higher education more easily than the state and local governments can. The needs of higher education for support would not loom so large in the Federal budget as they do in the budgets of state and local taxing authorities. Compared with the cost of a project to send a man to the moon, the total needs of higher education would appear modest indeed. What is needed, however, is broad, unrestricted support for educational and general purposes in institutions of higher education, rather than a continuation of piecemeal support for sharply limited purposes only.

The extensive provision of higher education in the United States by privately controlled colleges and universities poses a difficult question in the provision of support from Federal funds. Should public funds from the Federal government be used to support privately controlled—in many cases church-related—colleges and universities? Opinions differ sharply, even bitterly, when the issue of church-state relationships is considered. Many conscientious citizens feel strongly that government funds should not be used to support any church-sponsored activity. Authorities in some privately controlled colleges do not want to accept Federal funds for support (loans are a different matter), believing that if they accept support, their programs might eventually come under some objectionable form of Federal control. At the same time, leaders in most privately controlled colleges and universities would be unhappy to see large Federal funds granted *only* to publicly controlled institutions, for they fear this might ultimately relegate the privately controlled colleges and universities to a relatively minor place in American higher education.

The question of Federal aid to privately controlled institutions was the principal issue that defeated a promising bill for aid to higher education in the closing weeks of the Eighty-seventh Congress in 1962. A year later, however, differences that had existed among educators on this point were compromised. Near the end of the first session of the Eighty-eighth Congress in December, 1963, a bill was enacted providing Federal funds for grants and loans to institutions of higher education for buildings needed to care for the expanding enrollment. The signing of this bill by President Johnson marks an important breakthrough in the history of the financing of higher education. There are hopes that this is a first step toward a truly comprehensive program of Federal support for higher education. Many observers believe that the brightest prospect for obtaining the needed support for higher education is found in the Federal government. Achievement of this goal cannot be long delayed if institutions of higher education in the United States are to meet their obligations to the rapidly expanding numbers of students seeking a college education in the 1960s and 1970s.

SUMMARY: THE YEARS AHEAD

Higher education in the years immediately ahead faces the necessity of unprecedented increases in financial support. Four factors are affecting this situation:

1. The rapidly increasing enrollments will require at least a doubling of current annual operating budgets within a decade.
2. Research, long recognized as a prime function of universities, currently is being popularly regarded as highly essential to the national welfare and security. Institutions are under tremendous pressure to expand their research activities, and support for this function is being demanded on a scale undreamed of in the past.
3. Besides the expansion in the volume of teaching and research, the quality of institutional programs urgently needs strengthening. Particularly necessary is a substantial and rapid rate of increase in faculty salaries.
4. The accelerating rate at which new discoveries are adding to the store of human knowledge has greatly increased the demands for graduate and advanced professional studies. These levels of education are very expensive to maintain.

Especially striking is the need for new capital funds for financing building programs to house the expanded enrollment and the increased volume of research activity. Diligent, even all-out, effort over the past fifty years has been required to provide the present physical-plant space. But in the next ten years, the additions that will be required are equal to the total volume of plant facilities now in use.

To a limited extent, the financial requirements now faced by the institutions of higher education may be met by economies in operation. By improved utilization of physical plants, the demands for new buildings can be scaled down a bit. By cautious pruning of the curriculum, snipping off here and there some courses not much in demand by students and not essential to the purposes of the institution, a better use may be made of the time and energy of some faculty members. There are promising prospects of both improvement in the quality and, ultimately, some savings in the cost of instruction through the use of television and programed learning devices. Administrators are earnestly seeking means by which the dollar income in their institutions may be stretched to cover some of the necessary expansions and improvements in programs. Special offices of institutional research are being introduced rapidly in well-managed colleges and universities to assist by providing information about the operations of the institution itself.

Despite all the efforts for improved efficiency in the use of available resources, there will remain needs for very large increases in supporting funds for higher education. At present it seems that these increased funds must come mainly from the same sources that are now providing the bulk of the support. Endowment earnings, long considered a prime source of stable income, are not increasing as rapidly as the total demands for expenditure, and there is little prospect of reversing this trend. Philanthropic gifts for current purposes, on the contrary, exhibit a most encouraging tendency to increase faster than the total budgets for higher education. Current-fund gifts, however, have always provided a relatively small percentage of the total income of colleges and universities in the United States. Though the prospects are that this percentage will increase, it will doubtless remain relatively small.

Student fees have long been a mainstay in the support of higher education, quite in contrast with the situation in the public schools of the country at the elementary and secondary levels. The trend in fee charges to college students has been steadily upward for a long time, and increases in recent years have been steep. Yet it is manifestly contrary to public policy in the United States to allow higher education to become the privilege chiefly of those in the upper economic brackets. There seems to be a growing tendency to question the wisdom of expecting to increase the percentage of the support of higher education borne by student fees. Particularly in publicly controlled institutions, there is a tendency to resist further fee increase for residents of the area served. Some leaders are bold enough to suggest a return to the older ideal of free public education at the college and university level. The junior or community college seems the most likely kind of institution to be responsive to such a policy.

The only remaining source of support of substantial size is governmental appropriations. The three levels of government—local, state, and Federal—vary in their ability to provide additional support. Local governments may be expected to increase their contribution through the expansion of community colleges and by continuing the trend toward the establishment of many additional institutions of the community college type. Additional support from state governments seems dependent on the invention of some new and acceptable tax for raising the needed revenues. The prospects for such a breakthrough are not bright. The Federal government, with a long history of very minor support for sharply limited purposes in higher education, seems to have entered on a new phase in policy development with the passage in 1958 of the National Defense Education Act. Particularly promising is the enactment in

December, 1963, of the act providing Federal grants and loans for the construction of college building facilities.

To many observers, the Federal government seems to be the only agency that can provide quickly enough the relatively large sums needed for the support of higher education in the immediate future. Others caution that the prospects of support from Federal funds must not be relied on too exclusively. It will be necessary to exploit as fully as possible all the available sources of support if higher education is to meet successfully the demands for a rapidly expanding volume of service in programs of high quality.

SOURCES FOR FURTHER INFORMATION

Clark, Harold F.: *Cost and Quality in Public Education,* Syracuse University Press, Syracuse, N.Y., 1963.

Financing Higher Education, Southern Regional Education Board Bulletins, Atlanta, Ga., 1959–1964.

Harris, Seymour E.: *Higher Education: Resources and Finance,* McGraw-Hill Book Company, New York, 1962, pp. xxxviii, 714.

————: *Economic Aspects of Higher Education,* Organization for Economic Cooperation and Development, Paris, 1963.

Keezer, Dexter M. (ed.): *Financing Higher Education: 1960–1970,* McGraw-Hill Book Company, New York, 1959, pp. vii, 304.

Millet, John: "Financing Higher Education: Ten Years Later," *The Educational Record,* vol. 44, pp. 44–53, January, 1963.

Muskin, Selma J.: *Economics of Higher Education,* U.S. Office of Education Bulletin 5, 1962, pp. xviii, 406.

Norton, John K.: *Changing Demands on Higher Education and Their Implications,* National Committee for Support of Public Schools, Washington, D.C., 1963.

Ruml, Beardsley, and Donald H. Morrison: *Memo to a College Trustee,* McGraw-Hill Book Company, New York, 1959, pp. ix, 94.

Russell, John Dale: *The Finance of Higher Education,* rev. ed., The University of Chicago Press, Chicago, 1954, pp. xix, 416.

Tickton, Sidney G.: *Needed: A Ten Year College Budget,* Fund for the Advancement of Education, New York, 1961, p. 40.

JAMES G. RICE

13

the campus climate: a reminder

*T*he preceding chapters called attention to a number of recent
innovations in higher education. Many have important implications
for the twin problems of quality and quantity, which face
America's colleges and universities in the years ahead.

In such a time of accelerated change, it is important that we
remind ourselves that the undertakings reported, however important,
constitute only one phase of the educational process. In and of
themselves, they do not result in "education."

Within recent years, social scientists have been giving increasing
attention to some of the more subtle, but highly significant,
factors in student learning: the physical environment in which
the student lives, the social structures and processes of which
he is a part, and the kind of college-community, peer-group, and
other relationships in which he finds himself.

"The education of the student," writes Ralph Tyler, *"cannot be understood adequately just in terms of the courses he takes or the professors with whom he comes in contact. A student learns and develops in a complex environment, being influenced by and influencing the student groups of which he is a member, the friendships he forms, and the roles he plays in college affairs. He is also influenced by his teachers, advisors and the somewhat intangible climate of the college."*[1]

This chapter turns its attention to a discussion of the *"campus climate."* It is intended as a reminder of the role the total campus climate plays in the educational process.

INTRODUCTION

When the ancient and medieval philosophers focused their tools of inquiry on the world, they were able to agree with some consistency that it was constituted of four elements—water, earth, air, and fire. Although this was a neat, logical, and practical conclusion, it was not adequate to their sense of the inner life of things. They were led, therefore, to add to these four material elements a fifth. This fifth element, the *quintessence,* was said to permeate all the material world, giving it meaning, form, being, and purpose.

When all our modern analytical artillery, IBM machines, and batteries of tests have been brought to use in studies of the educative process and the educated person, we too end up with an itching suspicion that something quintessential has somehow escaped us. Despite the data provided by our charts, formulas, graphs, and measures, we sense that a quintessence in the educational process exists and needs identification if we are to understand fully the educative situation and its outcomes.

The preceding chapters reviewed a variety of new developments in higher education. Some cautionary remarks regarding these developments seem necessary, lest we assume too much for them and, in doing so, lose sight of the larger quintessence that permeates the education of the student. Put differently, there is a danger in our present preoccupation with numbers and costs in higher education

[1] *Personality Factors on the College Campus: Review of a Symposium,* The Hogg Foundation for Mental Health, University of Texas, Austin, Tex., 1962.

that we may be tempted—as Americans often are—to turn our "quality" problems into "quantity" problems and seek solutions only in these terms. While the picture that Raymond E. Callahan paints in *Education and the Cult of Efficiency*[2] may strike some readers as an overly pessimistic point of view, his warnings dare not go unheeded.

THE IMPORTANCE OF THE CAMPUS CLIMATE

In an article in the *College and University Bulletin,* Morris Keeton warns that all revisions of course content and improvement of teaching methodology may well prove a waste of time and effort unless such changes are "informed by a comprehensive theory about the climate of learning within which they are applied. . . . To design a college with only courses in mind is to overlook the most influential forces available for teaching: peer influences, direct experiences of the world around, responsibility-taking experiences in college affairs, and the influences of teachers upon their students in non-course relations."[3]

Edward D. Eddy, too, in *The College Influence on Student Character,* is quite explicit on the topic. A section of the book is entitled The Contagion of Intimacy, a phrase borrowed from Edmund Sinnott's volume *The Biology of the Spirit,* where it is used to summarize the idea that what is most intimate to us is apt to be most contagious. He observes:

An organism adapts itself to its environment; we "soak" up that which surrounds us. We found this obviously to be true of college students. We conclude that one of the most unfortunate mistakes in some colleges is the failure to realize the full potential of the contagion, the failure to come to grips with the student where he is found, and the tendency to leave to tradition, chance or student device all else but the purely academic.[4]

In recent years, a great deal of research has been directed toward studies of the undergraduate college environment or campus cul-

[2] Raymond E. Callahan, *Education and the Cult of Efficiency,* The University of Chicago Press, Chicago, 1962.
[3] Morris Keeton, "The Climate of Learning in College," *College and University Bulletin,* vol. 15, no. 4, p. 1, Nov. 15, 1962.
[4] Edward D. Eddy, Jr., *The College Influence on Student Character,* American Council on Education, Washington, D.C., 1959, p. 139.

ture.[5] These studies offer increasing evidence of the importance of the college's "climate of learning" as a major force in determining the quality of the college's educational program. The findings from these studies stress three sets of generalizations:

1. An educational institution does have its own distinctive climate or atmosphere. This climate remains fairly constant from year to year. It attracts with startling consistency the same kinds of students and has the same kind of impact on them.

2. Peer-group interaction and faculty-student interaction outside the classroom are important elements in the campus climate; *these have a stronger and more significant impact on student attitudes and values than the things that go on in the classroom.* Even narrowly defined academic achievement is affected by the en- vironment on the campus.

3. Many of the activities that go on outside the classroom—the advising program, the extraclass program, counseling services, a dormitory system and residence program, and a campus program of cultural events—enhance the motivation to learn and increase the perceived relevance of learning. They not only encourage but also facilitate the mastery of specific subject matter.

Taken together these conclusions and the studies that support them testify that the classroom teacher is not all that is on the other end of the log. They establish beyond doubt the fact that students learn from environment, from things, and from the kinds of sched- ules, routines, and interactions that exist in the college situation.

COMPONENTS OF THE CAMPUS CLIMATE, OR ETHOS

For purposes of analysis, the elements that constitute the campus climate or culture can be divided into several component parts: the quality of things present in the campus situation, the quality of per-

[5] See, for example, Philip Ernest Jacob, *Changing Values in College,* Harper & Row, Publishers, Incorporated, New York, 1957; C. Robert Pace, "What Kind of a College Environment Are Students Entering?" *The A.C.A.C. Journal,* vol. 6, no. 1, p. 6, Association of College Admis- sion Counselors, Evanston, Ill., Winter, 1961; Nevitt Sanford (ed.), *The American College: A Psychological and Social Interpretation of the Higher Learning,* John Wiley & Sons, Inc., New York, 1962; Paul Heist, "Diversity in College Student Characteristics," *Journal of Education Sociology,* vol. 33, pp. 279–291, February, 1960.

sons present, and the kind and quality of *interactions* among them. These factors do not, of course, operate as separate entities. They are, rather, part of an "ecology" and not a mere adding together of innumerable details: "The main lesson we can learn from animal ecology is the need for studying human communities as a whole and their total relationship to their physical and social environment."[6] The factors interact with each other in various ways to produce the ethos or climate of the institution. It is somewhat artificial even to discuss them separately. Nonetheless, it may be useful to do so as a means of achieving some perspective of the parts they play in the total impact of a campus.

Architecture and settings

Buildings, the kind of architecture and their organization on the campus, are important in the atmosphere of the place. The authors of *The College Influence on Student Character* noted this fact:

In attempting to analyze and identify the components of what constitutes a right learning environment we found that this contagion appeared to begin with the very physical arrangement of the campus as a whole. The thoughtful planning which goes into the design and placement of buildings, the care with which physical facilities are kept, and the opportunity for expressing love of beauty in the whole as well as its parts are of importance. A college president mentioned this when he told us, "We think the students ought to be surrounded by the kind of campus arrangements which indicate an order, a peace, an appreciation of the richness which can be found in life." As might be expected, many students with whom we talked viewed their physical surroundings as a symbol of their education, the tangible expression of their own aspirations in learning.[7]

Many campus buildings seem to be designed with the janitor and maintenance staff in mind rather than the student. The simplest building for a janitor is one built on the model of a hospital or a bathroom—tile floors and walls tiled 2 or 3 feet up make it possible for janitors to approach their task with a hose and mop. Too many

[6] William L. Thomas, Jr. (ed.), *Man's Role in Changing the Face of the Earth,* The University of Chicago Press, Chicago, 1956, p. 7.
[7] Eddy, *op. cit.*

classrooms have this sanitary quality. They look as though they were built to be flushed as soon as the present occupants leave.

Buildings can be authoritarian and formal. They can be informal, friendly, and residential. They can be separated at great distances from one another or closely related in a constellation. A constellation can be dominated by a single, tall, authoritarian structure— the administration building—or it can have several points of interest. In their external treatment they can reflect love, care, pride, or indifference. They can face inward to the campus and serve as a kind of bulwark against the surrounding town, or they can face outward and, like Wordsworth's hedgerows, send wild, reaching arms into the surrounding community.

Inside, also, some buildings look sterile, sanitary, and cold. Others look as though they were intended to be lived in. Fabrics, warm colors, and the use of wood give them a friendly feeling.

Walter McQuade asks a question and gives his own answer:

Must *classrooms all have the same size, shape, color, fenestration, and furniture? Must a school corridor—which is not just a traffic artery, but is also a very major social center, especially for teenage children—always run absolutely, relentlessly, inhumanly straight, without turn or indentation, for 300 yards? (Well, it sometimes seems 300 yards.) The answer is that of course it doesn't have to.*

Variety is, after all, stimulating. If a person is subjected to differences around him, in a subtle kind of way he naturally becomes more sensitive to differences of all kinds; and isn't the understanding of differences the very heart of education?[8]

Architecture plays on our sensitivities throughout our lives. From the time man is born and first gazes into a glaring light, to the time of his death, he is in the hands of architects, and this is not just a visual affair. It also involves all the things that act on our millions of sense receptors. Dr. Carl Menninger, a psychiatrist, has noted that beauty is a "psychological necessity." He believes that "mental illness can be prevented by design. The quality of structure may make the difference between being ill or mentally healthy. . . ."[9] Other equally strong statements could be marshaled, but for our purpose here these must suffice to illustrate a growing awareness

[8] Walter McQuade, "Environment for Individuality," *Saturday Review,* vol. 41, pp. 18–19, 54, Sept. 13, 1958.
[9] As quoted in the *St. Louis Post Dispatch,* July 8, 1962.

that "good college education does not happen by accident nor can it be carried out in an atmosphere of large, corporate enterprise."[10]

Administrators, teachers, and students

Administrators, faculty, staff, and students are the personal element in the campus environment. Each has an important contribution to make to the tone or spirit of the campus climate.

Of course, teachers should be selected who have competence in the subjects they profess. Of course, administrators should know about organization and how to administer the things they are responsible for administering. But these abilities, important as they are, neither ensure acceptance by such persons of the philosophical commitments of the institution nor measure their potential impact —positive *or* negative—on the sense of community and the atmosphere that characterizes it. Huston Smith states well a concern hopefully shared by educators:

Education is accustomed to giving advice: The time has come for it to inspire conduct. If the faculty and administration set the right tone, its vibrations will spread over the entire campus and become established in what sociologists call patterns of prestige. The motivations in question become objects of general esteem. Honor societies look for them. They are mentioned over beer or coffee and in the midnight bull sessions. A student entering such a college will absorb almost unconsciously a sense of what makes for greatness. He will hear names spoken of with respect, listen to incidents recounted with lament or affection, derision or pride, until gradually there creeps over him a sense of what makes for greatness. If this atmosphere supports the attitudes desired, it can be a powerful constructive force which releases among students motivations hitherto untapped. The process is all the stronger for being effortless and unself-conscious. It is a kind of education by osmosis, a learning through the pores as an adjunct to learning through the intellect.[11]

[10] Stanton Leggett, "The Educational Effects of College Architecture," *Columbia College Today,* vol. 10, no. 1, pp 24–27, Fall, 1962.
[11] Huston Smith, *The Purposes of Higher Education,* Harper & Row, Publishers, Incorporated, New York, 1955, pp. 190–191.

The college years are critical years for psychic development and for the development of ego functions. The young person at this period is looking for, and trying out, people as models for his own self-centering.[12] Good models strengthen his development; bad ones, immature ones, serve only to "fix" him in his immaturity. The teacher's contribution to the campus climate is therefore conditioned by his willingness and ability to be a person in the learning situation and not merely a distributor of information.

In earlier chapters of this book, both Bruce Dearing and Russell Cooper tell us something of the new role the teacher is assuming when they suggest that the teacher and the administrator are becoming more alike in their functions. This new emphasis on the organizing of knowledge and the supervising of learning is only one facet of the teacher's potential contribution in the emerging situation. It moves in the direction of detachment, of environmental preparation, and of manipulation. If, however, we are to take seriously the proposition that a college education should produce change in students, and if we are to take seriously the current thinking as to how change is brought about, the teacher must develop himself in the other direction as well. This is the direction of personal encounter (the authentic participation), of shared endeavor, and of playing an active role in the drama of exploration.

In addition to administration and faculty, there is another important part of the campus ecology—the students. It is indeed for them that the environment exists at all. The buildings, the campus, the administration, and the faculty were assembled in the first place to move students from adolescence to adulthood. The environment itself is likely to be relatively stable. A new group of students applies for admission to the environment each year. If, as is beginning to be commonly accepted, students get a significant part of their education—values, attitudes, appreciations, and motivations—as much from other students as from faculty, the kinds of students admitted into the environment have an impact on and can actually change that environment. The admissions policies and the processes of admitting students into the environment, therefore, are important in

12 Edgar Dale, "The Educative Environment," *The News Letter,* vol. 206, no. 8, May, 1961. "An educative environment must not only have heroic figures to admire; there must be models at hand to be imitated. Man may be the measure of all things, but what shall be the stature of the man whom we imitate?"

maintaining or changing a given environment. The faculty and the administration have some control over this. The degree of control will, of course, vary, depending on the kind of institution. Nonetheless, within the range of freedom the college has in accepting students, there is the possibility for influencing the environment in significant ways.

Within whatever freedoms colleges have in accepting or selecting students, they should not succumb to the recent tendency toward a one-dimensional criterion—a trend in the direction of accepting only students who rank in the upper ranges of the College Board exams or some other standardized measurement of intellectual ability. The best climate is one in which there is a range of talents, interests, and intellectual potential. This "mix" is important to the environment.

Once again, we shall draw on ecology for clarifying analogies. It is a rather common practice in the South to plant a field with a mixture of several kinds of useful plants. For example, a field may be planted with corn, beans, and squash or pumpkins—all mixed together. The squash vines spread over the ground, conserving the moisture; the cornstalks grow tall; and the beans climb up the stalks. The total plot is therefore well protected by plant coverage which intercepts the rain to prevent washing and which absorbs the sun in the leaves where it is useful and prevents it from evaporating the moisture in the ground where it is needed. This is the kind of efficient, productive human ecology that can result from a planned mixture of student interests and abilities and their meaningful interaction. The disadvantages, waste, and risk of a one-crop economy are coming to be generally recognized by farmers, and I think it must eventually be recognized by educators.[13] C. Robert Pace, in an article in *The A.C.A.C. Journal,* put the argument this way: "If in our zeal to improve education we are tempted to concentrate on one type of education and to mold our college environments to that type, let us remember that we will rather quickly find ourselves giving that education to only one type of student. Diversity itself provides some of the tension which keeps the system in movement and makes it responsive to new needs and new generations."[14]

[13] The ecological base of this analogy has been adapted from some remarks by Dr. Carl O. Sauer, professor of geography at the University of California.
[14] Pace, *op. cit.*

Interaction of the components

We turn now to the kind and quality of interaction among the elements involved in the campus climate. Interaction is the essence of environmental impact. For a campus to have some consistency and to make the maximum impact, there must be shared understandings.

The total staff of the institution must be a team; otherwise, one part of the staff can cancel the effect of another. Research in mental hospitals has shown that the attitudes of janitors, aides, and secretaries can have a significant bearing on the progress of patients. There are clearly implications from this research for colleges and universities.[15]

Do secretarial staff members feel that they are a vital part of the college? These people are likely to be the first ones to greet campus guests, and they have at least as much and perhaps more contact with students than faculty members do. Do they understand the college's objectives? What steps have been taken to make them feel that they are part of a group effort? Do the night watchmen or campus police sit with the student personnel staff when they discuss campus behavior problems? Do they feel a responsibility for what really goes on or simply a responsibility for carrying out someone's orders without any understanding of the reason for their being given? These people—buildings and grounds crew, secretarial staff, night watchmen—are all a part of the human ecology. If they are not functioning as a creative, contributing part of the team, some of the best college resources are being wasted.

It is possible to communicate with the faculty in many ways, for example, at faculty meetings, committee meetings, conferences, and social gatherings.

[15] Jacob Cohen and E. I. Struening, "Opinions about Mental Illness in the Personnel of Two Large Mental Hospitals," *Journal of Abnormal and Social Psychology,* 1962, vol. 64, p. 349. "This newer outlook is based on the general assumption that the well-being of mental patients is at least to some extent influenced by the social context. Derivations from this assumption include the more specific hypotheses that mental patients are sensitive to and influenced by the attitudinal atmosphere created by hospital employees, that the success of reintegrating former mental patients into society is affected by the attitudes of the general public toward mental illness, and that these attitudes play a role in determining the support of mental health programs by the general public as voters and tax payers."

One of the most useful devices for keeping faculty and staff moving as a team is the faculty bulletin, a daily mimeographed bulletin that goes to all faculty and staff. In it are included short news items about the college program, items to be discussed in the faculty meetings, matters that call for faculty attention at given points in the year, reports on faculty publications and honors, and so on. Faculty members on a campus are entitled to know college news before they read it in the local paper. To discover through some other source news having to do with the college does not make for teamwork, for a feeling of shared endeavor.

Committees that are conducted according to Roberts' *Rules of Order* are not going to be very creative. If committees are to move beyond the platitudinous, meetings must be conducted in such a way that spontaneity prevails. There must be a sense of hearing and of being heard. Committee meetings should never be called to tell people things. They should be called so that questions may be asked or problems posed and so that those present can listen to a variety of ideas and answers.

In addition to the spoken and written word, there is another kind of communication that is more subtle. This is what Andrew W. Halpin has called the "unvoiced message,"[16] what Reusch and Kees have called "nonverbal communication,"[17] and what Edward T. Hall has called the "silent language."[18] It is especially important to the administrator and to the faculty member as they deal with each other and with students. This language is made up of those subtle mannerisms and behavior patterns that either support or flatly and silently contradict all else that the person says or does. There are no how-to-do-it rules for managing the nonverbal dimensions of interactions of persons. The harder one attempts to reduce them to a Dale Carnegie "how-to" formula and the greater one's sense of need to do so, the more likely such procedures are to become self-defeating. What, then, can one do to sensitize himself to this muted behavior language? As a start, he can read the books mentioned and ponder them. These will help him sense what he is *really* saying or,

[16] Andrew W. Halpin, "The Unvoiced Message," *Midway*, no. 3, pp. 77–79, The University of Chicago Press, Chicago, July, 1960.
[17] Jurgen Ruesch and Weldon Kees, *Non-verbal Communication*, University of California Press, Berkeley, Calif., 1956.
[18] Edward T. Hall, *The Silent Language*, Doubleday & Company, Inc., Garden City, N.Y., 1959. Paperback edition: Fawcett-World Library, New York, 1961.

rather, acting out, as well as what other people are saying to him. Furthermore, he can try to come to know himself, his real needs, commitments, and convictions. These may not always be the same, but to know that they are not can provide the basis for an inner honesty and integrity that will without contrivance or manipulation communicate themselves to those dealing with him.

When we speak of campus climate, we speak of a very special quality or atmosphere that surrounds the place. It is a matrix of many elements, which interact with one another. It is a quality that is not easily identifiable or definable. But it is a quality that is very real. It exists in all settings. And it is a quality that has, in its own unique way, a very special and persuasive influence, on the education of the student.

SUMMARY

Most of this chapter was devoted to a discussion of the campus climate and the elements that constitute it. A major aim was to make the reader sensitive to the ways in which these elements of campus climate bear importantly on the education of the student.

The study of the campus climate is as much a study of what is there as it is a concern for what is not there. Unlike matter, it has no chemical formula, and it cannot be replicated by the simple expedient of mixing the proper elements in the proper quantities under the same conditions of pressure and heat. It is a subtle thing —a kind of mystique in the educational process—that can produce results not readily attributable to what goes on in the classrooms, to any particular subject matter, or to any new (or old) methodology of teaching.

Higher education faces a tremendous task in the decade ahead. It will need to find ways of educating at least twice the number of students that it is now accommodating in its colleges and universities, and it must do so at a time of rising costs and insufficient number of qualified faculty members.

There is no question but that higher education must continue to search for ways of organizing the student's educational experience so as to achieve more effective and more economical education. It must continue in its search for quality while handling greater numbers of students than ever before.

New media and technology, independent study, year-round calendars, off-campus research and study programs, and many other developments discussed in this volume all have important implications for higher education in the years ahead. But we must remind ourselves that they do not tell the whole story. There are many and complex forces that bear on the education of the student. It would be a mistake to assume *too much* for any of these developments and, in so doing, to ignore or discount the importance of the larger *climate of learning* in which they must take place.

SOURCES FOR FURTHER INFORMATION

"Creating the College Climate," *Proceedings of the Second Junior College Administrative Teams Institute, July 30, August 3, 1962,* Florida State University, Tallahassee, Fla., 1962.

Eddy, Edward D., Jr.: *The College Influence on Student Character,* American Council on Education, Washington, D.C., 1959.

Elfin, Mel, Bernard Asbell, Alvin Toffler, Margaret Farmer, and James J. Morisseau: *Bricks and Mortarboards: A Report on College Planning and Building,* Educational Facilities Laboratories, Inc., New York, 1964.

Keeton, Morris: "The Climate of Learning in College," *College and University Bulletin,* vol. 15, no. 4, Nov. 15, 1962.

Leggett, Stanton: "The Educational Effects of College Architecture," *Columbia College Today,* vol. 10, no. 1, pp. 24–27, Fall, 1962.

McQuade, Walter: "Environment for Individuality," *Saturday Review,* vol. 4, pp. 18–19, 54, Sept. 13, 1958.

Pace, C. Robert: "Evaluating the Total Climate or Profile of a Campus," paper read at the sixteenth National Conference on Higher Education, sponsored by the Association for Higher Education, Chicago, Mar. 6, 1961.

———: "What Kind of a College Environment Are Students Entering?" *The A.C.A.C. Journal,* vol. 6, no. 1, p. 6, Association of College Admission Counselors, Evanston, Ill., Winter, 1961.

Sanford, Nevitt (ed.): *The American College: A Psychological and Social Interpretation of the Higher Learning,* John Wiley & Sons, Inc., New York, 1962.

Stern, George G.: "Characteristics of the Intellectual Climate in College Environments," *Harvard Educational Review,* vol. 33, no. 1, pp. 5–41, Winter, 1963.

Ten Designs: Community Colleges, Department of Architecture, Rice University, Houston, Tex., 1962.

Thomas, William L., Jr. (ed.): *Man's Role in Changing the Face of the Earth,* The University of Chicago Press, Chicago, 1956.

Wilson, Everett K.: "Effecting Change in the College Student: Who Teaches What?" *Antioch College Reports,* no. 4, March, 1963.

SAMUEL BASKIN

14

summing up

*T*his book has reviewed a variety of developments in higher
education. Particular attention has been given to developments in
the four-year undergraduate institution. Developments discussed
included programs and emphases of the new colleges; effects of
curriculum revisions; new and expanded uses of independent
study, off-campus experience, and new media and technology;
programs for the abler student; study-abroad programs; the
improvement of college teaching and administration; year-round
use of college facilities; the design of college buildings and
facilities; possibilities in interinstitutional cooperation; and the
financing of the college. A number of these developments hold
particular import for higher education in its struggle to achieve
quality and quantity in the years ahead. These are reviewed
in this chapter.

OVERVIEW

In recent years, there have been a number of new developments in higher education. Some involve new organizational and structural uses of the college, such as the plans now under way for the use of the dormitory as a center for learning and the establishment of small colleges within the framework of the larger university. Some focus on curriculum revision. Some give principal attention to the problem of better utilization of the college's staff and plant resources, such as the adoption of year-round-calendar plans by a growing number of colleges and universities. Some center on the development of new teaching and learning methods, such as the uses now being made of new media and technology, independent study, and off-campus experience. And some deal with such long-standing concerns as the development of more effective programs for the improvement of college teaching and administration, the special program needs of the superior student, and the problem of educating the student for better international understanding in a world grown small.

This chapter highlights a number of key trends and developments as these evolve from a study of the earlier chapters of this report. It does so mindful of the cautions that James Rice has posed for us in his discussion of the *climate of learning* and the role it plays in educational process.

Maintaining smallness within the large university

As the press of numbers has continued, institutions of higher learning have sought to find ways of maintaining the qualities of smallness while continuing to grow. Some dimensions of the problem are seen in the following statistics: The University of Minnesota had 49,228 degree candidates in attendance during the 1963–1964 school year; the University of Wisconsin showed 38,883 students on its roster; Ohio State University had 34,184; and Indiana University had 34,032 students in attendance who were taking work toward the bachelor's degree.

Several institutions have dealt with this problem by establishing small autonomous colleges, each with its own faculty and student body, within the larger parent body. The programs at the Monteith College of Wayne State University and the New College at Hofstra, Long Island, are illustrative. Each builds on the concept of a college within a college, the student taking the bulk of his work within his *own* small college, while drawing on the facilities of the larger university for advanced courses and library and laboratory needs. Similar efforts to achieve smallness in the face of increasing numbers are seen in Wesleyan's establishment of a federation of small colleges within the framework of its university; the complex of small residential institutions being developed at the University of California, Santa Cruz, and the University of the Pacific at Stockton, California (with students "crossing over" to the other colleges to take advanced courses or special-area courses not available in their own college); Michigan State's use of living-learning centers; and the Florida State University proposal for the establishment of an experimental college as a separate unit within its university.

Independent study

While undergraduate institutions have long made use of independent study, these programs have generally been reserved for the superior or honors student only. There are several new elements in the way independent study is now begin employed in a number of institutions: (*1*) as an experience common to all students rather than the superior or abler student only; (*2*) at the very beginning of the student's college career, i.e., the freshman year, as contrasted with the usual practice of reserving these experiences for the senior or upper-division years only; and (*3*) the incorporation of procedures which make use of new media and technology (programed texts, single-concept films, playback of video tapes, etc.) in connection with the student's independent studies. Of note also in connection with the move toward the increased use of independent study are developments in building design which incorporate student individual study or Q spaces as basic structural components of the college's independent study program. Grand Valley College is developing its program around a cluster of four general-purpose buildings. A special feature of these buildings will be the individual study stations, or carrels (to be equipped with video and audio playback facilities), to provide comfortable study space for every student on campus. Similarly, the new Florida Atlantic University plans to make extensive use of individual study stations as a core element in its instructional programs.

Certain programs are of special note in that they are finding increased use in college undergraduate curricula. These include winter-term programs—such as that at Florida Presbyterian College, in which all classes are suspended during the month of January, during which time all students undertake individual study or research projects—and the independent study quarter programs in effect at Antioch and Kalamazoo Colleges, in which students may devote an entire quarter, *on or off campus,* to independent studies. Other institutions that give prominent attention to the use of independent study as a *regular* part of the student's undergraduate experience are Monteith College of Wayne State University, New College at Hofstra, Grand Valley State College, Florida Atlantic University, Goddard, Macalester, Colby, Earlham, Bard, and St. Andrews. New College at Sarasota, which opened in the fall of 1964, and the University of California at Santa Cruz, which is scheduled to open in the fall of 1965, also plan to make major use of independent studies in their programs.

The residence hall as a center for learning

For some years, a number of institutions have provided some instruction in their residence halls, sometimes through tutorial relationships, sometimes in the form of informal seminars, and sometimes through occasional lectures by resident and visiting faculty. In general, these programs do not include offerings from the college's regular instructional program and are often regarded as extracurricular rather than as an integrated part of the college's academic program.

In recent years several institutions have been giving consideration to ways by which they might make fuller use of the dormitory as a center for learning as well as living. These programs have the advantage of building on the natural cohesiveness of the hall unit for achieving certain educational gains, for example, developing closer student-faculty relationships and serving economy through the multiple use of the dormitory for both teaching and residential purposes. In several cases, faculty office space as well as large-group teaching, seminar and library spaces, and in some instances laboratories are located in the residence hall itself. The programs under way at

Michigan State University and Stephens College are representative of this development.

The system at Michigan State University presently includes three living-learning units, the first of which was built in 1962. Each of these units houses 1,200 students. They include a total of fourteen classrooms, six laboratories, forty-seven faculty offices, an auditorium, a kiva (a large room used for teaching, recreational, and cultural activities), a library, and five conference rooms. In the fall of 1963, seven colleges and sixteen departments were offering 101 sections of nineteen different courses in the in-hall academic programs. The present program houses freshmen and sophomore students only. Several upper class units are now being planned. It is hoped that these units will in effect serve as a base for department majors in different fields.

Under the House Plan in effect at Stephens College, some one hundred first-year students take all five of their required general education courses in the dormitory in which they reside. Lounges on the upper floors of the dormitory have been attractively furnished so that they serve equally well as lounges or informal classrooms. Faculty members who teach the courses serve as advisers to the students and have their offices in the residence hall grouped around a conference room. The House-plan assignment constitutes the teacher's entire load.

New media and technology

No development has received more attention in recent years than the new media and technology. Of particular note have been developments in the use of television and programed instruction; the growth of language laboratories; the development of new media materials, such as 8-mm film loops and single-concept films (which thread and rewind automatically); the development of facilities for the automatic playback of lectures in both audio and video form, using remote-control telephone dial or push-button systems; and the development of new teaching auditoriums, which often combine facilities for daylight, rear-screen, and multiple-screen projection, video- and audio-tape presentations, various types of film slides and other graphic materials (frequently controlled by punched tape or some other method of automation), and student response stations which provide for immediate feedback analyses of student learning.

Of special note also are developments in the use of the learning resources center as a core unit in the college's instructional program and the use of computer technology for teaching, information storage and retrieval, and the handling of various administrative, registration, course-scheduling, and research functions.

The learning resources centers bring together a wide variety of resource materials and production and distribution facilities for use in the college's instructional program. These centers usually include videotape and closed-circuit television, specially equipped rooms for audio and/or video playback, books and other library materials, programed materials, motion-picture films, kinescopes and video tapes of recorded courses, audio tapes and other instructional aids, still visuals, different types of graphic materials, and a variety of presentation and projection devices. Libraries and classroom buildings are usually tied into the center by an electronic system to permit telecast and radio broadcast of lectures to almost any part of the college campus. The new learning center at Stephens College, known as the James M. Wood Quadrangle, is a complex of five buildings that includes a four-story resources library, a TV-radio-film and audio-visual center, a fine arts center, and instructional, laboratory, and office spaces for the humanities, religion, philosophy, language, communications, and science departments. Provision has been made in the center for Q spaces for individual study as well as for small- and large-group instruction. Walls that can be moved are provided in several areas, making it possible to vary space size with minimum effort. At the heart of the center is a dissemination system designed to provide maximum transfer of information from the TV-radio-film and audio-visual center to various parts of the campus: classrooms, individual study areas, laboratories, exhibit corridors and lobbies, and even residence halls. Programing can originate from any point on campus, and all audio and video facilities can transmit to, and receive from, individual study spaces. Similar programs for the development of learning resource centers, although these vary in design, are under way at Florida Atlantic and Michigan State Universities.

Several developments in the use of the computer hold significant possibilities for higher education. Project Plato (Programed Logic for Automated Teaching Operation), at the University of Illinois, makes use of a computer-controlled system of slides, TV displays, and student response panels for teaching a number of students simultaneously, while still allowing each student to proceed through the lesson material individually. The computer also keeps detailed records of student performance and provides immediate feedback and analyses of student responses. Similar studies in the use of the computer of teaching and learning are under way at Massachusetts Institute of Technology, the New York Institute of Technology, the Systems Development Corporation, and IBM. In addition, substantial research is in process on the use of the computer for storing and disseminating information and for handling student registration and course scheduling. Under its Project Walnut, IBM has been developing a data storage and information retrieval system for the Central Intelligence Agency, which allows for almost instant retrieval of information through the use of certain key words (with each word coded to identify certain areas of the literature). Still other studies are under way at the University of Illinois, UCLA, the National Library of Medicine, and the National Science Foundation.

MIT's project GASP (Generalized Academic Simulation Program) illustrates some of the ways in which the computer can be used to handle registration and course scheduling with substantial advantages in terms of economy and speed and with the avoidance of conflict in classroom scheduling. It makes use of a 7090 computer in buildiing its entire course schedule as well as that of neighboring Nasson College.

Facilities for learning

Much experimentation is now going on in campus architecture and building design. A number of the developments are concerned with the more effective use of the college's teaching and learning spaces, particularly in the employment of new media and technology. Examples are seen in the learning resources centers developed at Stephens College and Florida Atlantic University. Other developments stress new uses and flexibility in the employment of what heretofore have been "specialized-use" spaces: Webster College in St. Louis, Missouri, has built a divisible auditorium (employing movable partitions) which can be used for small- or large-group classes as well as for theater-auditorium purposes; Chicago Teachers College North has planned its classrooms so that they can be easily converted to large-group, small-group, or individual study spaces; Southern Illinois University has developed "plug-in" cabinet equipment for various kinds of laboratory experiments, thus enabling it to use a *single* laboratory for biology, chemistry, physics, and other sciences by simply "plugging in" the appropriate equipment; Colorado College's new circular infirmary will provide for individual study spaces right within the infirmary for both ambulatory and nonambulatory patients (with study areas convertible to ward spaces as needed); and the new University of Illinois physical education building lends itself to multiple use for recreation, large conventions, student assemblies, and theatrical performances. Still other developments are reflected in the design of new libraries and other buildings so as to make use of new developments in computer technology (Florida Atlantic University) and in the incorporation of classrooms in the residence hall, as in Michigan State's use of living-learning centers (see above). Two groups, the Educational Facilities Laboratories of New York (a unit of the Ford Foundation) and the U.S. Office of Education's Media Branch, have had an especially prominent role in encouraging research and development in this area.

Seminars at the freshman level

Paralleling developments in the use of independent study, several institutions employ or plan to employ tutorial and seminar type of programs during the student's freshman year.

These programs seek to provide the student with an experience in depth at the very beginning of his college career, as contrasted with the large-size, broad, survey-type courses in which he frequently finds himself during his first year in college. As in the independent study programs, the intent here is to capitalize on the motivation and excitement that should come with the student's first year in college.

Some examples are seen in the freshmen seminar programs tried out at Mount Holyoke and Smith Colleges; in the programs at New College, Sarasota, Monteith College, and New College at Hofstra, which make use of small seminar groups in connection with the student's first-year courses; in Stephens College's use of freshman seminars in the dormitory; and in the plans now being developed for the University of California, Santa Cruz.

Year-round study

Many colleges are moving toward year-round operation, staying in session for a total of forty to forty-eight weeks, as contrasted with the usual two-semester plan, under which the college year runs for a period of thirty-two to thirty-six weeks. Several types of programs have been developed: quarter-type plans, which divide the school year into four quarters of ten to twelve weeks each; trimester programs, which make use of three terms of about fifteen weeks each; and semester-type plans, which employ two semesters of about sixteen weeks with an abbreviated summer session. A 1963 report of the Fund for the Advancement of Education lists a total of forty institutions that have recently adopted year-round programs.[1]

A number of arguments are advanced in favor of year-round calendars: the student may graduate in 2⅔ to 3 years (by attending three rather than two terms in each academic year), thus enabling him to enter graduate school earlier and thereby shortening the total number of years he would need to be in school; year-round calendars generate greater seriousness of purpose on the part of the student; colleges can accommodate more students, thus at least partially meeting present demands for more undergraduate facilities; and some financial gains may result from the more efficient use of the college's plant facilities and from long-term savings in capital outlay for buildings and equipment. Questions raised about year-round calendars relate to the speed-up aspects of these calendars and the effects they may have on the instructional programs, problems posed in relation to achieving a balance of students in each study term (with the summer session posing special difficulties), and problems associated with faculty recruitment and pay schedules, if they are to work a ten- or eleven-month year.

Some illustrative examples of year-round-calendar plans are seen in the trimester programs being employed at the University of Pittsburgh, Chicago Teachers College North, Columbia College (South Carolina), Parsons College, the California State College (California, Pennsylvania), and the State Universities of Florida; the quarter plans in use at the Pennsylvania State University, Allegheny College, Emory University (Atlanta, Georgia), the George Peabody College for Teachers, Kalamazoo, and Kent State University; and the semester-plus-summer-session programs in use at Wheaton College (Wheaton, Illinois), Baylor University, the University of Southern California (Schools of Education and Business Administration), Vanderbilt University, and the University of North Carolina.

[1] Sidney G. Tickton, *The Year-round Campus Catches On,* Fund for the Advancement of Education, New York, January, 1963.

Study abroad: education for world affairs

There is little question that undergraduate programs of study abroad have become an increasingly important part of the student's undergraduate college experience. The objectives of these programs can be grouped under three major headings: (*1*) the general education of the student, (*2*) the student's intellectual and professional development, and (*3*) the furthering of international understanding. The programs vary in type, patterns of operation, and time spent abroad. While many of the earlier programs were based in European countries (with Paris as a favorite site), a number of colleges are now turning their attention to the development of programs in other areas of the world, particularly in Mexico, Latin America, Asia, and Africa. In Mexico, Antioch has its own study center in Guanajuato; San Francisco College for Women and the University of Arizona offer programs at Guadalajara; and the Southern Association of Colleges sponsors a program at Monterrey. In Latin America, Colgate has a program in Argentina; Indiana University has developed a program in Peru; the Great Lakes Colleges Association has a center in Bogotá, Colombia; and Fordham has a program in Chile. Adelphi offers undergraduate study opportunities in Asia; the University of Wisconsin has developed an undergraduate year program in India; Princeton and the Great Lakes Colleges Association have opened centers in Lebanon; Stanford administers an interuniversity program in Taipeh and Tokyo; and a second GLCA center has been recently established at Waseda University in Japan. In Africa the University of Southern California sponsors an undergraduate program in Tunisia, and Kalamazoo College operates a program in Sierra Leone for the GLCA.

Complementing the developments in programs of study abroad are new course developments and special-area offerings designed to increase the student's knowledge of world affairs. A number of these courses are designed as introductory experiences, to come in the freshman or sophomore year. Many are directed toward non-Western studies. Illustrative are the two-year sequence in Oriental civilization offered at Columbia College, Harvard's program on Far Eastern civilization, and the University of Michigan's and the University of Minnesota's offerings in Asian civilization.

Off-campus experience

An increasing number of colleges are making use of some form of off-campus experience as a part of the student's undergraduate program. The trend here is not so much toward the adoption of alternating programs of work and study, as in colleges operating under the cooperative plan (although these have also increased in number in recent years), as it is toward the development of flexible calendar plans that require or encourage the student to spend one or more quarters in some kind of off-campus or field experience. This experience might be of several sorts: a job; extramural study, often tied into a related work or community experience; a research-oriented experience; a service activity; seminars in the field; or a period abroad.

Beloit College's new program, begun in the fall of 1964, provides for a three-phase calendar as follows: an "under-class year," in which the student spends three consecutive periods on campus; a "middle-class period" of five trimesters, two on campus, one off, and two that may be used for vacation, off-campus experience, or study; and an "upper-class year," in which the student spends his final three trimesters on campus. The off-campus terms may be spent in a variety of ways: for independent study, study abroad, work, a research project, or participation in one of several off-campus programs (the Argonne Laboratory program, the Chicago Urban Education Program, the Wilderness Field Station Project) sponsored by the Associated Colleges of the Midwest.

The new four-quarter plan adopted by Kalamazoo College in 1961 makes use of a total of fifteen quarters, ten of which are on campus and five off. Under this plan a student normally spends three quarters studying on campus during his first year, has two quarters of work experience during his second year, spends two quarters abroad during his third year, and spends one quarter in independent study during his fourth year.

In still other uses of off-campus experience as a way of learning, Goddard College makes use of a Comparative Cultures program, under which students spend two months in French Canada in work and in related project and seminar studies; Antioch has experimented with off-campus "trailer" courses, under which students can take the second half of an on-campus course while on their cooperative jobs in the United States or abroad (making use of the special opportunities and resources available in the field, such as visits to certain historical sites, studies of selected communities, interviews, and specialized libraries); and Earlham College has made use of a variety of community service projects as a part of the student's undergraduate educational experience.

Programs for the abler student

Few changes in higher education have come more rapidly than the dramatic increase in programs for the abler or gifted student.

Most of the new honors programs make use of a wide variety of procedures in the accomplishment of their objectives. These include seminars, colloquia, independent study, theme groups, senior theses, research projects, waiver of course requirements, advanced placement and credit by examination, use of student honors committees in program development, honors centers (libraries, lounges, special reading rooms, etc.), and the use of honors students, where feasible, in teaching, research, and counseling roles. They stress the importance of full faculty involvement in the programs in both teaching and counseling and in budgeting for these programs so that they become an integral part of the total college program. Of special note is the attention being given in these programs to the early identification of the honors student and the development of programs which *begin* at the *time of the student's admission to college* and carry through his entire college career. Many of the programs now being developed, such as those at the University of Illinois, Michigan, and Oregon State, are being designed as all-university programs, in which students from all schools of the university and all departments may participate, as contrasted with earlier developments in which certain selected departments established their own programs, usually limited to departmental majors. Of note also are developments in various professional schools, such as schools of agriculture, home economics, business, engineering, nursing, medicine, music, fine arts, and education, where a number of new honors programs have been established. Of particular interest are the M.A.-3 education programs (a specially designed three-year master's degree program which begins in the student's junior year). Some thirty-nine of these programs, underwritten by the Ford Foundation, are now in operation on campuses throughout the United States. They have as one of their principal objectives the early identification and selection of able students and the planning of programs, beginning with the students junior year, that will most effectively enable these students to prepare for and enter a career in college teaching.

Interinstitutional cooperation

Institutions of higher learning are giving increasing attention to possibilities in interinstitutional cooperation. Several such groups have been formed in recent years: the consortium of graduate schools founded in 1964, comprising American, Catholic, Georgetown, George Washington, and Harvard Universities; the Great Lakes Colleges Association, a grouping of twelve institutions of higher learning in Indiana, Michigan, and Ohio, which began in 1962; the College Center of the Finger Lakes, an aggregation of seven small colleges in south and central New York State, formed in 1961; and the Associated Colleges of the Midwest, founded in 1958 and consisting of ten colleges from the neighboring states of Minnesota, Iowa, Wisconsin, and Illinois.

These groups have joined together for a variety of reasons: to improve the educational programs of the colleges through the sharing of facilities, joint course offerings, faculty development programs, and a variety of other undertakings; to achieve economies of operation through joint purchase plans and the joint use of expensive laboratory, library, and research facilities and to provide a framework to exchange educational ideas and encourage cooperative research and new program developments within the member colleges. In large part these cooperative groups seek to do together what an institution may not be as well equipped to do singly. Several program examples will illustrate.

Under a program developed by the Associated Colleges of the Midwest, faculty members in such disciplines as physics, biology, chemistry, and mathematics are able to gain access to rare and highly expensive equipment while doing research at the Argonne National Laboratory. Similarly, advanced students in the same fields are able to spend a full semester in study and research at the laboratory. While no single institution could support or man such a program by itself, the program does become feasible through the cooperative efforts of the ACM member colleges.

Another case in point is the arrangement worked out by the New England Board of Higher Education (an interstate compact designed to promote cooperation among colleges in six New England States). Under this program, students attending one of the state universities in the New England region may enroll at any of the other state institutions to take advantage of specialized course offerings not offered in his own university. In the past year, some fifty courses of study were available under the New England regional program, with about 350 students enrolled in regional curricula.

Other illustrations of the kinds of activities in which the associations have engaged are the joint undertaking of education-abroad programs, as in the Latin-American Center being developed at Bogotá, Colombia, for students and faculty of the Great Lakes Colleges Association; various cooperative research undertakings, such as the programed instruction project of GLCA and the language research studies of the Associated Colleges of the Midwest; "traveling-scholar" programs, such as those developed by the Committee on Institutional Cooperation (a grouping of large Middle Western universities known as the "Big Ten"), the Richmond Area Center, and the Great Lakes Colleges Association; and the large-scale purchasing plans developed by several of the groups, such as ACM's joint insurance purchase plan, which has resulted in a lower insurance cost per college than was the case when insurance was purchased by the individual college.

CONCLUDING REMARKS

Institutions of higher education have long been criticized for their resistance to change. One frustrated administrator is supposed to have put the problem this way: "It is easier to move a cemetery than to overhaul a curriculum."[2]

No claim has been made in this book that all the developments discussed in the foregoing chapters represent "first ideas" in higher education. Some, like the concept of the small autonomous college within the larger university, the idea of the learning resources center, and the use of computer technology in teaching and learning, are

[2] Philip H. Coombs, "Education's Greatest Need: A Vice-president in Charge of Heresy," *Phi Delta Kappan*, Homewood, Ill., March, 1960.

relatively new. Others, like the use of new media and technology and independent study, have been talked about for some time in higher education. This however, is not the point. What is the point is that higher education has begun to move, and many ideas have begun to take hold—in new and expanded ways—in a variety of settings, both public and private.

Few would argue for experimentation for experimentation's sake. But also, few would deny that if we are to truly understand what we are about in higher education then we will need to take a hard and critical look at how we go about our business and to ask ourselves what we seek to do, how we do it, and how we might do it better.

There is good evidence from the developments cited in this book that we have finally begun to do so.

Surely higher education has much to worry about in the years to come, in terms of numbers of students, shortages of dollars, insufficient numbers of teachers, and far too few spaces for teaching and housing our college-age population. But the picture is not all bleak, and one might even hope that the very problems which now beset higher education may yet evolve into its best opportunities.

index